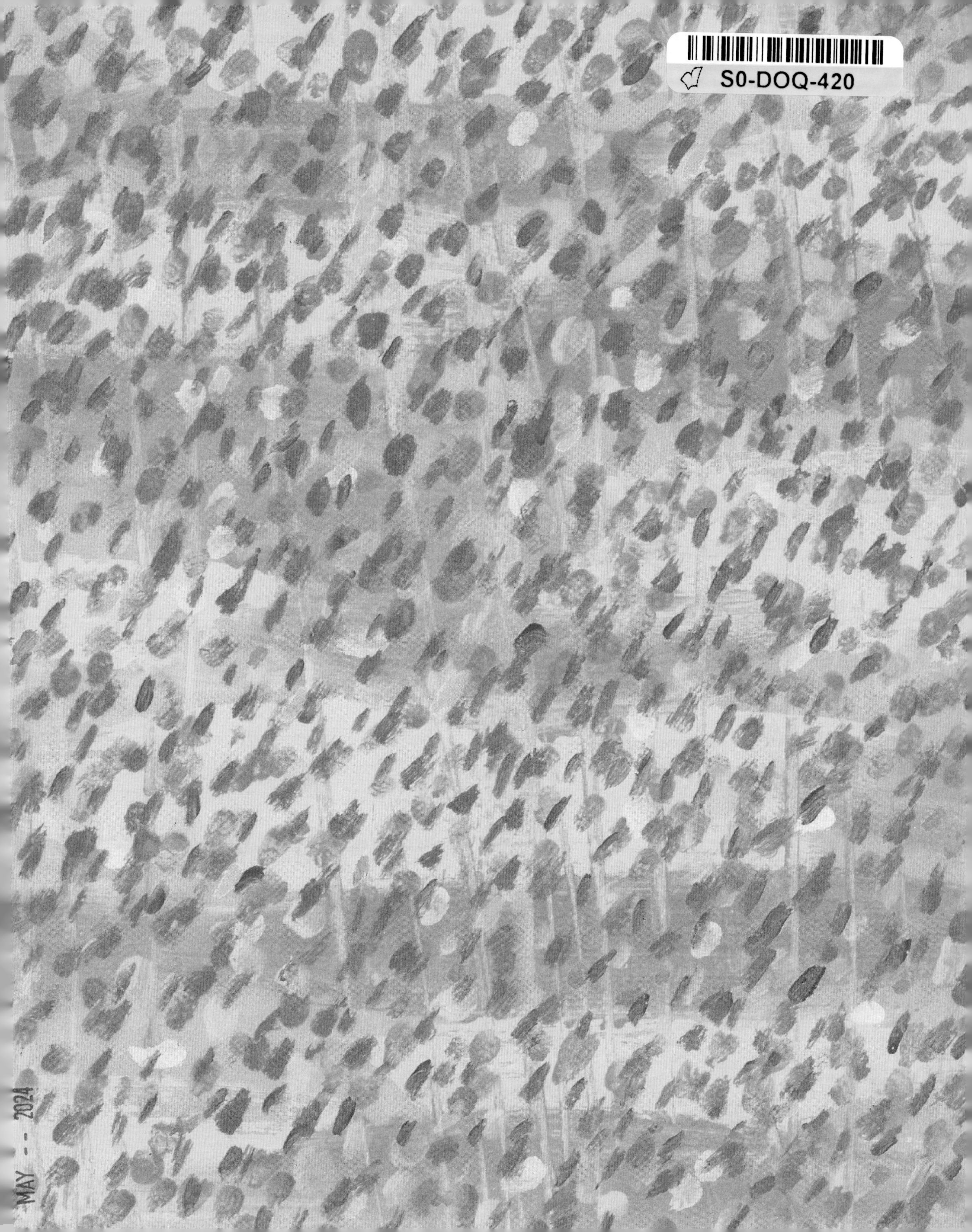

world of ERIC CARLE

DK

The Very Hungry Caterpillar's VERY FIRST ANIMAL ENCYCLOPEDIA

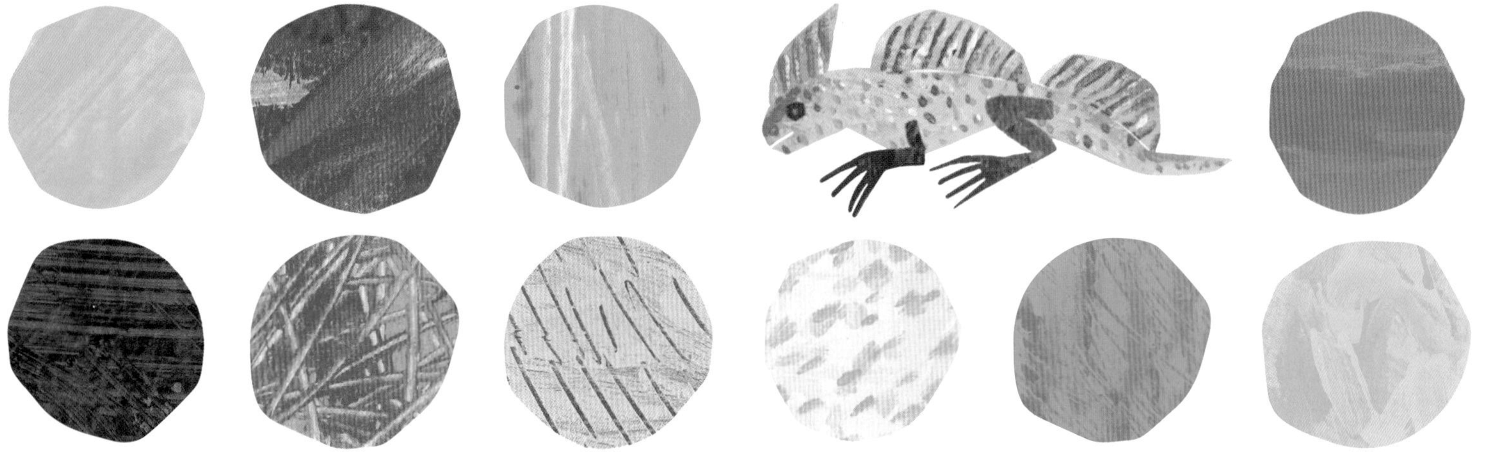

The Very Hungry Caterpillar's

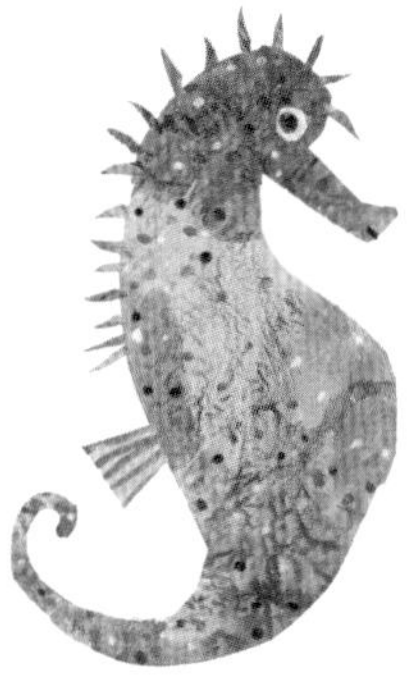

VERY FIRST ANIMAL ENCYCLOPEDIA

Contents

All about animals

Marvelous mammals

Beautiful birds

Remarkable reptiles and amphibians

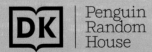

DK | Penguin Random House

Author Andrea Mills
Editor Rona Skene
Designer Bettina Myklebust Stovne

Additional design Charlotte Milner, Hannah Moore
Additional editorial Kieran Jones

Consultant Cathriona Hickey
US Editor Margaret Parrish
US Senior Editor Shannon Beatty
Managing editors Jonathan Melmoth, Marie Greenwood
Managing art editor Diane Peyton Jones
Senior production editor Nikoleta Parasaki
Production controller Isabell Schart
Picture researcher Rituraj Singh
Publishing coordinator Issy Walsh
Deputy art director Mabel Chan
Publishing director Sarah Larter

First American Edition, 2024
Published in the United States by DK Publishing
1745 Broadway, 20th Floor, New York, NY 10019

10 9 8 7 6 5 4 3 2 1
001-328020-May/2024

Fantastic fish

Incredible invertebrates

Animal activities

Published in Great Britain by
Dorling Kindersley Limited

A catalog record for this book
is available from the Library of Congress.
ISBN 978-0-7440-9763-4

DK books are available at special discounts when
purchased in bulk for sales promotions, premiums,
fund-raising, or educational use.
For details, contact: DK Publishing Special Markets,
1745 Broadway, 20th Floor, New York, NY 10019
SpecialSales@dk.com

Printed and bound in China

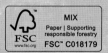

MIX
Paper | Supporting responsible forestry
FSC™ C018179
www.fsc.org

This book was made with Forest Stewardship Council™ certified paper - one small step in DK's commitment to a sustainable future.
For more information go to www.dk.com/our-green-pledge

www.dk.com

All about animals

Living things

Our world is full of life. Just look at the towering trees, beautiful blooms, and green grass growing all around. There are animals great and small, from whopping whales to tiny termites and, of course, humans like us. So, what does it mean to be truly alive?

That's life!

All living things share some important features. They all breathe air, grow, and can create new life. They also need food and water to stay alive.

Plant power

Plants are living things, but they are not animals. They need to take in water to survive. They use sunshine to make energy that helps them grow. They produce seeds that grow into new plants. Unlike most animals, plants can't see or hear, and they can't move themselves around.

Amazing animals

All animals stay alive by drinking water and by eating plants or other animals. Nearly all animals have eyes to see and ears or sensors to hear. They have tongues to taste or feelers to feel. They can move their bodies. Some animals grow their babies inside them, while others lay eggs that hatch into babies.

Baby chick

The animal kingdom

The world of animals is full of different creatures, including you. Scientists put animals into groups, to make them easier to study.

Animal families

All animals belong to one huge group called a kingdom. The kingdom is split into smaller and smaller groups, until each one contains just one type of animal, called a species.

Invertebrates

Animals without a backbone are called invertebrates. Their soft, squishy bodies are often covered by a shell or skeleton on the outside.

Starfish

Echinoderms

"Ee-kai-no-derms"
Sea stars, sea urchins, and sea cucumbers belong in this group.

Jellyfish

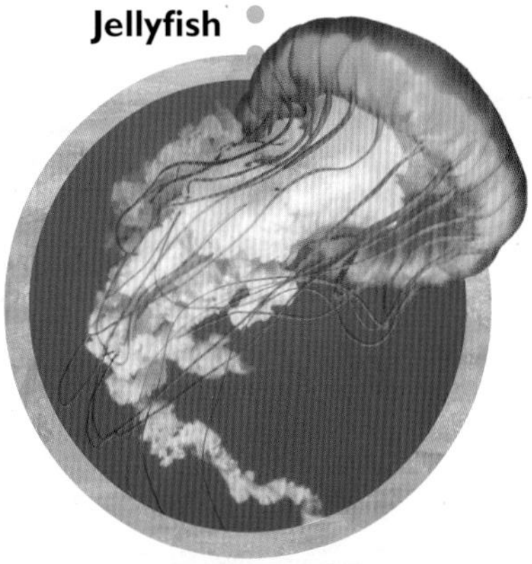

Cnidarians

"Nye-dare-ee-anns"
These simple sea creatures include jellyfish, corals, and anemones.

Earthworm

Worms

Flatworms and roundworms are species in the wriggly worm group.

Ladybug

Arthropods

This group of creepy-crawlies includes insects, spiders, scorpions, and crabs.

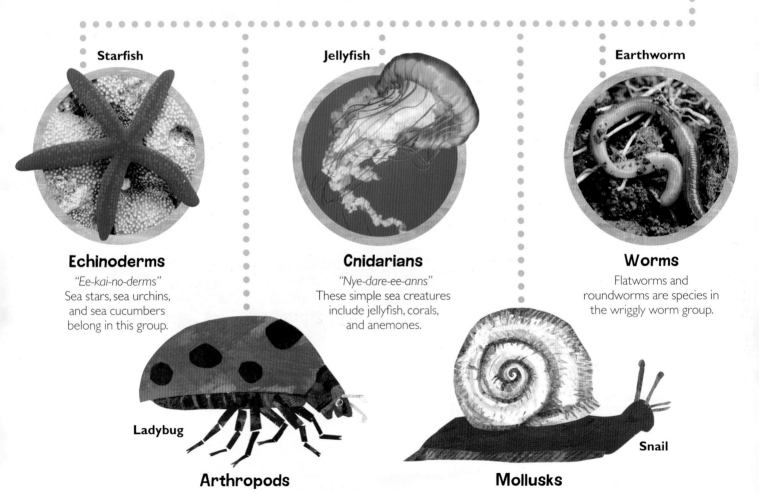

Snail

Mollusks

Slugs, snails, and octopuses are all types of mollusk.

Two million different species of animal have been named so far, so don't try to count them!

Vertebrates

Animals that have a backbone are called vertebrates. Although they share this feature, members of the five main groups look very different from each other.

Mammals

This group includes bears, elephants, whales, monkeys, and humans, too!

Fish

These swimming superstars include sharks, rays, and clown fish.

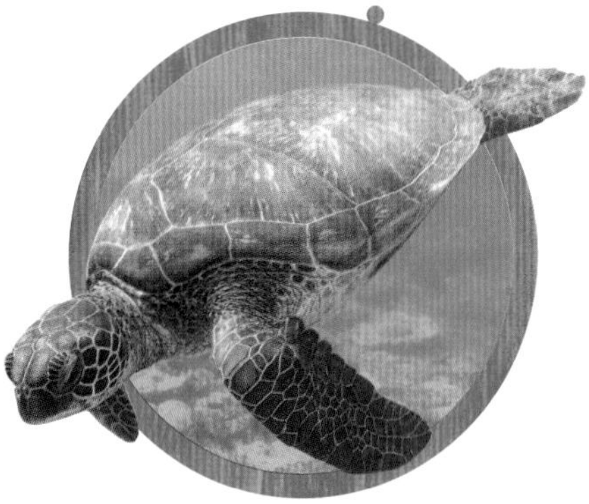

Reptiles

Turtles, tortoises, snakes, and crocodiles belong in this group.

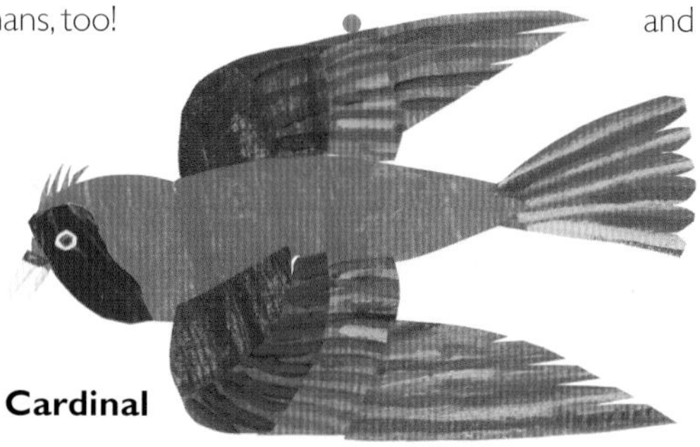

Birds

This group of feathered animals includes eagles, penguins, and ducks.

Amphibians

Frogs, toads, and newts are all included in the amphibian group.

High and low

Animals live all over the world, from dizzying heights to the forest floors. They set up home high on snowcapped mountain peaks, deep underground in the soil, and everywhere in between.

Wood thrush

Wild woodlands

Woods and forests make great homes for animals. Birds nest in the leafy treetops, squirrels leap from branch to branch, and insects scuttle along the ground through fallen leaves.

Red squirrel

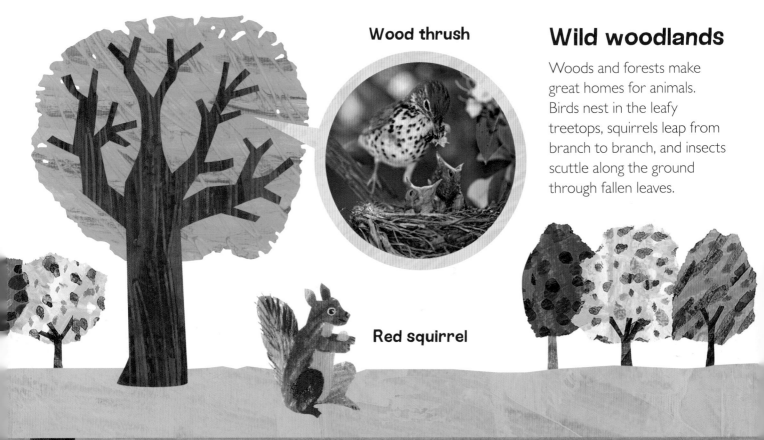

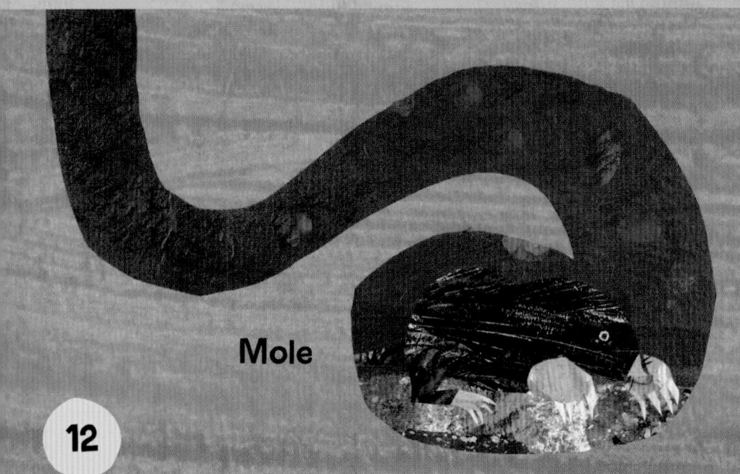

Mole

Under the ground

Some animals tunnel underground for safety. Rabbits create a network of burrows called a warren, while badgers dig homes called setts. Earthworms feed on the goodness in the soil, but risk becoming dinner for hungry moles boring through the earth hunting for their favorite treat!

Eagle

Living the high life

The Himalayan jumping spider lives on the slopes of Mount Everest, the world's tallest mountain.

Mighty mountains

Mountain animals have to be tough to survive the rocky, cold, and windy conditions. Eagles soar the skies, snow leopards blend into the backdrop, and mountain goats leap easily over crevices and ledges.

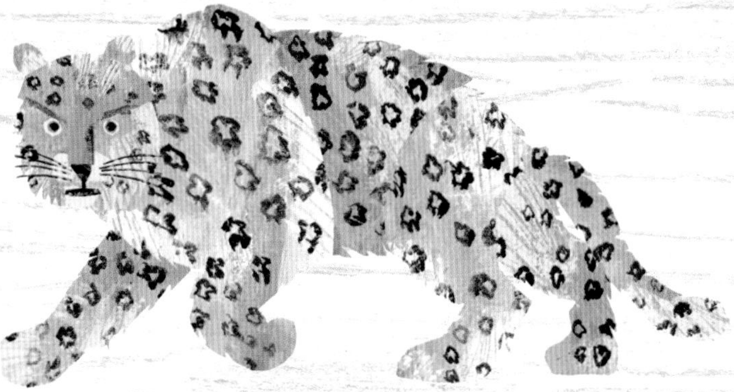

Snow leopard

Mountain goat

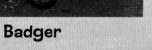

Badger

Rabbit

Earthworm

Under the ocean

The different levels of the ocean are called zones. They range from the sun-kissed surface to the darkest depths.

Watery world

Planet Earth looks blue from space because of its vast oceans. Beneath the calm surface is an underwater world swimming with all kinds of incredible sea life.

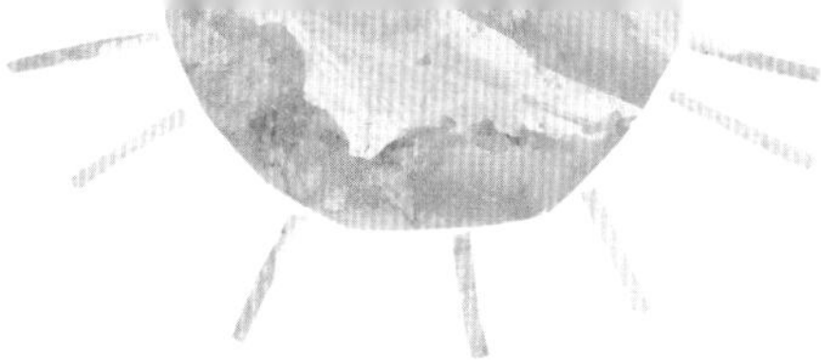

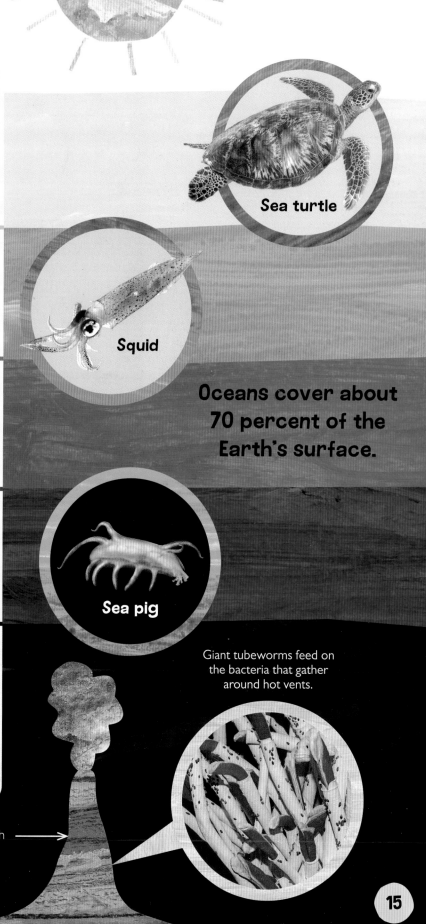

Sunlight zone

The sun helps keep the top layer of the ocean warm, light, and full of food, such as small fish and seaweed.

Twilight zone

Less sunlight reaches this level, so the water is colder and darker. Many twilight-zone animals have big eyes to see better in the darkness.

Midnight zone

In this dark zone, animals have to withstand pressure from all the water pressing down from the zones above.

Oceans cover about 70 percent of the Earth's surface.

Abyss

Not many animals live at such a great depth because of the extreme water pressure and freezing cold. Brrr!

Hadal

Hardly any animals live here because there is nothing to eat on the ocean floor, except for a few waste scraps and tiny living things called bacteria. It is completely dark, so some hadal animals have no eyes at all!

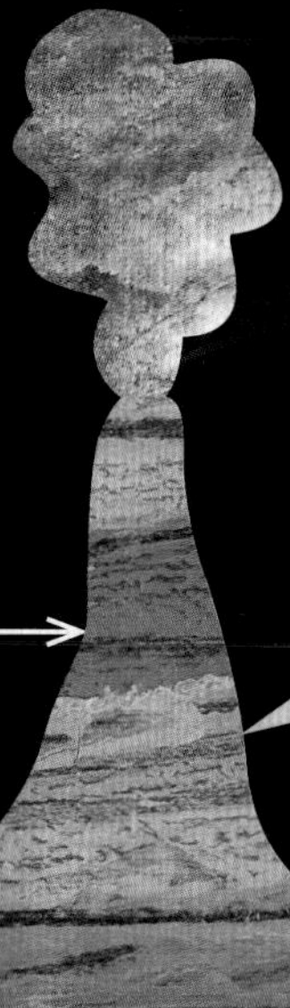

Vents on the seabed gush out steaming-hot water from deep inside Earth.

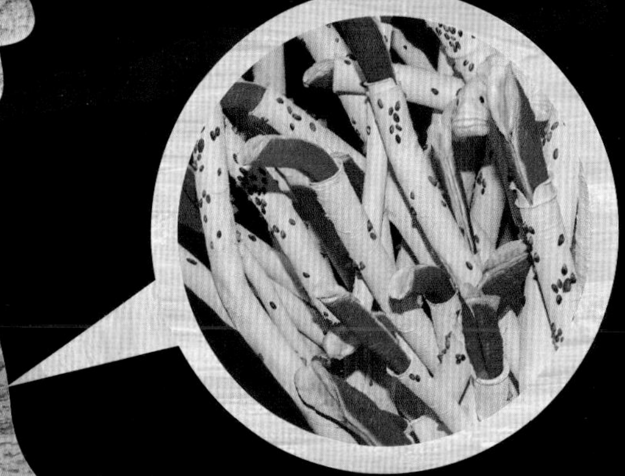

Giant tubeworms feed on the bacteria that gather around hot vents.

Rivers and wetlands

Wherever there is water, there is life. From flowing rivers and shimmering lakes to soggy swamps and muddy marshes, watery habitats attract animals of all kinds.

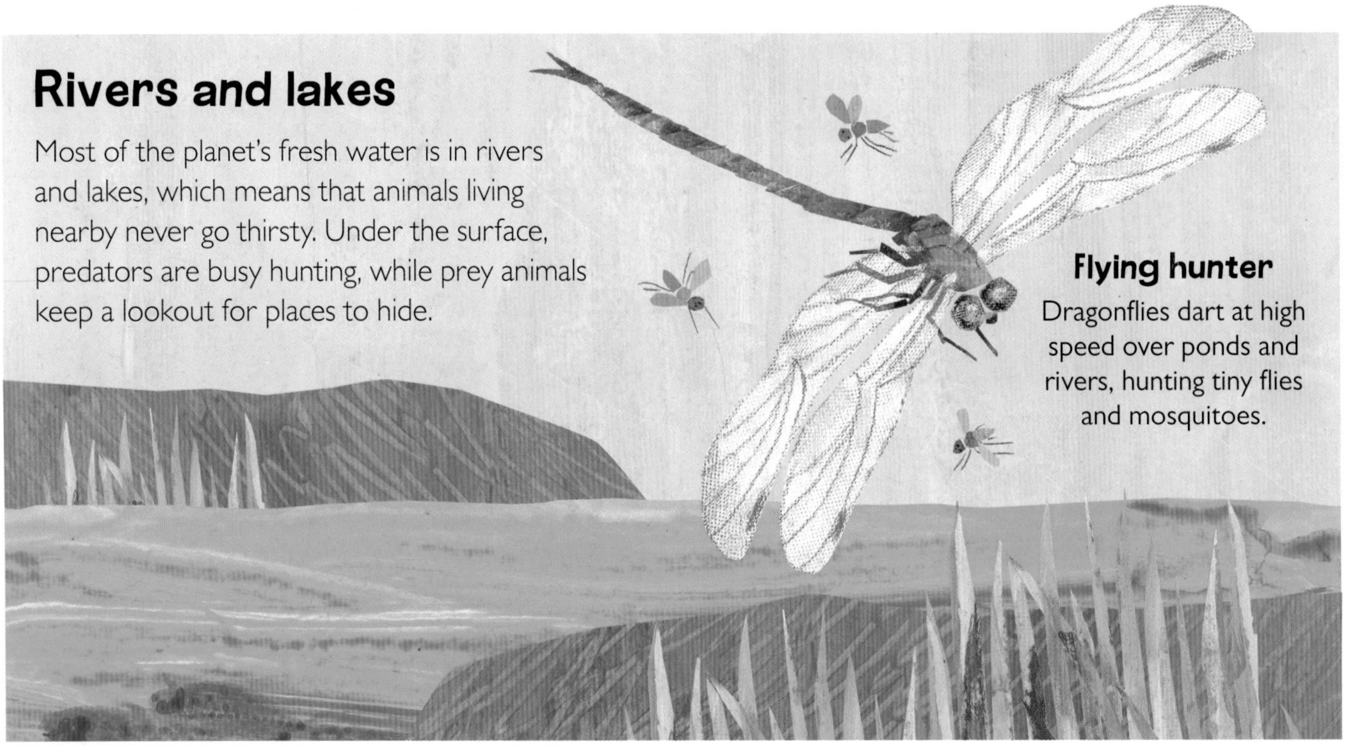

Rivers and lakes

Most of the planet's fresh water is in rivers and lakes, which means that animals living nearby never go thirsty. Under the surface, predators are busy hunting, while prey animals keep a lookout for places to hide.

Flying hunter

Dragonflies dart at high speed over ponds and rivers, hunting tiny flies and mosquitoes.

Hunting bear

The grizzly bear waits patiently on the riverbank, ready to catch slippery salmon with its huge claws.

Diving bird

The shiny blue kingfisher dives from a low tree branch to snatch fish with its slim, sharp bill.

Skating insect

A pond skater has special hairs on its legs that help it to walk on the surface of the water.

Watery wetlands

Swamps, bogs, and marshes are all types of wetland. Wetlands provide plenty of water and food for many different animals.

Sneaky snapper

Crocodiles hide in swampy waters, ready to attack passing prey.

Best of both worlds

Frogs and toads can live both on land and in water, so wetlands make a perfect home for them.

Fishing for dinner

Long-legged herons wade through shallow waters searching for tasty fish to spear with their bills.

Stealthy predator

The anaconda is a huge snake that hunts in the water for caimans, which are members of the crocodile family.

Deserts and savannas

In the desert, very little rain falls, while on the sunbaked savanna, the long dry season means there is a shortage of food and water. Regardless, plenty of animals survive and thrive in these habitats.

Desert dunes

Life is hard in a hot desert. In addition to a lack of water, animals face sizzling-hot sunshine all day long. After sunset, the night is freezing cold.

Clever camels

Camels store fat inside their humps to help them survive long periods with little water or food.

Shade-seeker

Like most desert-dwellers, the rattlesnake heads for a shady spot during the day, when the sun is strongest.

Scorpion shelter

A scorpion will dig itself a hole in the sand to avoid the intense heat. Then at night, it comes out to hunt.

Desert antelope

The Arabian oryx is well suited to desert life. Its white fur reflects the sun's rays and helps to keep it cool.

Cold deserts

Deserts don't have to be hot. In frozen Antarctica, there is very little rainfall, so it is a desert, too.

Groups of grazers

Herds of zebra roam the savanna, feeding on the grass and staying close to each other for safety.

Hungry rhinos

Thick-skinned rhinoceroses have to munch stacks of grass every day to stay strong enough to fight predators.

Observant ostriches

An ostrich has lanky legs and a long neck to help it spot predators over the tall savanna grass.

Wide grasslands

In the African savanna, dry grasses grow thick and strong in the scorching sunshine. These plants provide food for grazing animals like antelopes, zebras, and gazelles.

Tropical grassland, like the African savanna, is hot all year round. Temperate grassland has hot summers and cold winters.

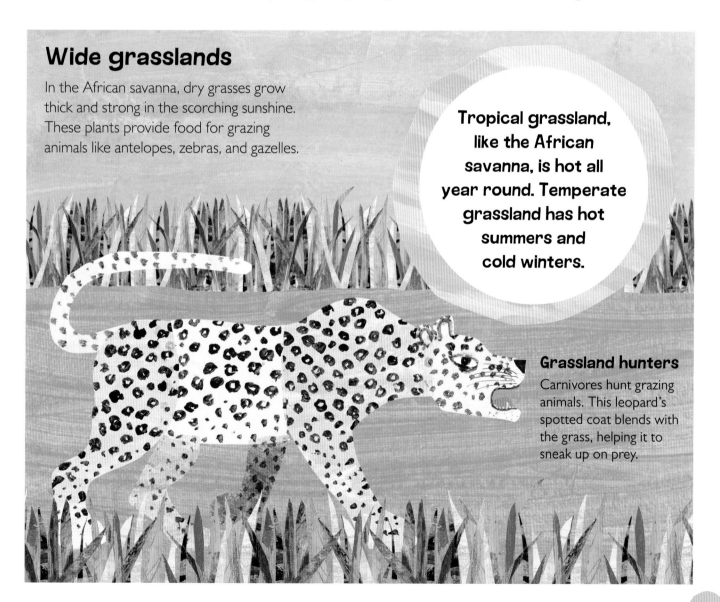

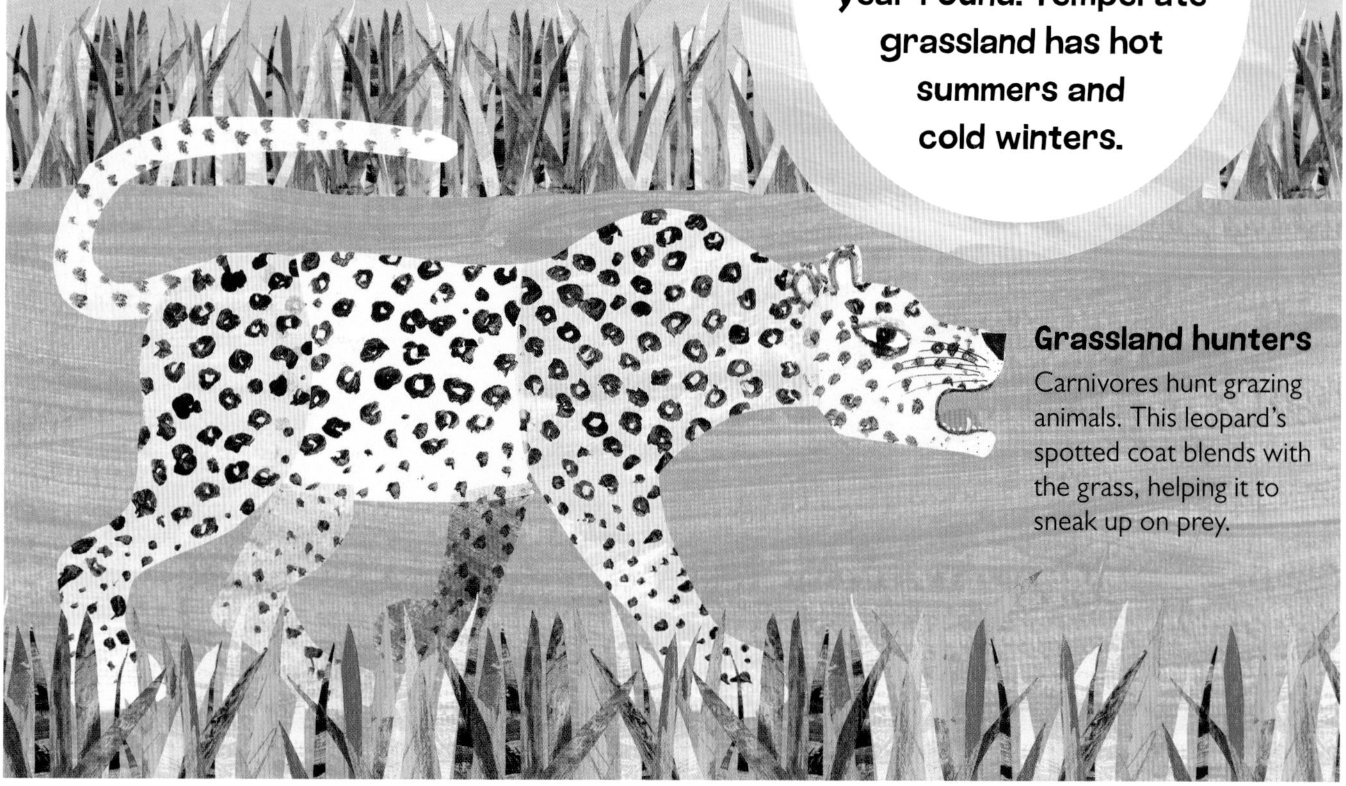

Grassland hunters

Carnivores hunt grazing animals. This leopard's spotted coat blends with the grass, helping it to sneak up on prey.

Bird's nests

Woodland birds fly back and forth, collecting materials to build their treetop nests. Twigs, moss, and grass make a cozy home for a bird.

Homes and hideaways

All animals, including humans, need a safe place to live. Many animals are expert builders, using things they find to create homes in different shapes, sizes, and styles.

Wasp nest

Insect homes

Birds are not the only animals to make nests. Wasps chew wood to make paper nests that hang from branches. Their wet mouths act as glue to seal the paper walls. Termites build giant mounds out of soil and animal droppings. Yuck!

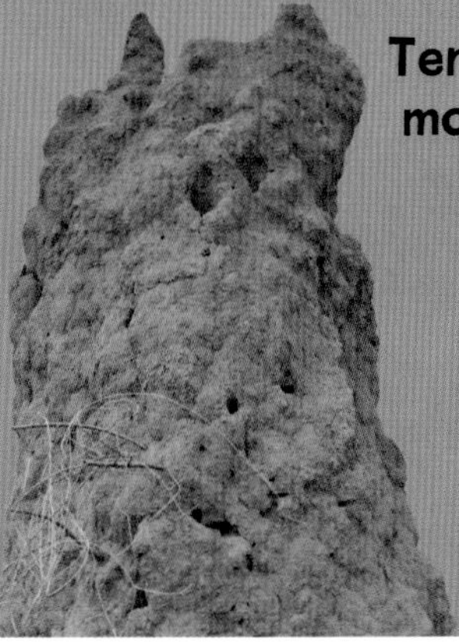

Termite mound

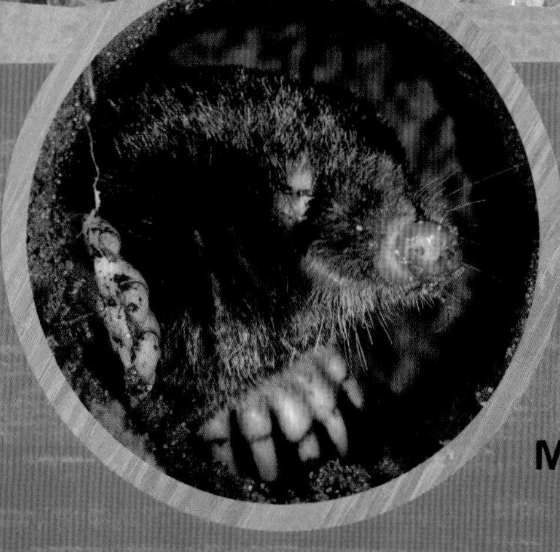

Mole

Cozy burrows

The safest shelter for small mammals like moles, rabbits, and chipmunks is underground. A mole digs a network of tunnels and underground "rooms" where it can sleep and eat in peace.

Beaver lodge

Beavers build floating homes, called lodges, using sticks, mud, and rocks. They make small underwater entrances so they can swim up and sneak inside without predators seeing them.

Secondhand shell

Some animals don't need a permanent home. The hermit crab uses another animal's empty shell as a temporary shelter. When the hermit crab grows too big for the shell, it simply finds a new one.

Cub care

Foxes and polar bears dig dens just below the ground. Inside, their cubs stay warm and safe until the youngsters are ready to venture into the outside world.

Fox den

Polar bear den

Amazing adaptations

Life can be a struggle for survival when animals are faced with extreme weather, scary predators, or a shortage of food and water. To stay safe, raise their young, and live long, healthy lives, animals need to be able to adapt to their surroundings.

Champion sprinter

The cheetah is the fastest animal on land, and the only cat that can't draw its claws back in. The claws act like built-in running spikes, similar to the shoes worn by Olympic sprinters.

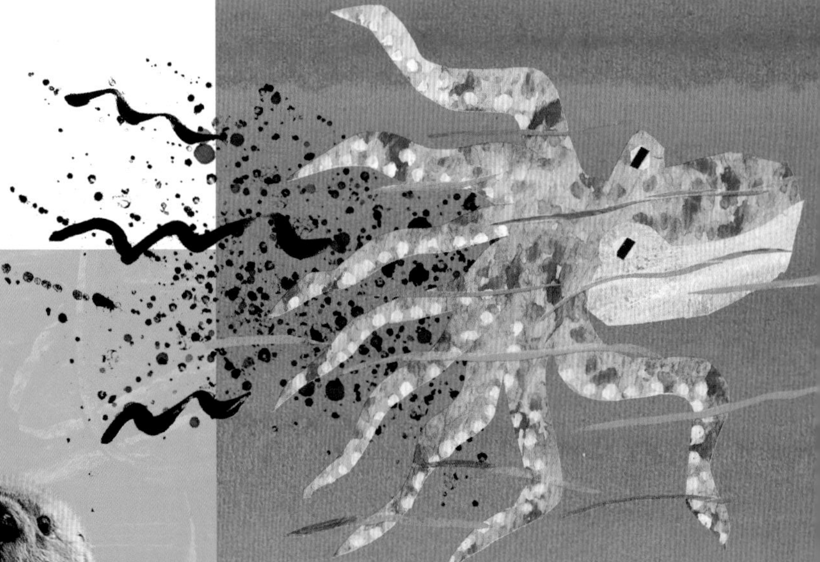

Snug in the sea

A furry coat is essential for mammals living in cold conditions. Sea otters have the thickest fur of any animal, keeping them warm even in the chilliest waters.

Disappearing act

Now you see the common octopus, now you don't! When under attack, it releases a puff of black ink, turning the water around it cloudy. This cunning trick confuses predators, giving the octopus time to escape.

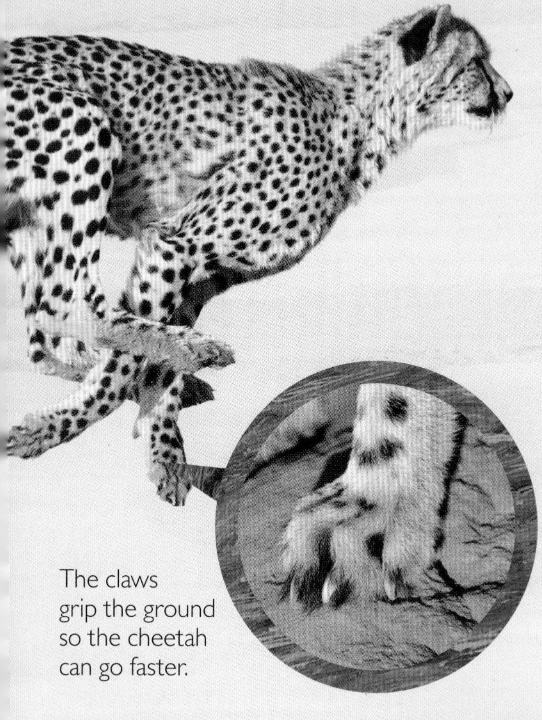

The claws grip the ground so the cheetah can go faster.

Saving energy

Koalas eat eucalyptus leaves, which don't provide them with much energy. So, a koala snoozes for up to 18 hours every day to save as much precious energy as possible.

Sand survivor

A camel is well equipped to deal with desert life. Long lashes blink away sand, while its nostrils can be shut tight to keep out sandstorms. Padded feet protect camels from the sizzling-hot sand.

Tongue tool

The giant anteater has a sticky, spiny tongue that is as long as your arm! This tongue is perfectly adapted to poking deep inside termite nests and slurping up hundreds of insects at a time.

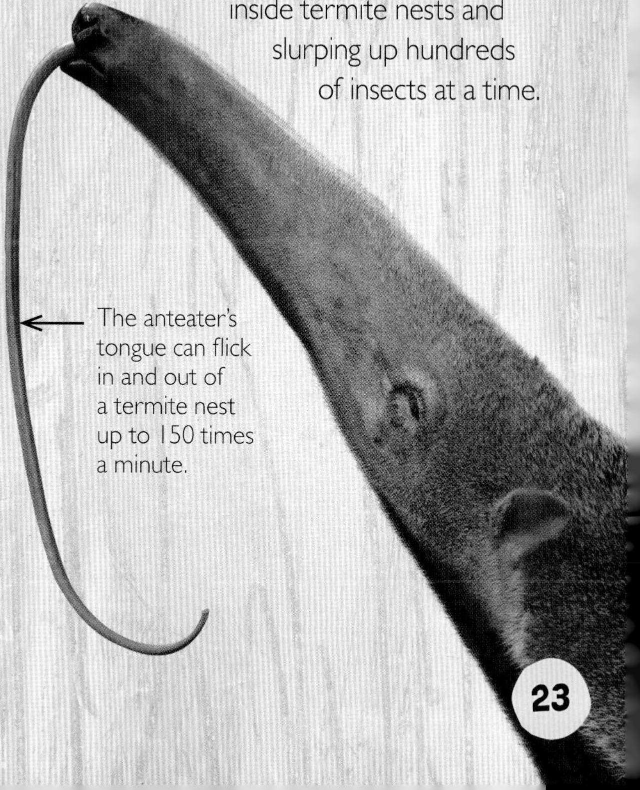

The anteater's tongue can flick in and out of a termite nest up to 150 times a minute.

Heads and tails

In the animal kingdom, there are thousands of different-shaped heads and tails, and each one is superbly suited to its owner's lifestyle.

Head starts

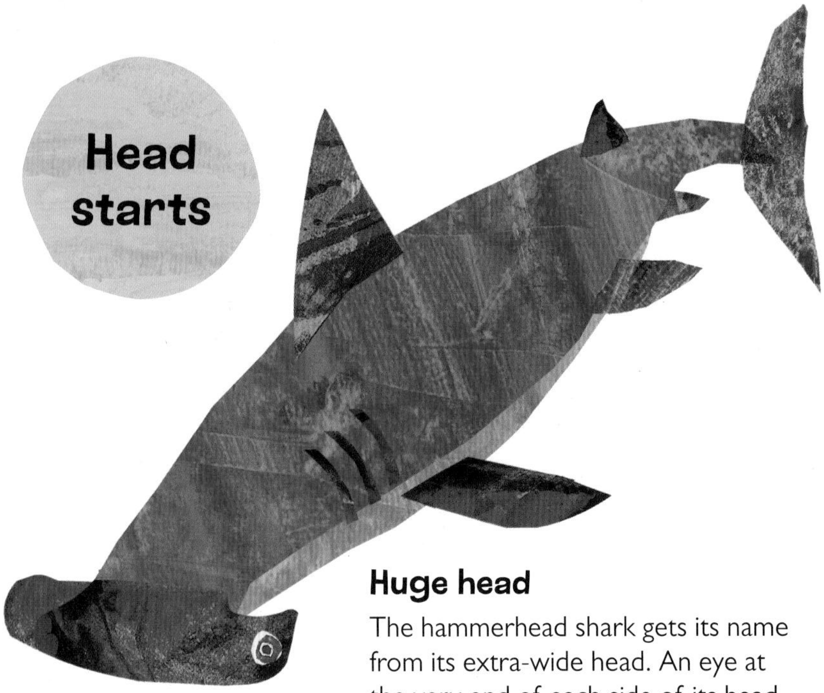

Huge head

The hammerhead shark gets its name from its extra-wide head. An eye at the very end of each side of its head allows the shark to see in all directions.

Hunter's vision

Like many land predators, a wolf's eyes face forward. This means wolves are able to spot prey that is far away. They can also judge distances very well, allowing them to pounce on fast-moving prey.

Alert to danger

Many animals that are hunted by predators, such as rabbits, have eyes on each side of their heads. This allows them to see clearly all around them, which is useful when watching out for hungry wolves!

Twisting neck

Owls are brilliantly bendy birds. They are so flexible that they can twist their heads almost all the way around. This means they can look behind them without having to turn the rest of their body.

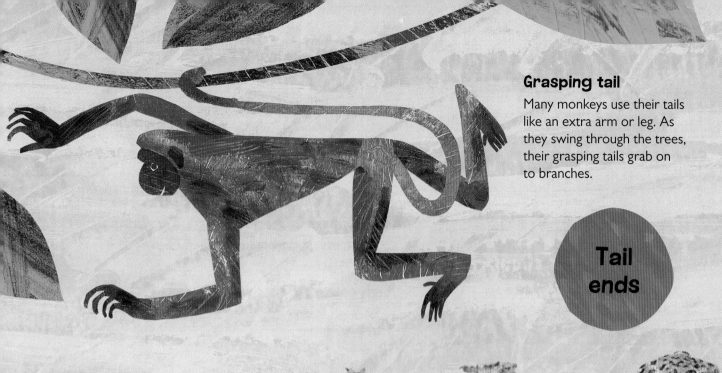

Tail ends

Grasping tail

Many monkeys use their tails like an extra arm or leg. As they swing through the trees, their grasping tails grab on to branches.

Quick getaway

Some lizards, such as this gecko, have a nifty escape tactic if an attacker grabs their tail. The tail separates from the body so the lizard can run off. Later, a new tail grows in its place.

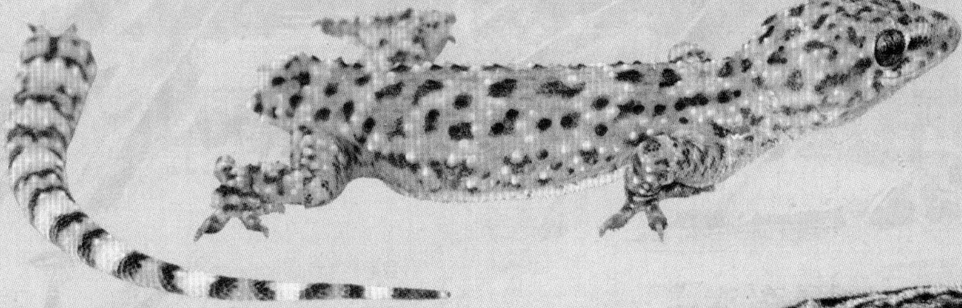

Tell-tail signs

A dog's tail gives humans and other dogs a good idea of its mood. A wagging tail suggests a happy dog. A tail held high shows confidence, while a low, tucked-in tail usually means the dog is scared.

Happy dog!

Furry blanket

The snow leopard uses its long tail to balance on narrow branches and steep rocks. On snowy nights, the tail acts as a soft blanket, keeping this big cat cozy.

Swimming aid

A beaver's flat, scaly tail is perfect for swimming. It acts like a paddle to steer the mammal through the water. If a beaver senses danger, it slaps its tail hard on the water to warn others.

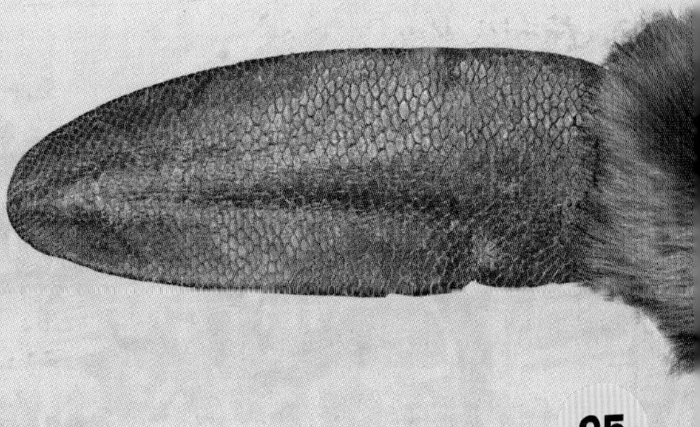

Paws and claws

Most animals don't have hands like we do, but they still have different ways to grasp, grab, and grip things.

Eagle's talons

Tearing talons

Birds of prey, such as eagles, have razor-sharp claws called talons. They are strong enough to keep hold of birds, rabbits, and even deer.

Lion's paw

Deadly combination

Ferocious big cats have large, padded paws with cutting claws. The pads help them to stalk their prey silently. The claws dig into prey and grip so tightly that there is no escape.

Thumbs up

Some animals have thumbs that can move around, just as ours do. The giant panda uses its thumbs to grip bamboo stalks while it chews the day away.

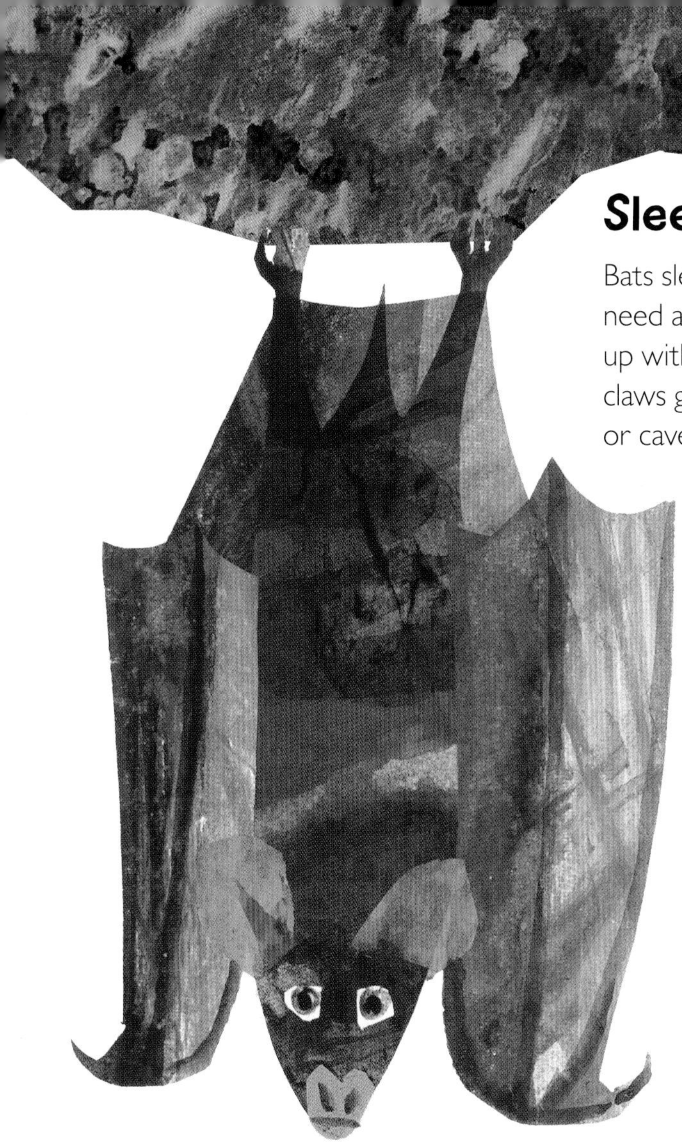

Sleep tight!

Bats sleep upside down, so they need a strong grip to avoid waking up with a bump! Their small, strong claws grip tightly to tree branches or cave roofs. Zzzz…

Flexible trunk

Elephants use their bendable trunks to grab branches, pick up food, and spray water. A trunk is so nimble it could even turn the pages of this book.

Blue crab's claw

Crunching claws

Watch out, worms and fish! A crab can give a nasty nip with its pair of powerful pincers. Once those claws get a grip, it can be very hard to break free.

Ocean heavyweight

The blue whale is the biggest animal alive. This mega mammal is the same size as a passenger airplane. Its huge heart is as big as a small car, and its tongue weighs the same as an elephant.

Land giant

The African elephant is the largest and heaviest animal on land. African elephants are much taller and chunkier than their relatives, Asian elephants.

Tallest of all

Giraffes are the tallest living animal. These long-legged, gentle giants have the world's longest neck. A full-grown giraffe is taller than three adult humans standing on top of each other.

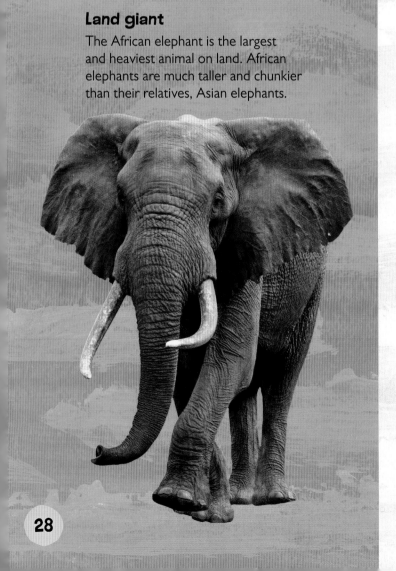

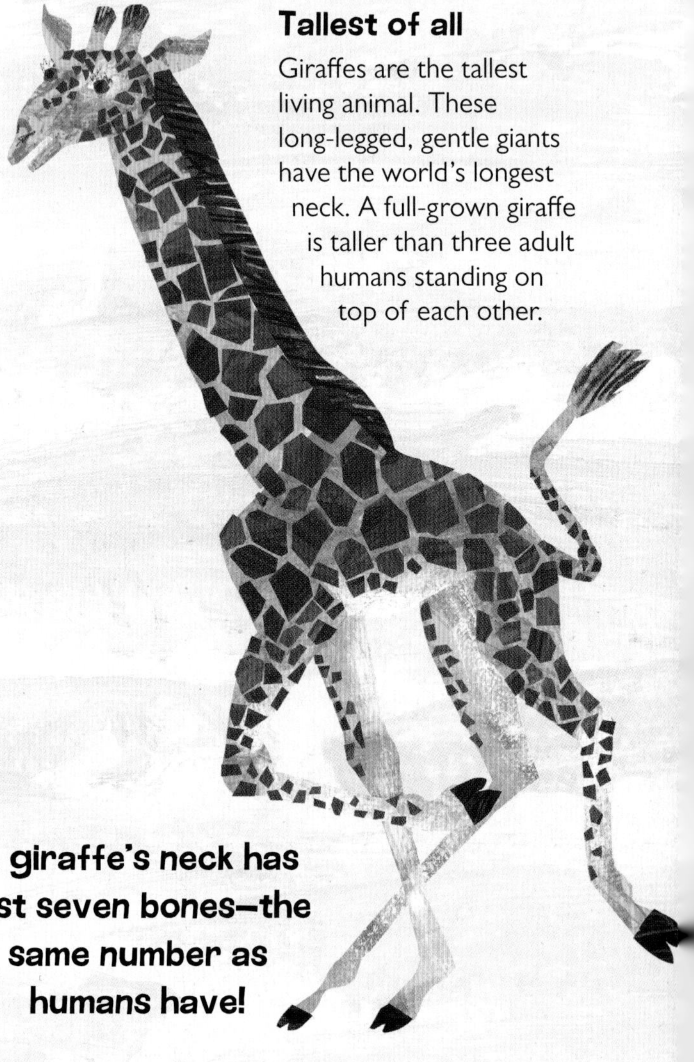

A giraffe's neck has just seven bones—the same number as humans have!

Big and small

Planet Earth is full of incredible animals whose size, whether massive or miniature, makes them record-breakers.

Tiny flier

The world's smallest bird is the bee hummingbird. As you can guess from its name, it's only the size of a bee. This bird is so small, it could sit on the end of a pencil!

This hummingbird flaps its wings 80 times every second!

A long stretch

The bootlace worm is the longest animal on Earth. Although only as thick as the laces on your sneakers, this record-breaking ocean-dweller is twice as long as a blue whale!

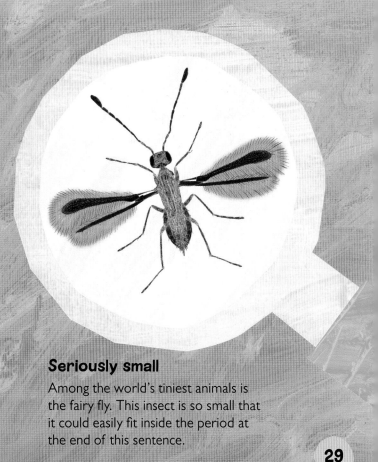

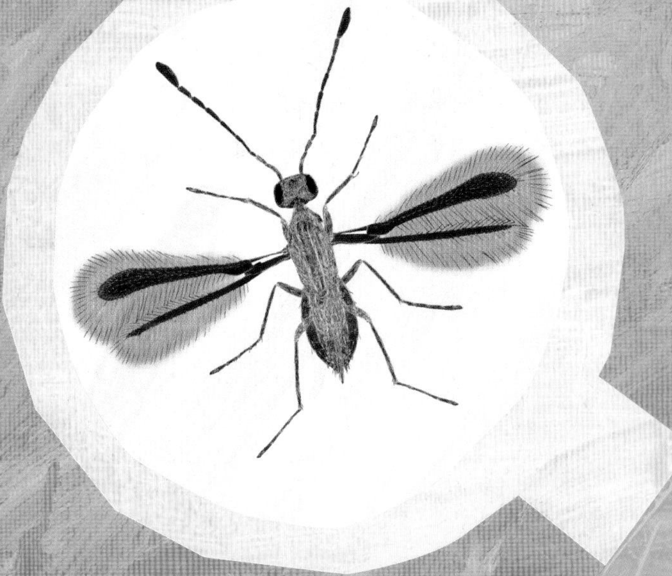

Seriously small

Among the world's tiniest animals is the fairy fly. This insect is so small that it could easily fit inside the period at the end of this sentence.

1 day

Shortest-living animal

Time flies for mayflies. They live for just one, very busy day. Within 24 hours, they are born, find a mate, make babies, and die.

6 months

Shortest-living mammal

The Müller's giant Sunda rat lives in the forests of Southeast Asia. It only lives for about six months.

Longest-living fish

The huge, slow-swimming Greenland shark lives in the Arctic and has a superlong life span of almost 400 years.

400 years

Animal life spans

Some animals live for many years or even centuries, while other creatures have to squeeze a whole lifetime into a single day!

Longest-living mammal

Bowhead whales live in the icy waters of the Arctic Ocean. Some have lived for more than 210 years.

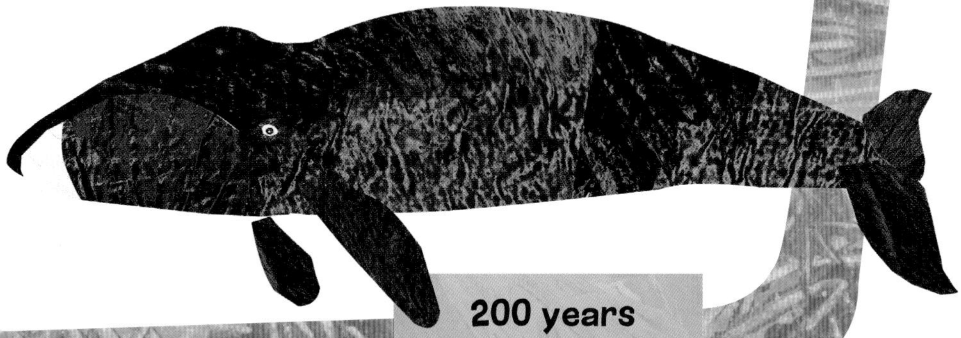

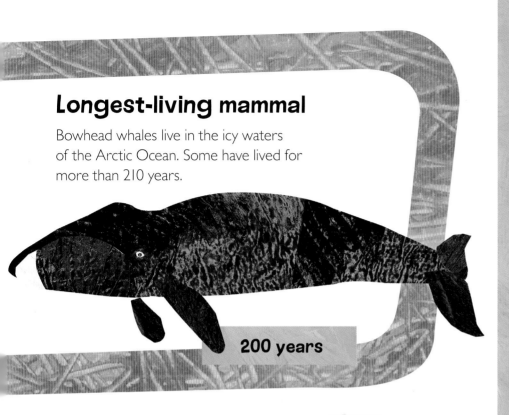

200 years

Longest-living animal

The giant barrel sponge can live for a mind-boggling 2,300 years! Despite looking like a plant, it is actually a slow-moving ocean animal.

2,300 years

Everlasting life

The tiny turritopsis, also called the immortal jellyfish, can regrow its whole body to repair itself. So, as long as it keeps from being eaten, this jellyfish could live forever!

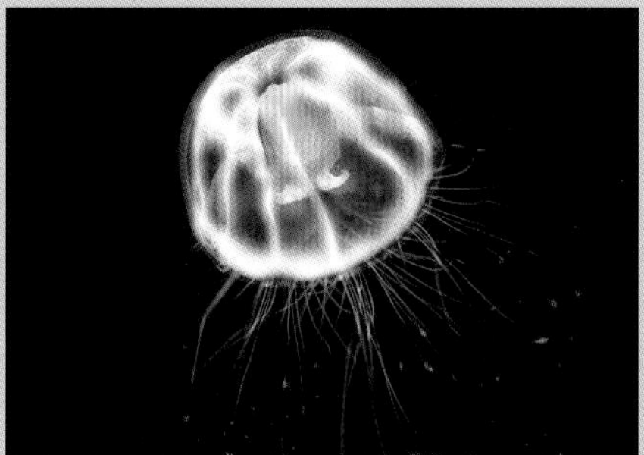

Happy birthday!

Here are two animals that have celebrated a LOT of birthdays...

Mighty Ming

The oldest animal ever found is Ming, a quahog clam that was pulled from the ocean in 2006. Experts calculated that Ming was 507 years old.

Tireless tortoise

Jonathan the giant tortoise is the world's oldest living land animal. He celebrated his 190th birthday in 2022 on Saint Helena, the South Atlantic island where he lives.

Fast and slow

In a race between all the animals on land, sea, and air, who would cross the finish line first and who would still be stuck at the start? Ready, set, go!

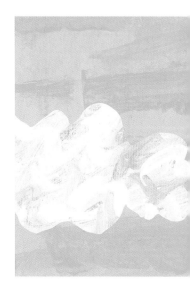

Slowest on land

The banana slug is one of the slowest movers on land. It travels about the length of a playing card every minute.

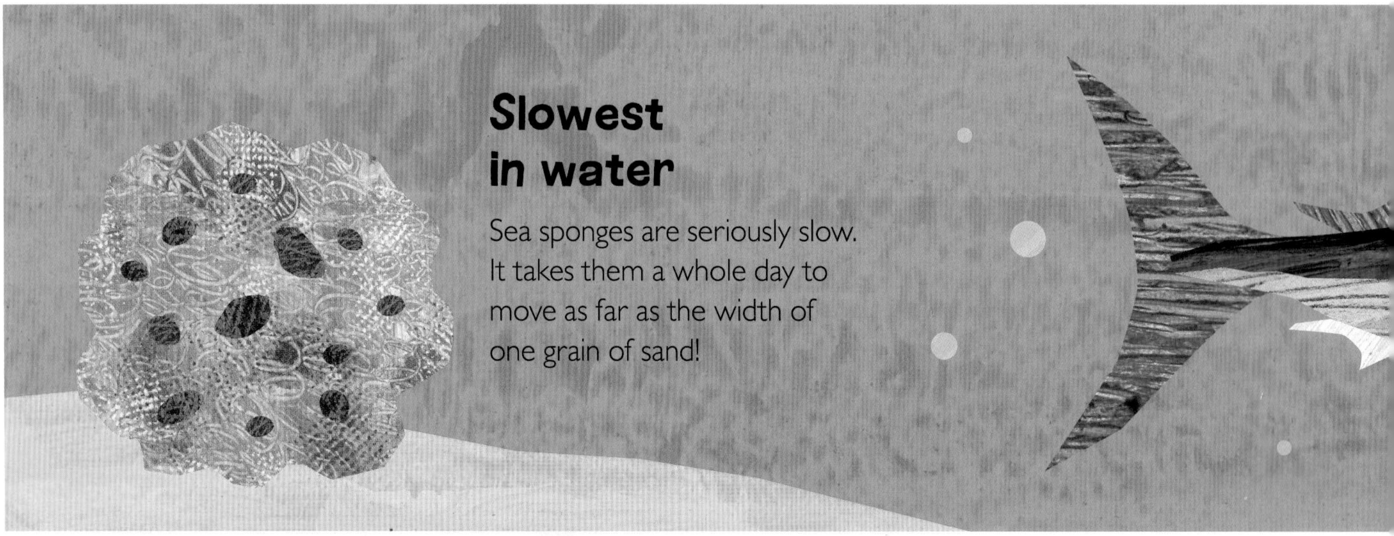

Slowest in water

Sea sponges are seriously slow. It takes them a whole day to move as far as the width of one grain of sand!

Fastest in the air

Flying into first place is the peregrine falcon. No other animal can beat this bird of prey. It can dive downward at the same top speed as a Formula 1 race car.

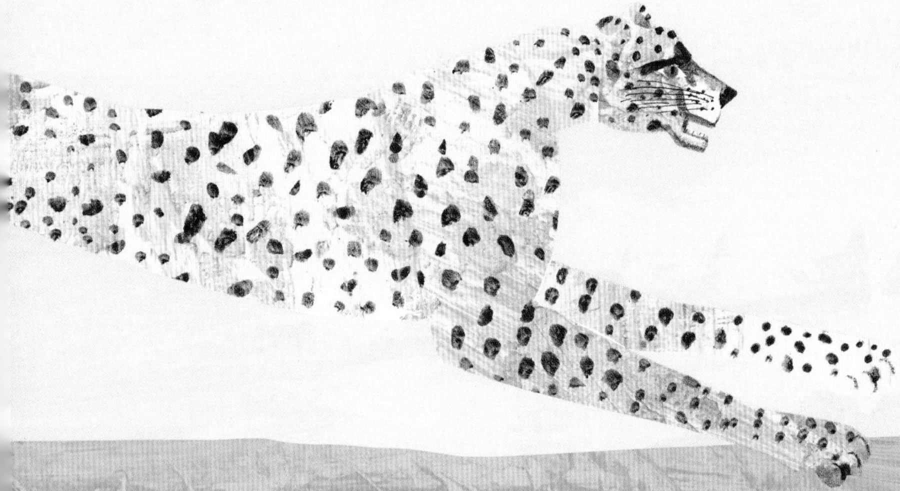

Fastest on land

The cheetah takes first prize for the fastest runner. Its flexible spine and long legs power this big cat through grasslands at the same speed as a car on the highway.

Fastest in water

The black marlin zooms through the water 10 times quicker than an Olympic swimmer. This fast fish is a high-speed hunter, slashing at prey with its sharp bill.

Spiked and smooth

From the prickliest porcupine to the smoothest snake, animals have an amazing array of skin types. This outer layer can protect against icy cold or burning heat, prevent predator attacks, or grow flight feathers for takeoff.

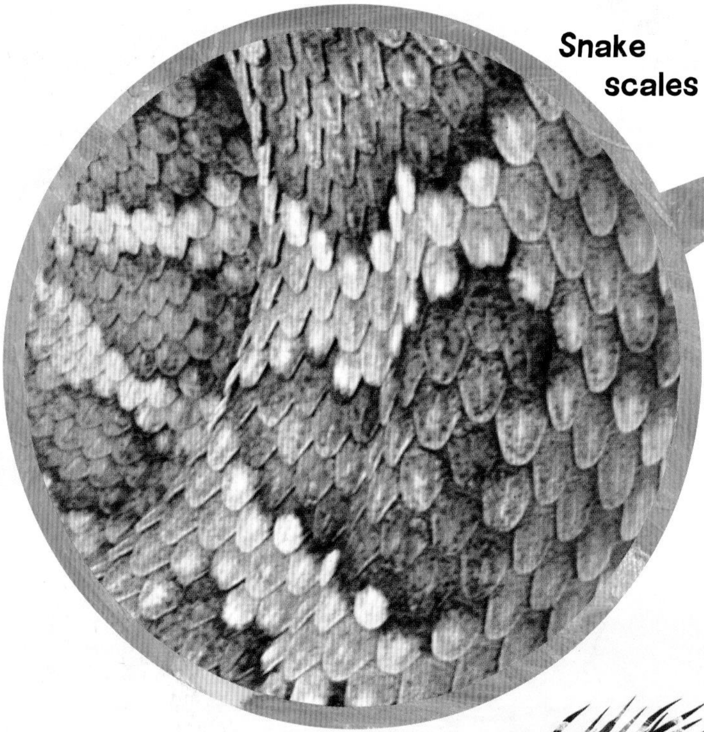

Snake scales

Scales

Many insects, fish, and reptiles have scaly skin. Hundreds of tiny, tough scales create a covering of body armor. Rattlesnakes like this one shake their tails so fast that the scales make a rattling sound.

Porcupine spikes

Spikes

Spiked skin makes an animal almost impossible to eat. Hedgehogs, porcupines, and thorn bugs put predators off by curling into spiked balls.

Feathers

Birds grow feathers out of their skin. A soft, strong layer of feathers gives a bird warmth and protection. Feathered wings also help many birds to fly.

Parrot feathers

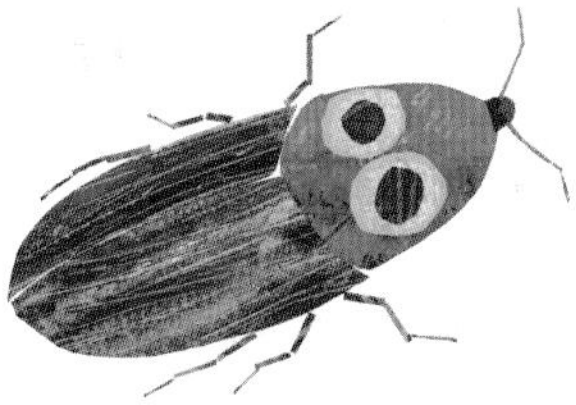

Insects are inside-out compared to us! Our skeleton is covered in skin, but insects have a skeleton on the outside, with a skinlike layer underneath.

Thick skin

Some large mammals, including hippopotamuses, rhinoceroses, and elephants, have thick, leathery skin. They cool off in water, using sloppy mud to block the sunlight. Hippos even produce their own oily, red sunscreen to protect their skin.

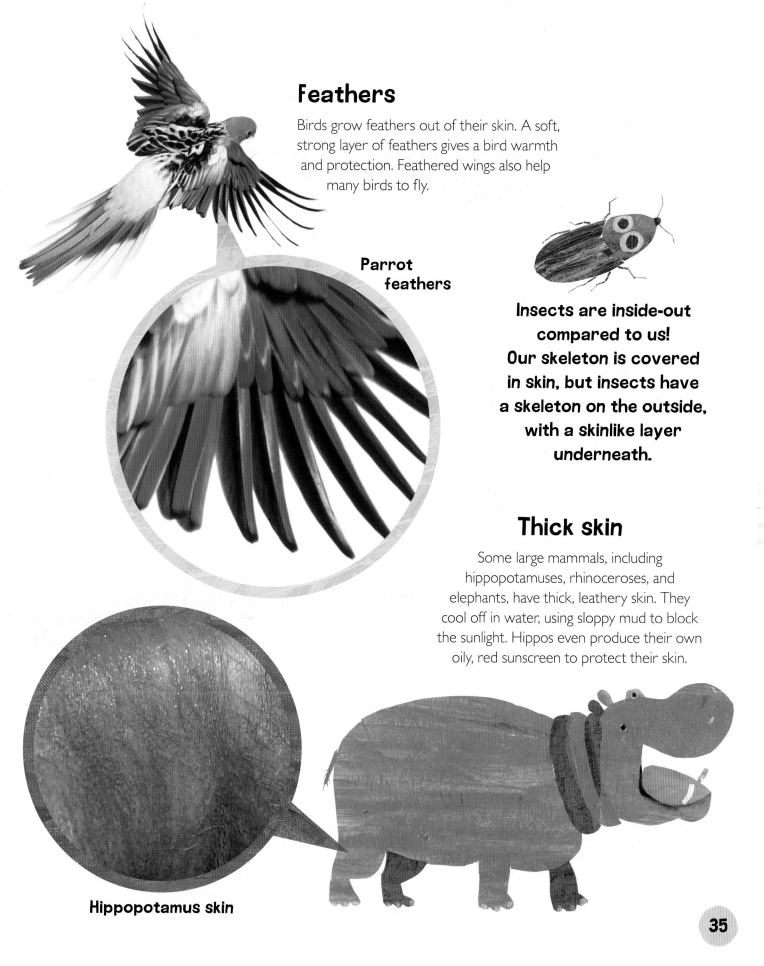

Hippopotamus skin

Blending in and standing out

Some animals are show-offs, while others prefer to stay out of sight. Here are some clever disappearing acts, incredible impersonations, and standout displays.

Stick insect

Is it a branch? Is it a bug? No. It's a stick insect! These insects merge with twigs and branches so well that predators assume they are part of the plant.

Hiding away

Avoiding the limelight is one way to keep safe. Animals pretend to be something else or simply disappear into the background.

Hoverfly

Despite looking just like a wasp, this flying fraudster is harmless. Predators assume that striped hoverflies must have a deadly sting, so they steer clear of them.

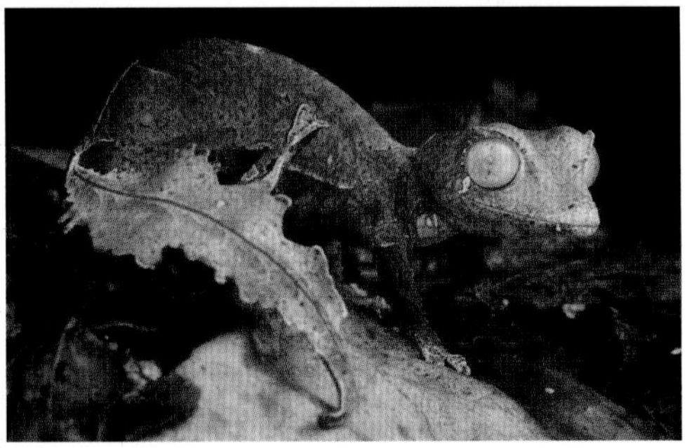

Leaf-tailed gecko

This little lizard has a mottled brown body and a tail that looks just like a dead leaf. It sits perfectly still on a tree, invisible to any predators that pass by.

Poison dart frog

You can't miss South America's poison dart frogs! Although they are tiny, their dazzling colors warn predators that their skin is poisonous.

Poison dart frogs make their poison from insects that they eat.

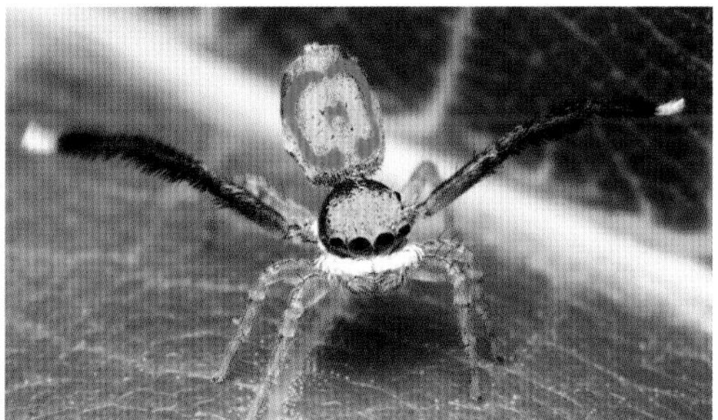

Peacock spider

Despite being the size of a grain of rice, this groovy mover wiggles its colored body flap and gets its eight legs going in a dance designed to attract females.

Frigate bird

The male frigate bird inflates a stretchy pouch under its throat like a big, red balloon. This unusual trick is performed to impress female frigate birds.

Showing off

These super show-offs are desperate to attract attention and find a mate.

Super senses

Animals survive in their different habitats by using their five senses, just like we do. Their hearing, touch, taste, eyesight, and sense of smell are often much better than ours.

Big ears

The tiny fennec fox lives in the deserts of North Africa, where its oversized ears are used to listen for prey animals scurrying around in the sand.

Feeling the way

The manatee, or sea cow, has a powerful sense of touch. The sensitive hairs on its body feel the surroundings and recognize other manatees.

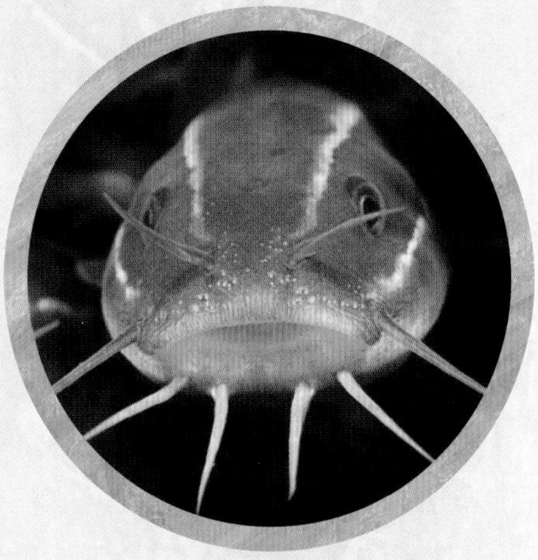

Taste test

The catfish has long whiskers that fan out from its face. These are covered with tiny taste buds that can detect fish and clams in the dark waters.

Types of teeth

Depending on the foods that tickle their taste buds, animals have different-shaped mouths and teeth. Fish and reptiles, like this gharial, have rows of identical sharp teeth. Most mammals have a mixture of sharp and flat teeth, so they can tear meat and also chew plants. Birds have a beak instead of teeth. Amphibians have no teeth at all.

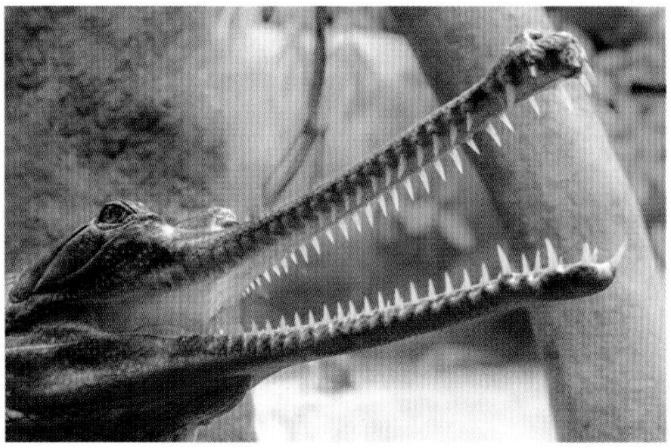

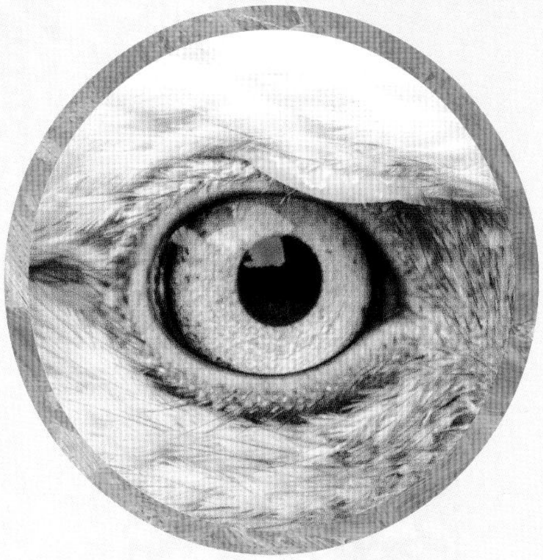

Eagle eyes

An eagle's eyesight is eight times better than human eyesight. This sharp vision helps the bird to spot prey up to 2 miles (3 km) away.

Nifty nose

A bear can smell things 2,000 times better than a human can, making it easy for this predator to sniff out food or possible mates over long distances.

Shooting skills

When the archerfish spots prey on an overhanging branch, it squirts a high-speed, pinpoint-accurate jet of water from its mouth to topple the insect from its perch.

Feet first

Butterflies use special sensors on their feet to check a flower's taste. If the flower passes the taste test, the butterfly settles and sucks up the sweet nectar.

Musical legs

Male grasshoppers make their own sweet song by rubbing their back legs against their wings. This unique tune attracts the attention of nearby females.

Whale song

The blue whale is one of the loudest animals on Earth. It swims along, singing its unique song, for hours at a time. These tunes can be heard by other whales hundreds of miles away.

Meerkat chat

Meerkats work as a team, taking turns defending their burrows. They communicate by squeaking, but this turns to loud shrieks if a predator comes too close.

Sending messages

Some animals use their voices to communicate with each other, filling the air with squeaks, songs, or screams. Others find more unusual ways to make themselves understood.

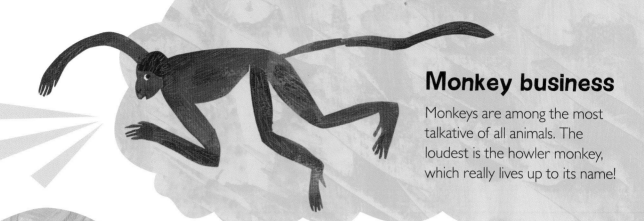

Monkey business

Monkeys are among the most talkative of all animals. The loudest is the howler monkey, which really lives up to its name!

The howler monkey's booming call can be heard more than 3 miles (5 km) away!

Chameleon colors

Without making a sound, chameleons can still communicate by changing color. This tells other chameleons if they are feeling calm, annoyed, or looking for love!

Call of the wild

Lions are known for their deafening roar. This terrifying sound is a warning to rival males to back off from the family group, called a pride.

Wild and tame

The pets that share our homes are very different from animals that live in the wild. This is why you might welcome in a domestic cat, but not let a prowling panther through the door!

On the farm

Some animals are cared for by people, but do not live indoors with them. Instead, they live on farms. Farm animals include cows, donkeys, horses, chickens, sheep, pigs, and goats.

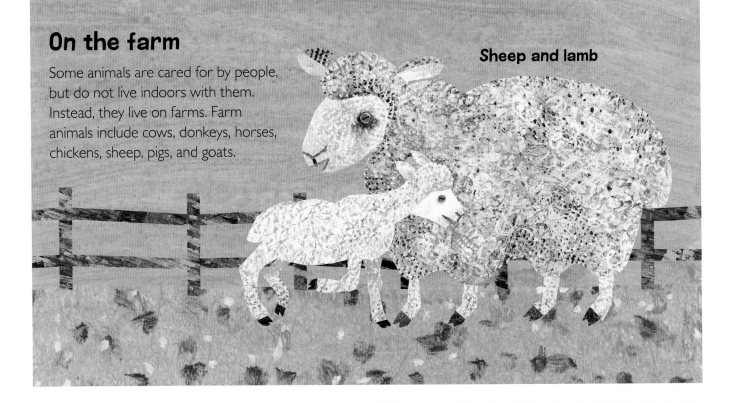

Sheep and lamb

Part of the family

Animals that live in our homes are called pets. Some animals have developed over time to prefer being with humans. Popular pets include cats, dogs, rabbits, hamsters, fish, and tortoises. More unusual pets, such as lizards, snakes, and spiders, need expert care and attention to keep them healthy.

Hamster

In-betweeners

Sometimes, farm animals or pets escape or get lost. This means that they are no longer cared for by people, but instead live in the wild and have to fend for themselves. They are called feral animals. Some animals that can become feral are wild boar, goats, and deer.

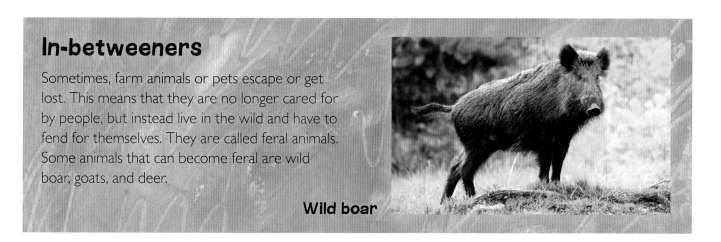

Wild boar

Wild ones

Most animals on Earth live their lives in their natural surroundings, without interacting with humans. Wild animals, such as this red panda, survive by finding their own water, food, and shelter.

Red panda

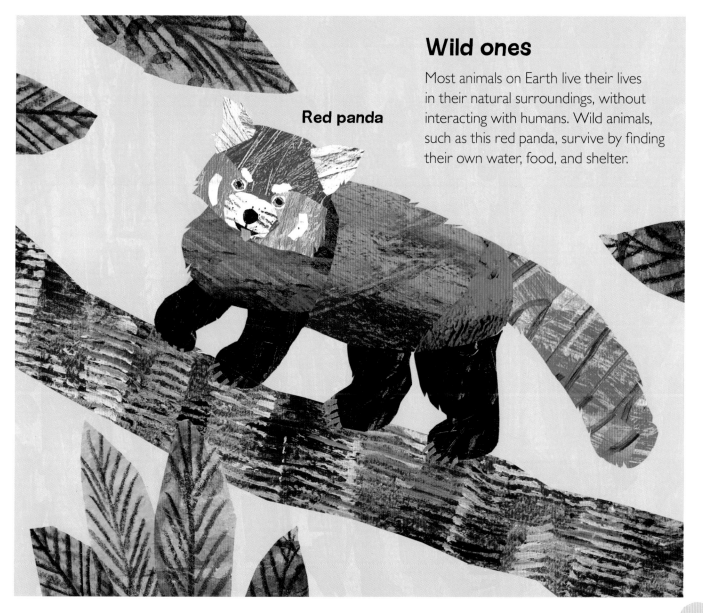

Elephant seal

Monarch butterflies

Seal swim

Northern elephant seals make a marathon swim of 13,000 miles (21,000 km) from the United States to the North Pacific Ocean to find prey. Their long journey is rewarded with lots of delicious squid and fish. Yum!

Long-haul flight

Monarch butterflies leave cool Canada and head south to mild Mexico. Exhausted upon arrival, they take a long sleep, wake to lay their eggs, then die. The baby butterflies then fly 3,000 miles (4,800 km) all the way back to Canada.

Animal travelers

Some animals make regular journeys, called migrations, to escape cold winters, find food, or have their babies.

Newly hatched monarch butterflies often fly to the exact tree their mothers started out from!

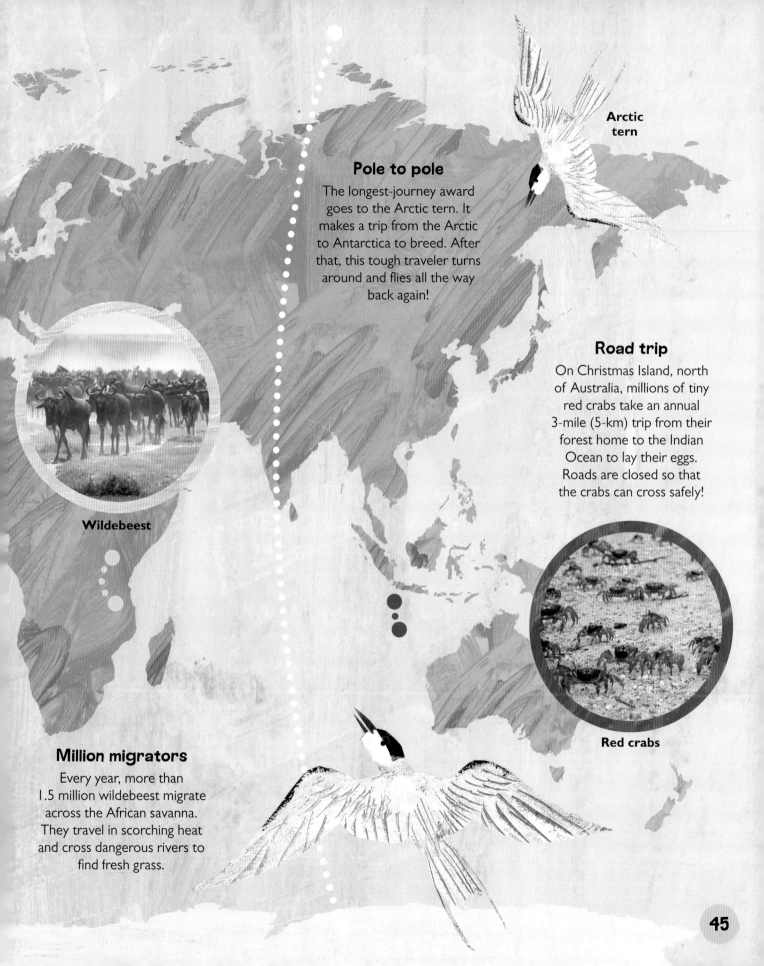

Arctic tern

Pole to pole

The longest-journey award goes to the Arctic tern. It makes a trip from the Arctic to Antarctica to breed. After that, this tough traveler turns around and flies all the way back again!

Wildebeest

Road trip

On Christmas Island, north of Australia, millions of tiny red crabs take an annual 3-mile (5-km) trip from their forest home to the Indian Ocean to lay their eggs. Roads are closed so that the crabs can cross safely!

Red crabs

Million migrators

Every year, more than 1.5 million wildebeest migrate across the African savanna. They travel in scorching heat and cross dangerous rivers to find fresh grass.

Marvelous mammals

Milk supply

Mammal mothers produce milk inside their bodies to feed their babies. Young mammals feed on this nourishing milk for months or years to help them grow.

Cow and calf

Giving birth

Most mammals grow inside their mother's body until they are ready to be born. Female rhinos are pregnant for almost a year and a half before they give birth to their babies.

Rhinoceros and calf

All about mammals

What is a mammal? You, for starters! Humans are one of more than 5,000 different types of mammal. They might not look the same, but all mammals have important things in common.

Musk ox

Furry friends

Almost all mammals have fur or hair. Some have a thick, all-over covering, while others have light hair on some parts of their bodies. Either way, this fuzzy layer keeps mammals warm and protects their skin.

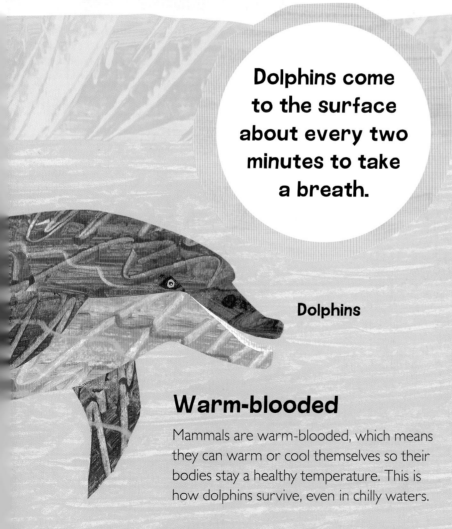

Dolphins come to the surface about every two minutes to take a breath.

Dolphins

Warm-blooded

Mammals are warm-blooded, which means they can warm or cool themselves so their bodies stay a healthy temperature. This is how dolphins survive, even in chilly waters.

Unusual mammals

Some mammals break the rules by looking or behaving differently from most other members of the group.

Pangolin

This predator is the only mammal with scales. When it senses danger, it curls up into a tight, armored ball.

Naked mole rat

This small African rodent is almost totally bald. A fantastic burrower, it spends most of its time underground.

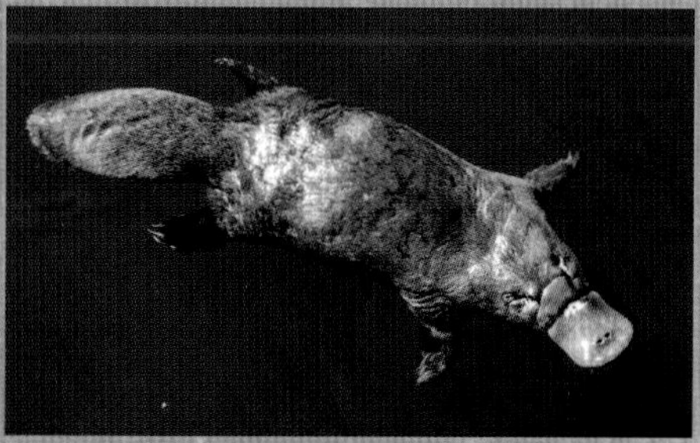

Platypus

Almost all mammals give birth to live babies, but the Australian platypus is different, because it lays eggs.

Monkeys and apes

Forest-dwelling monkeys, apes, and lemurs all belong to the group of mammals called primates.

Clever climbers

Monkeys use their long arms to swing from branch to branch. Many sleep up in the trees and hardly ever come down to the ground. The baboon is one of the few primates that prefers life on the forest floor.

Spot the difference

Monkeys and apes are close relatives, but there are differences. Monkeys, such as baboons, capuchins, and macaques, are usually fairly small and thin, with long tails. Apes, including orangutans, chimpanzees, and gorillas, are bigger and broader. They stand upright and have no tail.

Family facts

Habitat
Mainly trees and forests

Location
Africa, Asia, Europe,
North America, South America

Diet
Almost anything! Leaves, flowers, insects, and meat

Family
Monkeys, lemurs, apes, and us—humans are in the ape family, too!

Leaping lemurs

Lemurs live on the tropical island of Madagascar. These slinky movers jump from tree to tree and scamper along the forest floor, stopping every so often to sunbathe.

Living together

Monkeys and apes love company. They hang out in groups called troops, usually made up of one male, plus lots of females and their babies. They eat and sleep together and groom each other to get rid of dirt and bugs.

Strong silverbacks

The biggest and strongest apes are gorillas. Fully grown males are called silverbacks because of the silvery-gray stripe on their backs. These peaceful apes are only aggressive when one of their group is threatened.

Clever chimps

Chimpanzees are so smart that they use tools, just like humans do. This chimp is poking a twig into a tree to reach a juicy insect.

Feline family

From mighty African lions and powerful Asian tigers to the cute kitties that live with us as pets, cats are all part of the same family of felines.

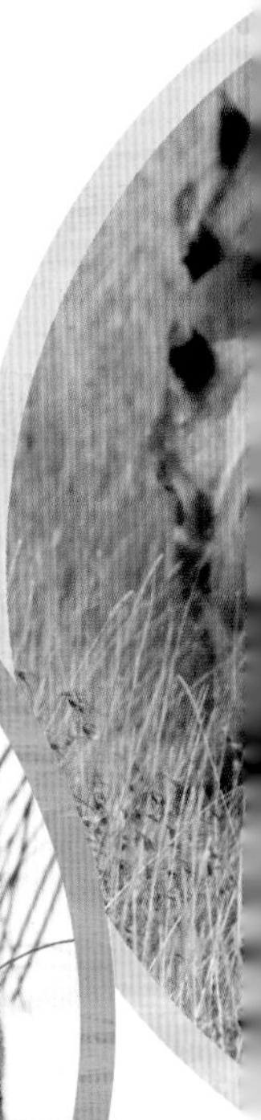

Family facts

Habitat
Forests, grasslands, human homes

Location
Every continent, except Antarctica

Diet
Meat, from large deer to tiny mice

Family
Thirty-seven types, including tigers, cheetahs, and domestic (pet) cats

Meaty menu

All cats eat meat, but wild cats, such as this lynx, have to catch their own. They use their strong eyesight and long legs to spot and chase prey. Their sharp teeth and claws tear the meat.

Biggest big cat

The striped tiger is the largest member of the cat family. This powerful hunter can carry prey twice its size.

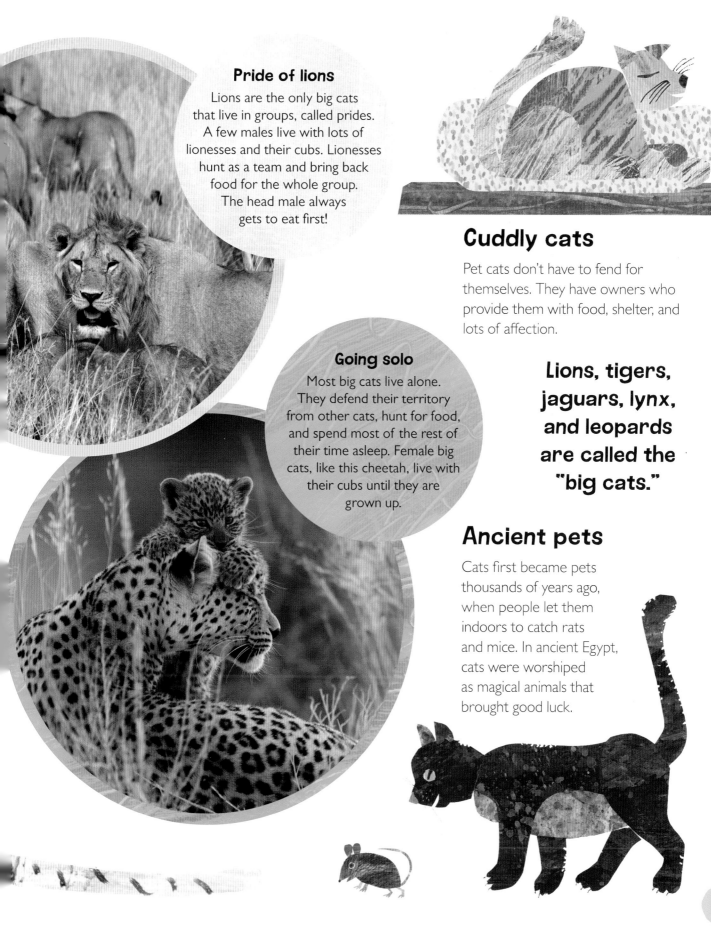

Pride of lions

Lions are the only big cats that live in groups, called prides. A few males live with lots of lionesses and their cubs. Lionesses hunt as a team and bring back food for the whole group. The head male always gets to eat first!

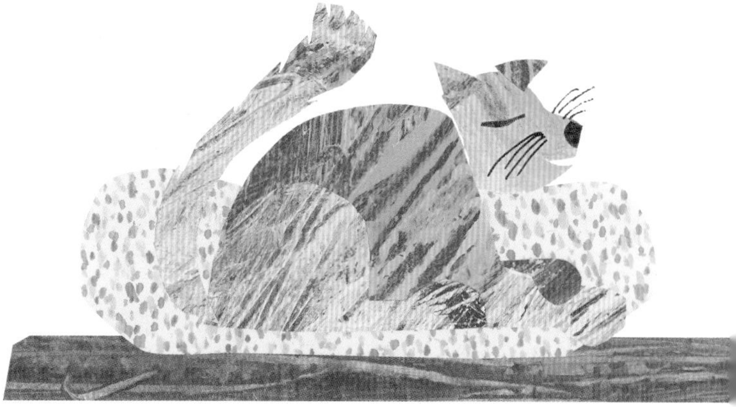

Cuddly cats

Pet cats don't have to fend for themselves. They have owners who provide them with food, shelter, and lots of affection.

Lions, tigers, jaguars, lynx, and leopards are called the "big cats."

Going solo

Most big cats live alone. They defend their territory from other cats, hunt for food, and spend most of the rest of their time asleep. Female big cats, like this cheetah, live with their cubs until they are grown up.

Ancient pets

Cats first became pets thousands of years ago, when people let them indoors to catch rats and mice. In ancient Egypt, cats were worshiped as magical animals that brought good luck.

Cool canines

The canine family has 34 members, from wolves howling in the wild to pet pooches barking for their dinner. All domestic breeds of dog share the same ancestor, the gray wolf.

Family facts

Habitat
Mountains, woodlands, grasslands, deserts, and human homes

Location
Every continent, except Antarctica

Diet
Meat, meat, and more meat!

Family
Includes wolves, coyotes, foxes, jackals, and domestic dogs

There are about 350 breeds of pet dog.

Heightened senses

Canines have excellent eyesight, sharp hearing, and a super sense of smell. They use their noses to sniff out prey or predators, and to check out other dogs.

Dogs with jobs

Often called our "best friends," dogs have a long history of helping humans. Their duties include rounding up sheep for farmers, pulling sleds in polar regions, and performing tasks for people with disabilities.

Leaders of the pack

Gray wolves live in large family groups called packs. The most dominant male and female are in joint charge of a team of other adults and their young pups. The wolves all work together to stalk and round up prey, then they move in to grab the animal with their strong jaws and sharp teeth.

Supreme hunters

African wild dogs are super-successful hunting mammals. These furry balls of energy are always on the go, making a kill every day. They live in big groups and work together to chase and attack prey.

Street scroungers

Not all canines hunt for their prey. Red foxes that live in cities have become expert scavengers, raiding garbage cans for leftover food.

Terrific teeth

Looking inside a mammal's mouth gives us clues about what it eats. Fearsome fangs help hunters tear into meaty meals, while rows of flat teeth make it easy for grazers to grind up grass.

Carnivores

Animals that eat only meat are carnivores. Their powerful jaws open to reveal long, sharp canine teeth, which slice through meat and shred it into chunks that are small enough to swallow.

Lion

The insect-eating armadillo has about 100 tiny teeth—more than any other mammal.

Teeth types

Mammals have three different types of teeth.

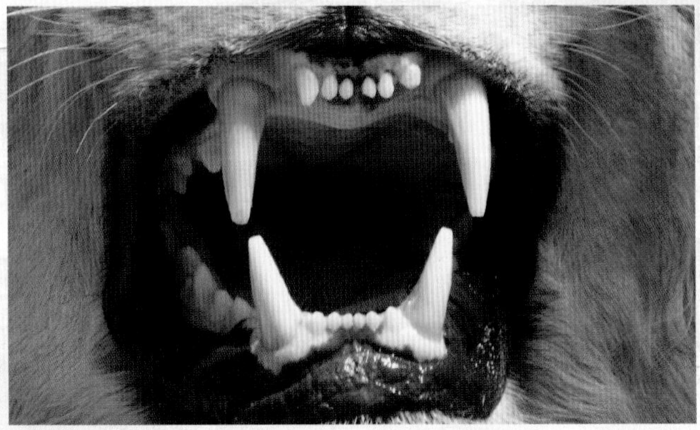

Canines

A carnivore's four, pointed canine teeth are used to stab and tear through chunks of meat.

Herbivores

Animals that eat only plants are herbivores. They have sharp incisors at the front of their mouths to cut through stalks and leaves. Broad molars at the back grind plants to a pulp.

Omnivores

Animals that munch a mixed menu of meat, plants, and fruit are omnivores. They have a combination of incisors, sharp canines, and flat molars to eat different types of food. Most humans are omnivores.

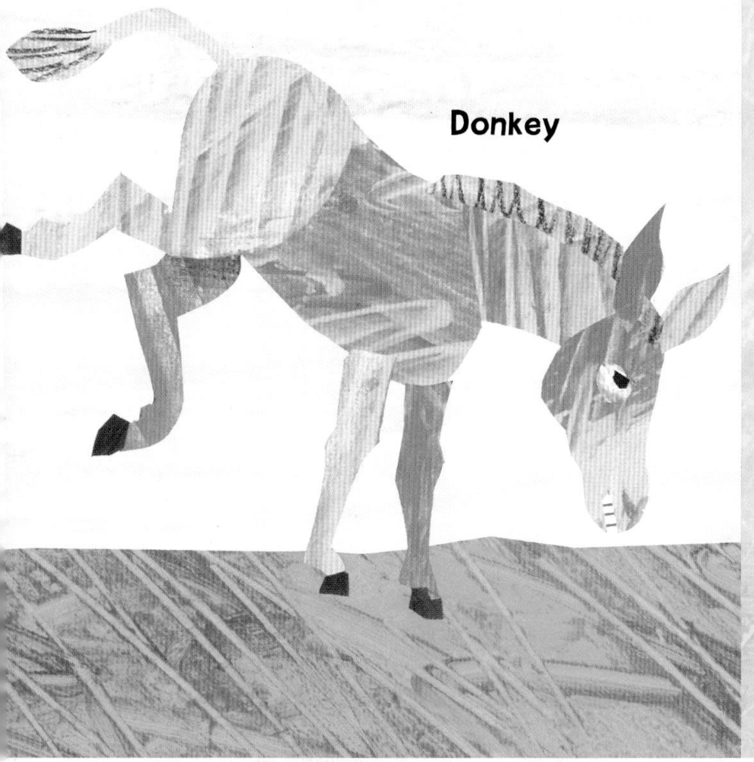

Chimpanzee

Chimpanzees are our closest relatives. They have 32 teeth, the same number as we do.

Incisors

The herbivore's large, sharp-edged incisor teeth can snip off stems, twigs, and leaves.

Molars

Broad molars at the back chew and grind bits of food until they are small enough to swallow.

Furry coats

Mammals are the only animals covered in hair. Our hair grows thickest on our heads, but other mammals have fur all over their bodies, to protect their skin and to keep them warm.

Thick coats

An all-over hairy coat is essential in colder habitats. Thick fur keeps the animals living there snug and dry.

Mountain gorilla

The mighty mountain gorilla has long, shaggy fur to keep out the cold and wet.

Changing seasons

The Arctic fox has gray-brown fur in the summer that turns pure white when winter comes. This helps the predator go unseen in the snow as it creeps up on prey.

Black and white

Polar bears have white fur and black skin. The fur makes them hard to spot in icy habitats. Black skin helps keep them warm because black is the color that absorbs the most heat from the sun.

Blurred lines

Zebra fur is patterned with black and white stripes. When zebras gather in a big herd, it becomes harder for predators to pick out a single animal because all they can see is one big, striped blur.

Cat coats

Big cats are famously furry. Their coats are a variety of colors and patterns to blend in with their different habitats.

Spotted cubs

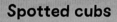

Lion cubs have faint spots on their golden fur for extra camouflage among the grasses.

Striped tiger

This huge hunter is well camouflaged as it moves through the grasslands and forests of Asia, thanks to its orange-and-black striped fur. Every tiger has its own unique striped pattern.

Spotted leopard

A spotted coat helps this big cat to move through the sunlight and shadows without being seen. Black leopards, called panthers, also have spots, but these are more difficult to see.

Bears

Bears may look cute and cuddly, but they are not toy teddy bears! These big, strong mammals will eat just about anything if they're hungry enough.

Brown bear

Claws for climbing

Like most bears, brown bears are skilled climbers. They leap up on a tree, then use their sharp claws to grip the trunk tightly.

Keeping warm

Grizzly bears are brown bears that live in colder places. They have thick fur to keep them warm. Through the winter, they stay snuggled up in their dens.

Grizzly bear

Family facts

Habitat
Forests, grasslands, mountains, deserts, and Arctic areas

Location
Asia, Europe, North America, South America

Diet
Small animals, fish, fruit, plants, and grasses

Family
There are eight different members of the bear family.

Meet the bears

The eight different types, or species, of bear live in all kinds of habitats, from high mountain forests to the frozen Arctic.

American black bear

Asiatic black bear

Brown bear

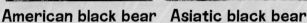

Giant panda

Polar bear

Sloth bear

Sun bear

Spectacled bear

The spectacled bear's name comes from its furry face pattern, which makes it look as if it is wearing glasses!

Strong swimmers

Polar bears are great swimmers. They hunt for seals in the icy Arctic Ocean and teach their cubs to do the same.

Polar bear and cub

Elephants

Elephants are the largest land animals. An African elephant can weigh as much as four cars! But, despite their size, they are peaceful plant-eaters.

Family facts

Habitat
Forests, grasslands, and deserts

Location
Africa and Asia

Diet
Leaves, plants, and fruit

Family
The two members of this family are the African elephant and the Asian elephant.

Friendly families

Elephants live in loving, caring family groups. On the move, they keep babies safe by putting them in the center of the herd. A baby stays with its mother for the first five years of its life.

Elephant and calf

Long tusks

Tusks are supersized, curved, ivory teeth. Elephants use them to dig up tasty plants and tear bark from trees.

Big ears

The shape and size of an elephant's ears can tell us where it comes from. African elephants have huge, flapping ears, but Asian elephants have much smaller and more rounded ears.

African elephant's ear

Terrific trunk

A trunk is a long, flexible nose used for breathing, smelling, and drinking. It also grabs plants and pops them into the elephant's mouth. Elephants need lots of food, so they chew and chomp for up to 18 hours a day!

An elephant's trunk is packed with more than 40,000 muscles.

Groovy hooves

Many fast-moving mammals have hooves. A hoof is a hard protective covering on the toes. Hooves wear down over time, but, luckily, keep growing back.

Tough covering

Hooves are made of a material called keratin. Your hair and nails are made of this, too.

Even-toed animals

Mammals that have either two or four toes that are covered by hooves are called even-toed mammals.

Hippopotamus

This giant has four toes, which help it balance and spread out the load of its great weight.

Camel

A camel's two widely spread toes are perfect for walking over hot sand.

Caribou

This deer's four toes act like snow shoes and keep it from sinking into the snow.

Hippo hoofprint

Camel hoofprint

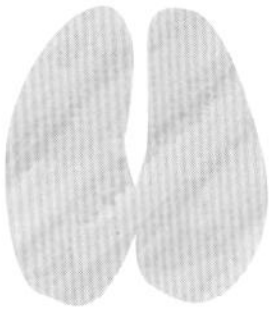

Caribou hoofprint

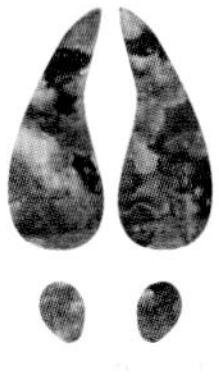

On the run

Hooves allow animals to run on their toes without hurting their feet. Most hoofed mammals are peaceful plant-eaters. They need long legs and strong feet to escape predators quickly.

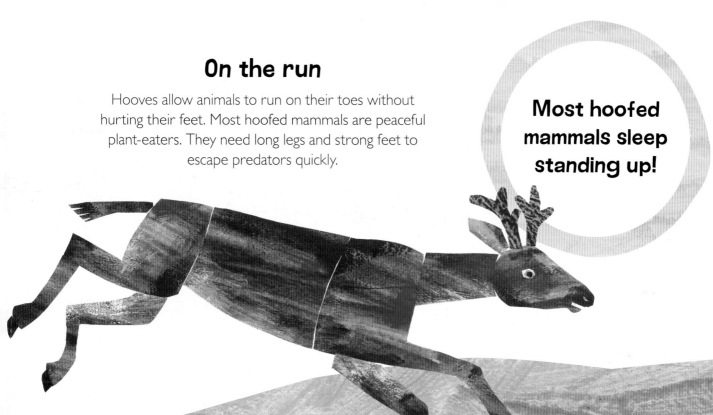

Most hoofed mammals sleep standing up!

Odd-toed animals

Mammals that have either one or three toes under their hooves are called odd-toed mammals.

Rhinoceros

A rhino's three chunky toes support its bulky body and help it move at high speed.

Horse

A horse has a single toe surrounded by a hoof, and runs on its tiptoes.

Tapir

The tapir is an unusual member of this family. It has four toes at the front and three at the back.

Rhino hoofprint

Horse hoofprint

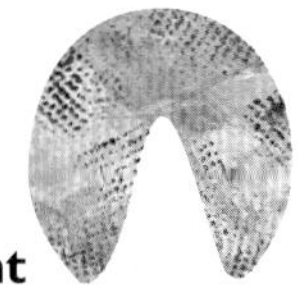

Tapir front hoofprint

Tapir back hoofprint

Horse power

Horses can walk, trot, canter, or gallop. This horse and foal are galloping, which means running at top speed. Metal shoes are often attached to hooves to protect horses' feet on hard roads.

Family facts

Habitat
Fields, forests, grasslands, and deserts

Location
Every continent, except Antarctica

Diet
Grass, grass, and more grass!

Family
Zebras, horses, and donkeys

Horses

These pointy-eared powerhouses are known for their strength and speed. Horses, ponies, and donkeys have lived with people for thousands of years, while zebras live in the wild.

Horseplay

There are more than 300 different breeds of horse. Racehorses are big and strong, with lots of stamina. Smaller, stocky ponies are perfect for children to ride.

Pony

Racehorse

Wild asses

Asses look different from horses, with longer ears and shorter bodies. They roam wild in the deserts and grasslands of Africa and Asia.

A donkey is a domesticated ass that lives with people.

Striped zebras

No two zebras look the same: each one has its own unique black-and-white striped pattern. Zebras live in herds on the African savanna and graze on grass.

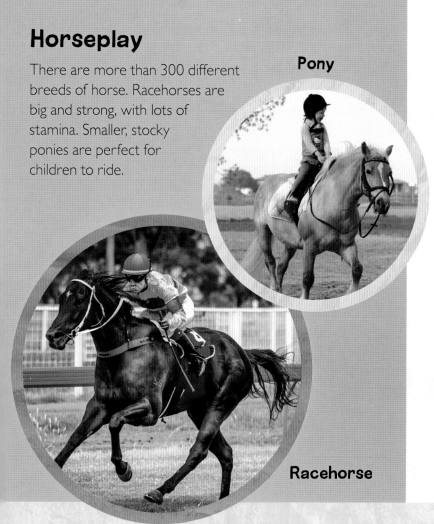

Farm animals

On a farm, the animals are kept and cared for by farmers. They either live outside in fields or shelter inside barns.

Cows have four stomachs to help them get all the goodness out of the chewy grass they eat.

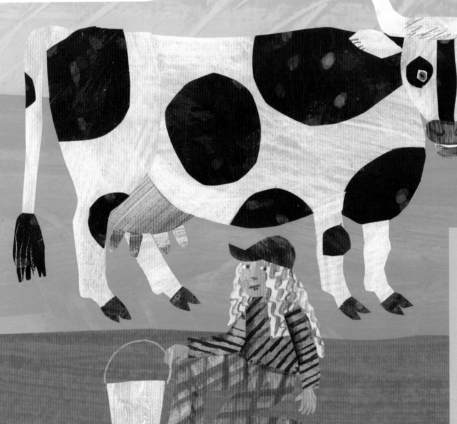

Farm food

Sheep, goats, cows, and pigs were once wild, but farmers tamed them for the food they provide. Cows, sheep, and goats produce milk for us to drink. Some farm animals are also raised for their meat.

Grazing cows

Moo! Cows that eat grass graze for at least six hours a day. They munch a mouthful of grass, swallow it, then bring it back up, and chew it all over again! This is called chewing the cud.

Woolly sheep

Baa! Fleecy flocks of sheep graze together. Their wool is used to make clothes. Farmers sometimes have a sheepdog to help round up or move the sheep.

Playful goats

Me-eh! Goats bring fun to the farm. These clever climbers are always on the lookout for tasty snacks. Their milk is often used to make cheese.

Muddy pigs

Oink! Pigs love to mess around in the mud. They use their snuffly snouts to root in the soil for snails, worms, and other treats to eat.

Baby mammals

Many newborn mammals are weak and helpless when they come into the world. They are cared for by their mothers until they are fully grown.

Baby seals

Baby harp seals are pure white. This helps them hide from predators. After a few weeks, they turn dark, just like their parents.

Kittens

Like most baby mammals, kittens are covered in fur when they are born. They can't see or hear at first. The mother cat produces nourishing milk that helps the kittens grow quickly.

Mothers and babies

Some baby mammals are mini versions of their parents, but these three look very different from their moms!

Giant panda

Giant pandas are famous for their black-and-white fur, but their babies are born with pink skin and hardly any hair.

Young dolphins

Many mammals are on the move from the moment they are born. A newborn dolphin has to swim immediately to the surface to take its first breath.

Whale babies

Blue whales have the biggest babies on Earth. A newborn calf weighs the same as a small car.

Orangutans

A baby orangutan spends up to nine years being cared for by its mother. That is the longest time any mammal takes to grow up, except for humans.

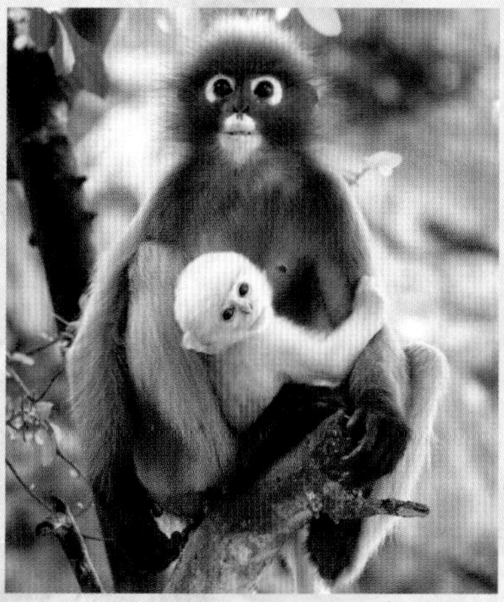

Leaf monkey

Adult leaf monkeys have dark fur. Their babies are bright orange, which makes them easier to keep track of!

Tapir

Tapirs are plain and dark-colored, but their babies are spotted and striped. This makes it harder for predators to spot them.

Marsupials

Marsupials are a group of mammals that have a special belly pouch for carrying their young safely.

Family facts

Habitat
Forests, grasslands, and deserts

Location
Oceania, North America, and South America

Diet
Plants or meat

Family
About 250 members, including koalas, kangaroos, wombats, and wallabies

Protective pockets

Newborn marsupials are teeny tiny. They crawl along their mother's fur until they reach the pouch. They stay here for months to drink milk and keep safe while they grow.

Kangaroo

Boii-nng! This big Australian marsupial use its long legs to make huge leaps over the ground. The baby stays snug and safe inside its pouch.

Tasmanian devil

Living up to its name, this small Australian mammal is a fierce, meat-eating marsupial. Its terrifying teeth can even bite through bones!

Opossum

Found in North and South America, opossums are unusual marsupials that don't have a pouch. Babies hang on tight to their mother's body to stay safe.

Baby koalas and kangaroos are called joeys.

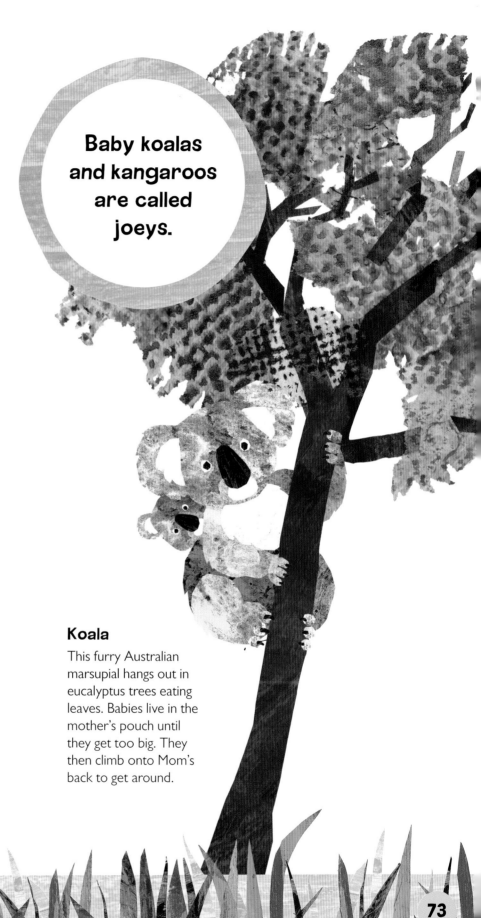

Koala

This furry Australian marsupial hangs out in eucalyptus trees eating leaves. Babies live in the mother's pouch until they get too big. They then climb onto Mom's back to get around.

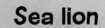

Narwhal

The narwhal uses its long, hornlike tooth to spear fish. Its nickname is "the unicorn of the sea"!

Sea lion

Although they can move around on land, sea lions find their food in the ocean. They swim at high speed to hunt down fish, crabs, or clams, then swallow them whole.

Ocean giants

Some of the biggest mammals on Earth hunt in water. From huge whales to powerful polar bears, these hungry heavyweights patrol the oceans looking for lunch.

Toothed whales

Meat-eating toothed whales hunt for fish, seals, and other animals. This sperm whale's favorite food is deepwater squid. Inside the sperm whale's huge head is the biggest brain of all animals.

Polar bear

The largest land predator is also a great swimmer, diving off floating ice into the sea to hunt seals. If a polar bear can't find any seals, it will feed on dead animals, such as whales, instead.

Baleen whales

Baleen whales, like this humpback whale, are some of the largest animals in the sea, but they feed on truly tiny creatures called zooplankton. They use their massive mouths to filter the food from the water.

Walrus

Big, blubbery bodies keep walruses warm in icy seas. They swim along the ocean floor, using their long whiskers to feel for crabs and sea urchins. They use their two massive tusks to break through ice or to fight rivals.

Dolphin

It's always playtime for dolphins! These curious mammals love to swim alongside boats. They jump clear out of the water, then land with a big splash.

Blowhole for breathing

A dolphin can hold its breath underwater for 15 minutes by closing the blowhole on its head.

Sea otter

These small sea mammals have thick fur to keep them cozy in cold waters. When sea otters are sleepy, they wrap themselves in layers of a seaweed called kelp. This stops them from floating away while they snooze.

Porpoise

These close relatives of the dolphin look similar, but are smaller and shyer. They have big appetites and are always on the hunt for fish to eat.

A porpoise's nose is shorter than a dolphin's.

Super swimmers

The oceans are home to swimming superstars. These marine mammals are smooth and sleek to help them glide, slide, and dive around their underwater habitat.

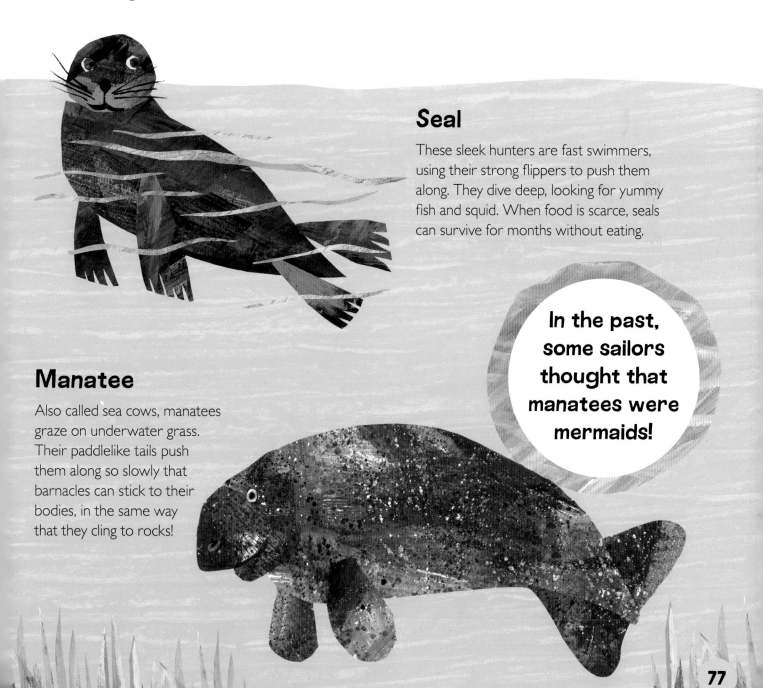

Seal

These sleek hunters are fast swimmers, using their strong flippers to push them along. They dive deep, looking for yummy fish and squid. When food is scarce, seals can survive for months without eating.

In the past, some sailors thought that manatees were mermaids!

Manatee

Also called sea cows, manatees graze on underwater grass. Their paddlelike tails push them along so slowly that barnacles can stick to their bodies, in the same way that they cling to rocks!

Bats

There are many types of mammal, but bats are the only ones that can fly. After dark, they wake up and flap out of their bat caves to feed on insects, flowers, fruit, or even blood!

In the dark

Bats live in dark caves or shady woodlands. They gather in huge groups called colonies and sleep all day, hanging upside down. One colony can include up to 20 million bats!

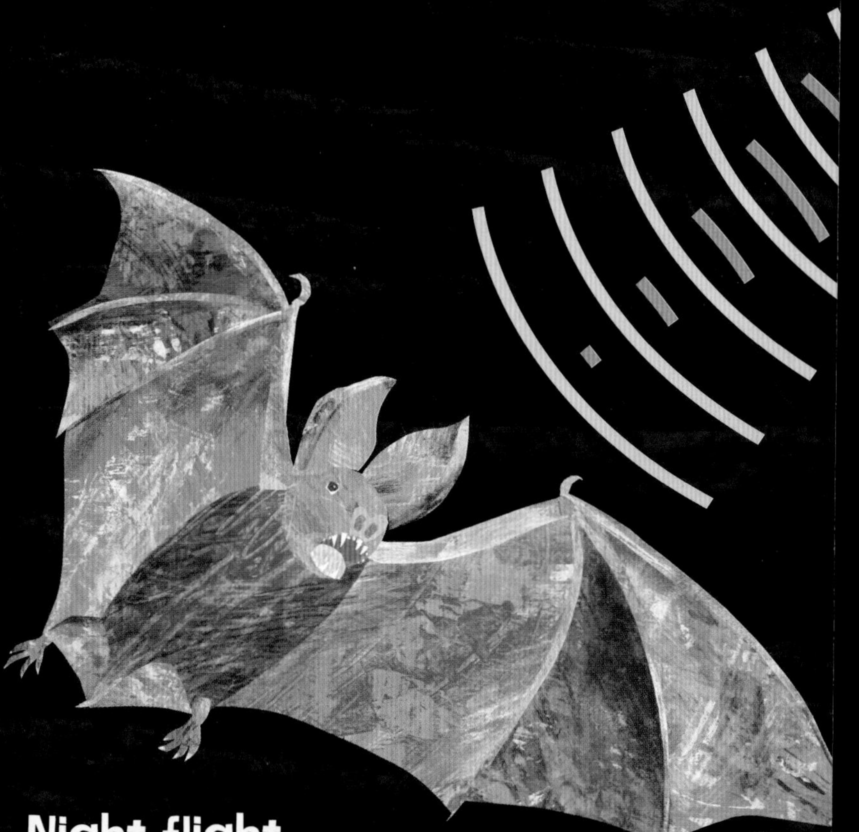

Family facts

Habitat
Woodlands, deserts, caves, and cities

Location
Every continent, except Antarctica

Diet
Meat, plants, or fruit

Family
There are at least 1,300 different types of bat.

Night flight

Most bats are nocturnal, which means they are awake at night. They use their strong wings and flexible joints to fly high and change direction as they hunt flying insects.

Listening for prey

Bats find their prey using echolocation. The bat sends out squeaks and listens for echoes that bounce back off a passing insect. It uses the echo to figure out exactly where the insect is, then attacks.

Sound waves from the bat's squeaks hit the fly.

The echo travels back toward the bat's sensitive ears.

The tiny bumblebee bat is the size of a bee and weighs less than a grape!

Flying squirrel

Despite its name, the flying squirrel cannot actually fly the way a bat can. Instead, this forest mammal spreads out its body and glides from one treetop to another. Without real wings, it can only travel short distances.

Different diets

Almost all bats eat insects, but a few prefer a very different menu...

Fruit bat

Also called flying foxes, fruit bats use their big snouts and long tongues to slurp nectar from flowers and suck on juicy fruit.

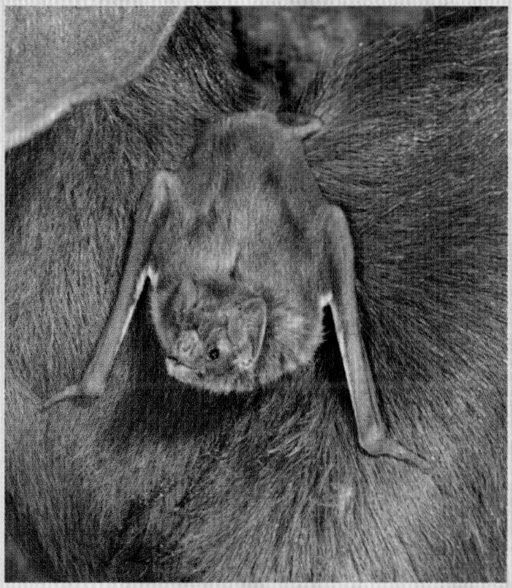

Vampire bat

Like the vampires in scary stories, these bats sink their teeth into their victims and suck up their blood. Don't worry though, they much prefer cows' blood to human blood!

Staying safe

Mammals avoid predators in all kinds of ways, from being part of a crowd to freezing like a statue and disappearing into the scenery.

Helping herds

Some mammals stick together for safety. Gazelles travel across the African savanna in huge herds because this makes it harder for predators to pick on a single victim to attack.

Playing dead

To defend themselves, opossums lie down, curl up, and stay still for hours. Playing dead helps trick predators into thinking they are rotten old meat to be avoided.

Stinky surprise

When skunks feel threatened, they lift their tails and release a cloud of super-smelly gas. This disgusting spray can also temporarily blind predators that get too close.

Racoons under threat make a real racket, shrieking and shouting to scare away predators.

Whiteout

The Arctic hare's pure-white winter coat blends in perfectly with the snowy landscape. When the hare sits still, even the sharpest-eyed predator cannot spot it.

Quick getaway

North American pronghorns are among the fastest land animals, and they can sprint long distances, too. They use their muscly legs to outrun coyotes, wolves, and bears.

Rodents

There are more types of rodent than any other mammal. They range in size from the chunky capybara to the thumb-sized harvest mouse.

Red squirrel

This bushy-tailed beauty loves climbing trees, chasing other squirrels, and nibbling tasty nuts.

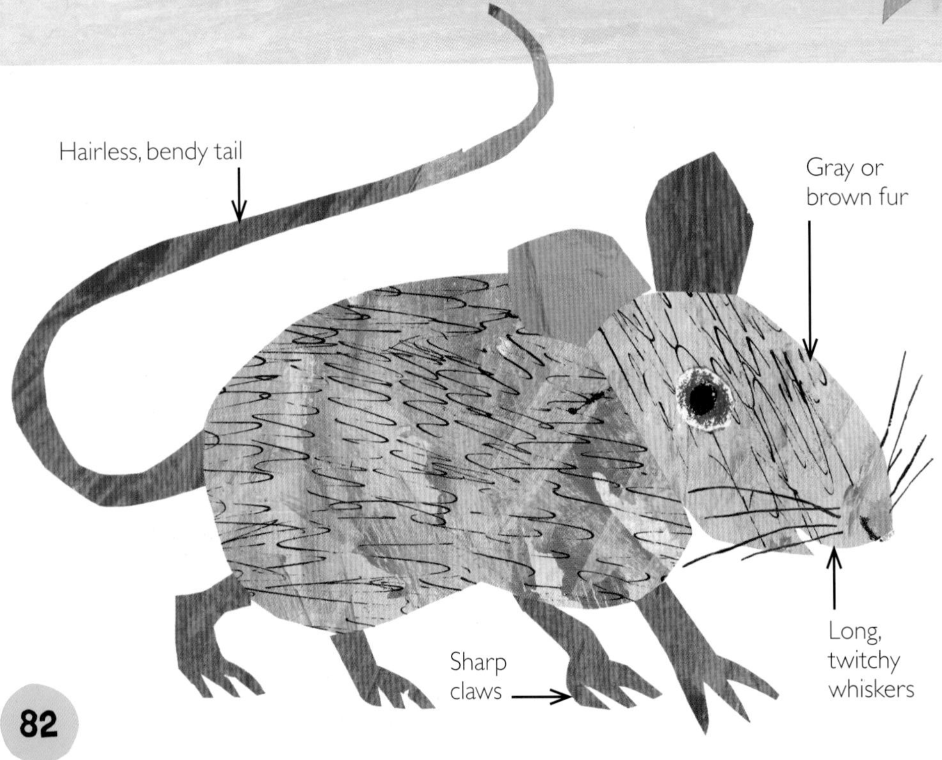

The European harvest mouse is so tiny it could easily sit in a teaspoon!

House mouse

The house mouse is the world's most common rodent. It scampers along on all fours, but often sits up on its back legs to eat or when it senses danger.

Gopher

Survival experts

Rodents can live in all habitats because, like this gopher, most rodents are not fussy eaters. Their strong teeth can gnaw through all kinds of food. Many rodents survive easily on human food and leftovers.

Rodents are everywhere! Almost half of all types of mammal are rodents.

A beaver's bright-orange teeth contain real iron! These toughened teeth can gnaw through thick tree trunks.

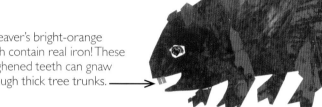

Beaver

Brown rat

Rats are excellent at climbing, burrowing, and swimming. They live almost anywhere they can find food, even in stinky underground sewers.

Guinea pig

Wild guinea pigs live in burrows in the mountains of South America. Guinea pigs also make great pets, since they are friendly and curious.

Capybara

The South American capybara is the world's biggest rodent. It grows as big as a labrador dog! Capybaras live in family groups on grassy riverbanks.

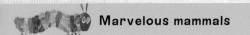

Going underground

Burrowing mammals dig deep into the ground. They create tunnels and chambers where they can sleep, eat, hide, or have their babies in safety.

Badger sett

This shy, secretive mammal's underground home is called a sett. Badgers come out after dark to feed on insects, fruit, and birds' eggs.

Rabbit warren

Bunnies live in groups and dig big burrows, called warrens, to escape from predators and cold winters. Here, they can also raise their babies in peace.

Armadillo den

By day, armadillos lie low in their underground burrows. At night, they clamber to the surface and go sniffing for fruits and insects.

Molehill

Look out for molehills! These mounds of dirt show where moles come out of the ground. Moles use their front paws like shovels to dig through the soil and find wriggly worms.

Animal architect

The busy mole works hard to create an underground mansion with separate rooms linked by tunnels. It has a bedroom for sleeping and even a special pantry for delicious dead worms!

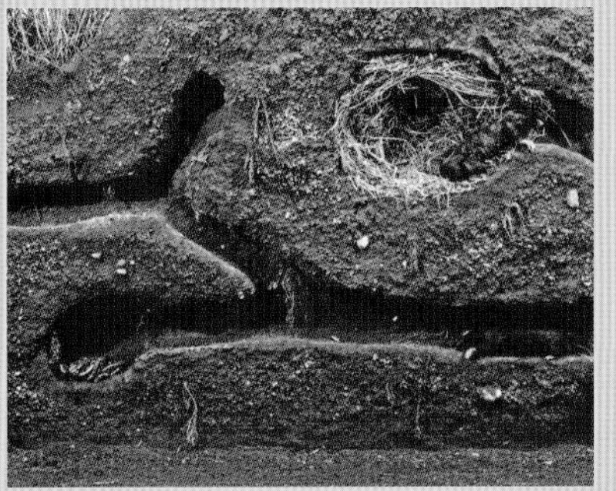

Aardvark tunnel

It only takes the sharp-clawed aardvark a few minutes to dig a tunnel, then disappear under the ground completely.

Beautiful birds

Breathtaking birds

These fabulous, feathery fliers come in a spectacular variety of shapes, sizes, and colors, but all birds have some important things in common.

Fancy feathers

Birds are the only animals that have feathers. They keep birds warm and dry and also help them to fly. Some birds have feathers in eye-catching colors to attract mates.

Most birds' bones are full of holes! This makes the bones lighter, so it is easier for the birds to fly.

Bills and beaks

Birds have beaks, which they use as tools to help them eat or keep their feathers clean. Beaks can be different sizes and shapes, depending on what a bird eats.

High fliers

Most birds can fly. They flap their feathered wings to keep themselves in the air and use their tail feathers to steer or slow down.

Golden eagle

There are about 10,000 different types of bird.

Warm bodies

Birds are warm-blooded, just like us. This means that their bodies can make their own heat. So, even when the surroundings are cold, birds like this siskin can stay warm.

Laying eggs

Baby birds hatch from eggs. First, the female bird lays an egg and keeps it warm and safe. When the time is right, the egg cracks open. Ta-dah! The chick is born.

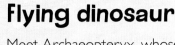

Living dinosaurs

Millions of years ago, dinosaurs stomped their way around the world. Did you know, though, that today's birds are living versions of those prehistoric animals?

Flying dinosaur

Meet Archaeopteryx, whose name means "ancient wing." It had wings and feathers, just like modern birds. It could even fly, although only for short distances.

Archaeopteryx

Wings had claws for climbing and gripping.

Prehistoric past

Some dinosaurs were mighty, meat-eating monsters with sharp teeth and slashing claws. Alongside them were smaller, feathered dinosaurs with winglike arms, such as the Velociraptor.

Velociraptor

Reptile bird

The hoatzin, from South America, is also called the reptile bird. Hoatzin chicks have small claws on their wings to help them grip branches, just like their prehistoric cousin, Archaeopteryx.

Tyrannosaurus rex

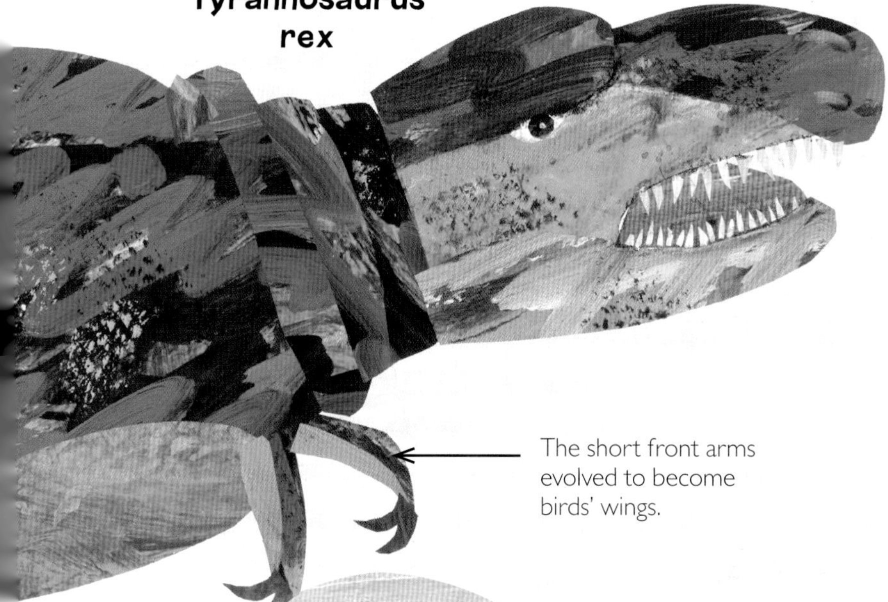

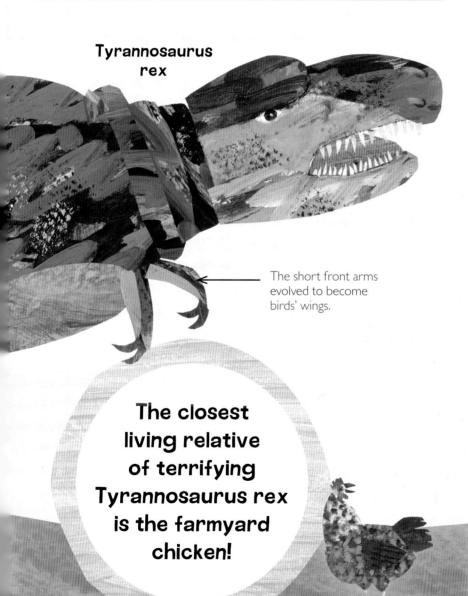

The short front arms evolved to become birds' wings.

The closest living relative of terrifying Tyrannosaurus rex is the farmyard chicken!

So similar!

Modern birds share lots of features with their dinosaur ancestors.

Feathery skin

All birds have feathers, and we know now that many dinosaurs in prehistoric times did, too.

Clawed feet

Birds' feet are covered in scaly skin, with claws on the tips of their toes. They look just like dinosaur feet!

Laying eggs

Like birds, prehistoric dinosaurs laid eggs, and many of them built nests to protect their young.

Songbirds

Almost half the world's birds are songbirds.

Every morning, members of this family of small birds fill the air with tuneful songs. If you get up early, listen for the dawn chorus!

Blue tit

The tiny, brightly colored blue tit has a loud, trilling song. It flies from tree to tree looking for tasty insects to eat.

European robin

The robin has a red chest and a loud, chirpy song. It visits our yards on the hunt for beetles and other insects.

Blackbird

High in the trees, male blackbirds sing to attract females. Males are shiny black and females are brown.

Singsong sounds

Each songbird produces its own unique tune. Male songbirds sing the loudest and most often to attract females and also to warn rival males to keep their distance.

Feet keep a tight grip while the bird is singing or sleeping.

Family facts

Habitat
Forests, woodlands, wetlands, farmland, and parks

Location
Africa, Asia, Europe, North America, Oceania

Diet
Insects, snails, spiders, and worms

Family
This huge group includes finches, tits, and warblers.

Sparrow

This friendly little bird lives all over the world. Males cheep and chirp to invite females to their nests.

Northern mockingbird

This clever mimic can copy the songs of other birds, and even the sounds of car alarms and squeaking doors!

Nightingale

The male nightingale sings at night, producing a loud, tuneful song to impress nearby females.

Forest birds

Leafy forests provide birds with branches to perch on, fruit and insects to eat, and places to hide from hungry predators.

Woodpecker

What's that loud drumming sound? It could be a woodpecker, hammering its strong bill against tree trunks to find insects or to make a hole for nesting inside.

White-throated tree creeper

This Australian bird whistles as it flits around the forest. Its favorite foods are butterflies, which it catches midair, and ants, which scuttle on the ground.

Northern cardinal

This colorful bird lives in North America. Its brilliant red feathers are partly due to the fruit and berries it loves to eat.

Seeds make trees!

When a bird leaves droppings on the forest floor, they often contain seeds that the bird has eaten. The seeds grow into new trees to fill the forest.

Victoria crowned pigeon

The forests of Asia are home to this big, blue pigeon. It lives in groups, rooting around on the ground for fruits, insects, and worms. If a predator gets too close, the pigeon escapes up into the nearest tree.

Kakapo

This New Zealand parrot is too heavy to fly. It hops around the forest floor and uses its sharp claws to climb trees, searching for fruits and nuts.

The kakapo was almost extinct, but now there are more than 250 birds, the highest number in 50 years!

Finding a partner

Male birds go all out to impress females! To attract a partner, they might sing, dance, offer some tempting gifts, or build a beautiful love-nest.

Slow dancing

Male and female swans bond by performing a graceful dance, intertwining their necks and gently nuzzling each other.

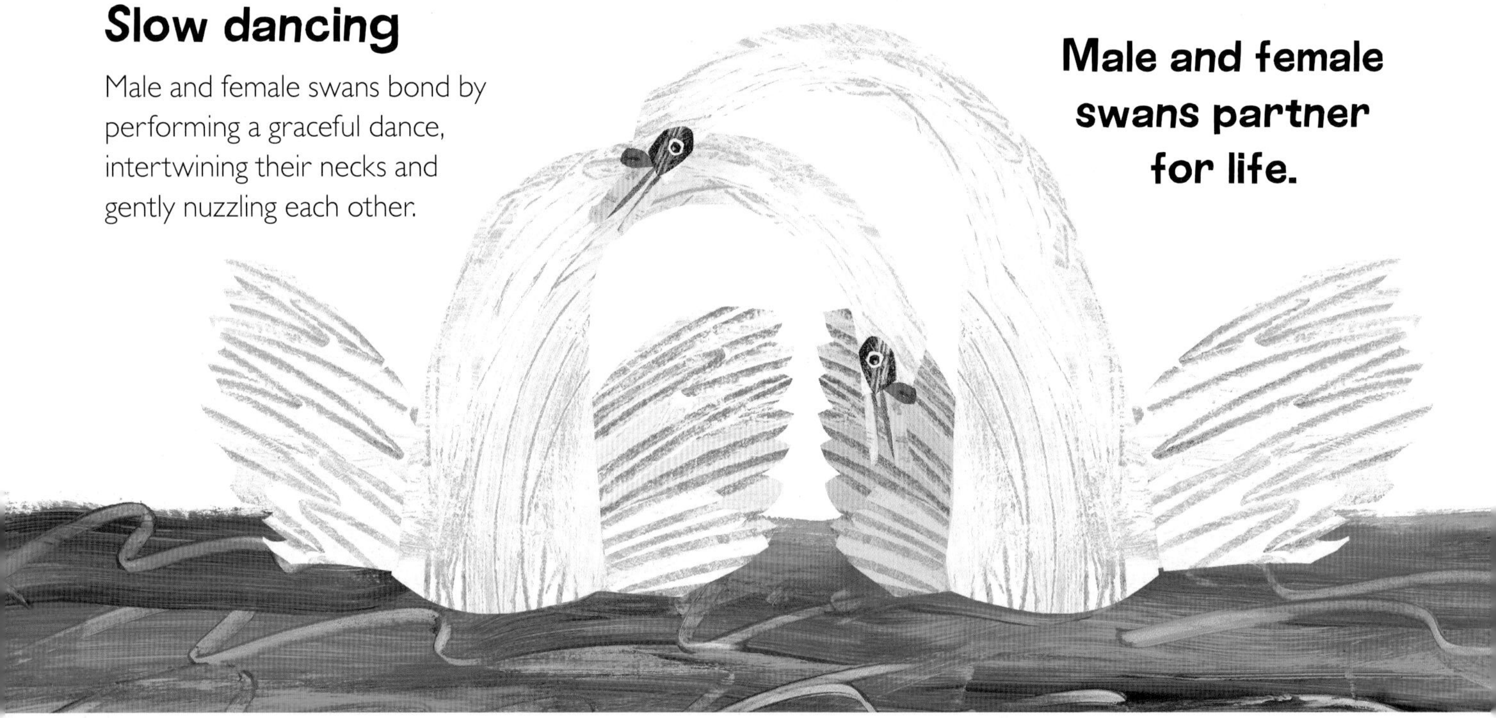

Male and female swans partner for life.

The dancer

The female blue-footed booby wants a mate with blue feet, and the brighter, the better! So the male performs a dazzling dance for her, to show off his colorful feet.

The collector

The male satin bowerbird of Australia gathers together a hoard of eye-catching treasures, such as shells, feathers, or pieces of string. Then he lays them out, hoping to impress passing females.

Showtime!

The male peacock puts on a dramatic display by spreading out his spectacular tail. He struts up and down, hoping that a passing female will like what she sees.

A peacock's tail can have 150 feathers.

The singer

The Australian lyrebird is a proud performer. First, he creates a mound of earth. Then he stands on top, waves his stunning tail feathers, and calls out to females at the top of his voice.

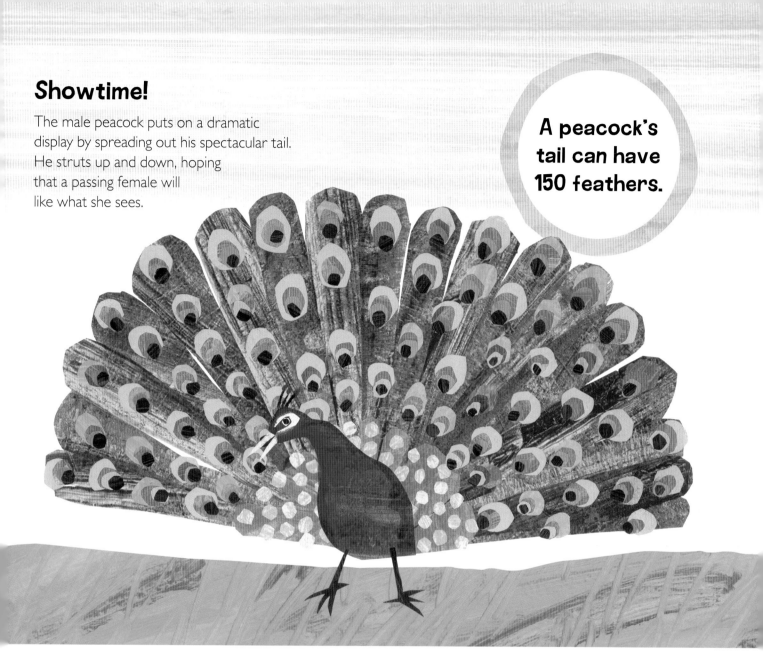

The builder

The male weaver bird builds an amazing show home. He takes his time, weaving together only the finest, freshest grass. Before she moves in, a visiting female will tug at the nest to test its strength.

Owls

When darkness falls, owls wake up, ready to go hunting. Special feathers allow them to fly in total silence before swooping down on their unsuspecting prey.

Family facts

Habitat
Forests, woodlands, deserts, and farm buildings

Location
Every continent, except Antarctica

Diet
Animals such as mice, birds, and insects

Family
There are more than 200 different types of owl.

Night hooters

Although owls fly silently, they know how to make a noise! Listen for their loud "woo-hoo, woo-hoo" sound in the night. This means that two owls are communicating or one is marking its territory.

A group of owls is called a parliament.

Cough it up!

Owls cannot break down fur and bone in their bodies. Instead, they cough up little pellets of undigested prey. Yuck!

Flight feathers

An owl's wings are covered in ultrasoft flight feathers. The wings spread out wide and flap without making a sound.

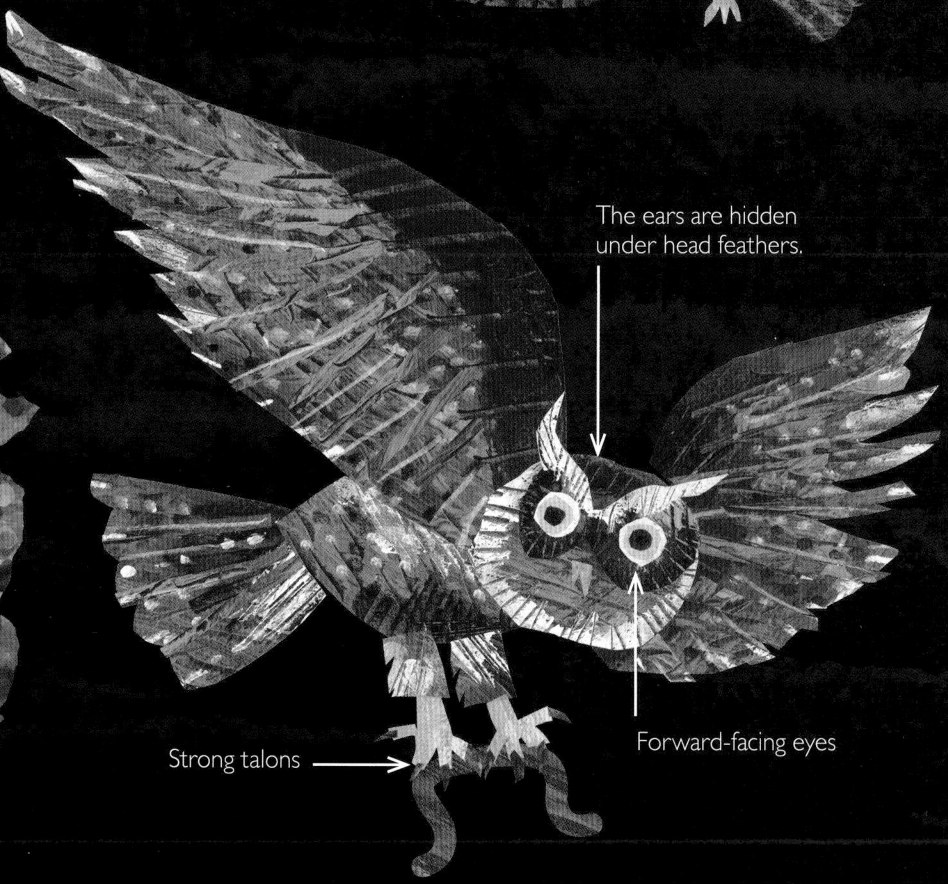

The ears are hidden under head feathers.
Strong talons
Forward-facing eyes

Fearsome hunters

Owls hunt using their extraordinary eyesight and hearing. They swoop in and grab prey with their sharp talons. They tear the flesh with their hooked beaks and gulp down the chunks.

Snow stalker

Unlike other owls, the snowy owl hunts in the bright sunlight of the Arctic summer. Its thick covering of white feathers blends in with the icy background, helping the owl to hide as it hunts.

Underground owl

Most owls live in trees, but the burrowing owl nests underground. It can dig its own burrow, but usually prefers just to move into another animal's empty nest.

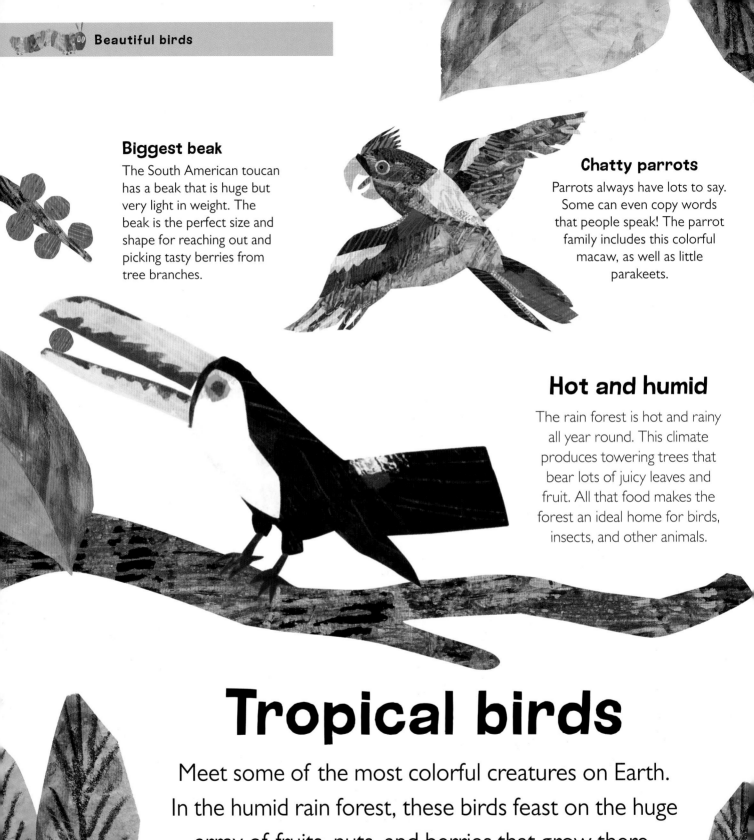

Biggest beak

The South American toucan has a beak that is huge but very light in weight. The beak is the perfect size and shape for reaching out and picking tasty berries from tree branches.

Chatty parrots

Parrots always have lots to say. Some can even copy words that people speak! The parrot family includes this colorful macaw, as well as little parakeets.

Hot and humid

The rain forest is hot and rainy all year round. This climate produces towering trees that bear lots of juicy leaves and fruit. All that food makes the forest an ideal home for birds, insects, and other animals.

Tropical birds

Meet some of the most colorful creatures on Earth. In the humid rain forest, these birds feast on the huge array of fruits, nuts, and berries that grow there.

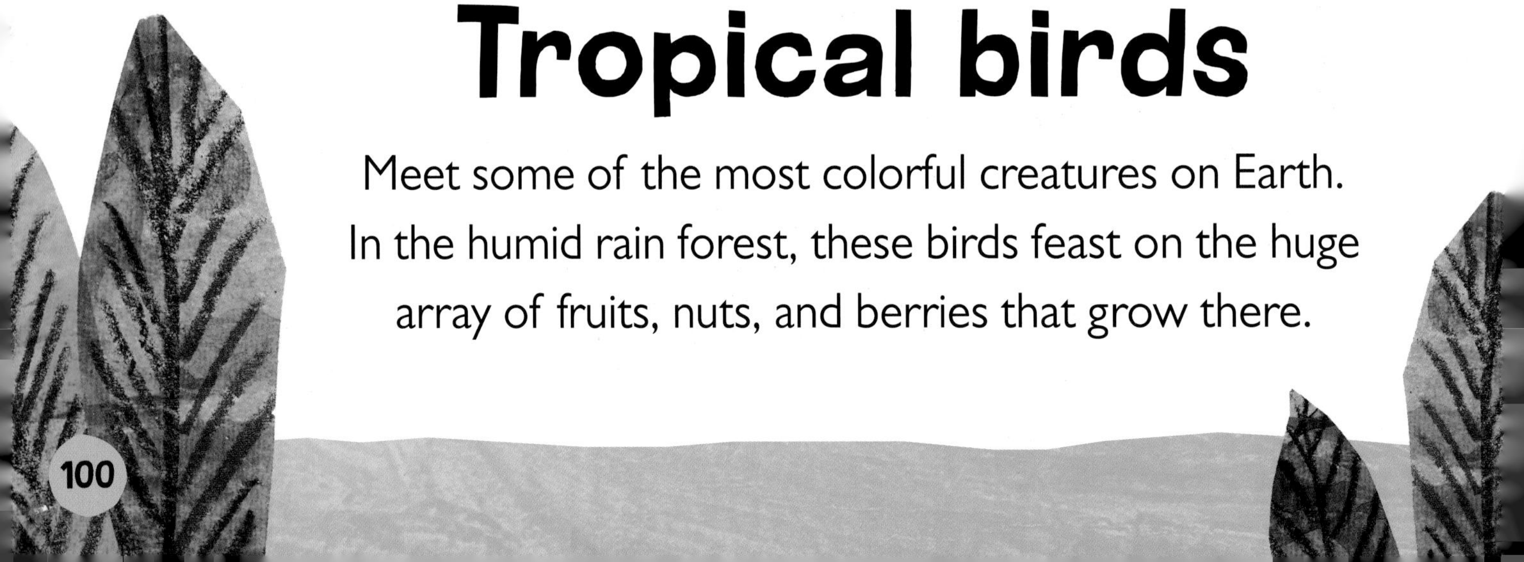

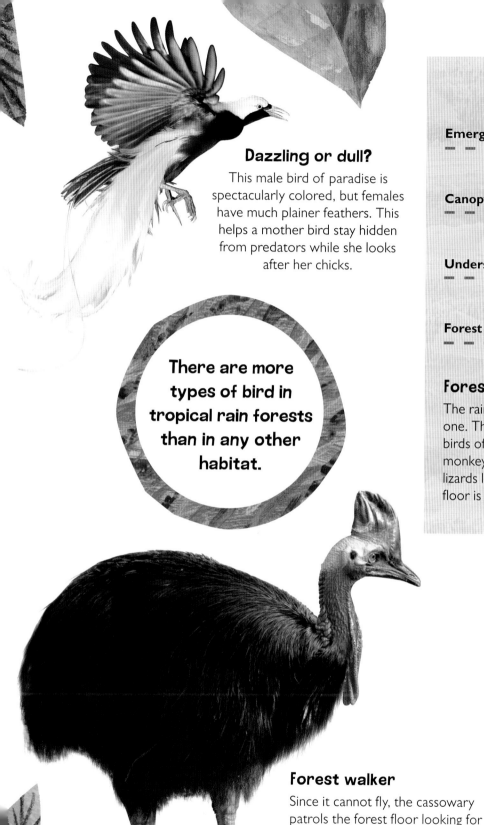

Dazzling or dull?

This male bird of paradise is spectacularly colored, but females have much plainer feathers. This helps a mother bird stay hidden from predators while she looks after her chicks.

There are more types of bird in tropical rain forests than in any other habitat.

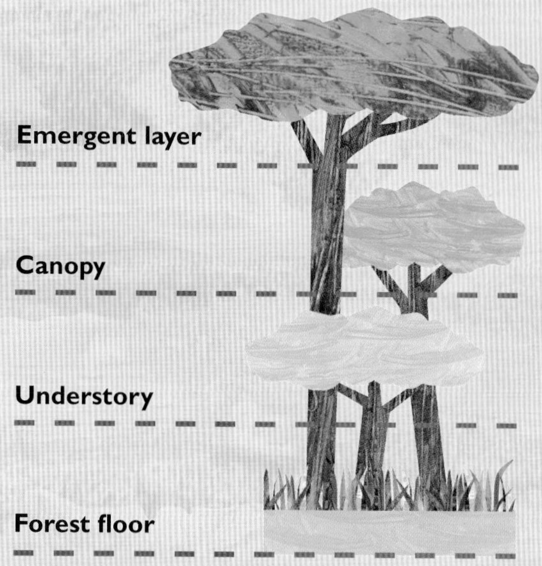

Forest layers

The rain forest is four different habitats in one. The top layer is home to butterflies and birds of prey. The canopy is full of parrots, monkeys, and reptiles. Jaguars, bats, and lizards live in the understory. The forest floor is alive with insects and huge spiders.

Forest walker

Since it cannot fly, the cassowary patrols the forest floor looking for fallen fruit. This bird can also run fast to escape predatory pythons and cunning crocodiles.

Frog fisher

The tiny, brightly colored African dwarf kingfisher hunts in the understory of the rain forest. It perches patiently, waiting to attack insects and frogs.

Ground birds

Look down to spot this type of bird! Ground birds feed and nest on the floor and prefer running to flying. They only take flight when feeling really threatened.

Male turkeys are called gobblers or toms, and females are called hens.

Wild turkey

Partridge

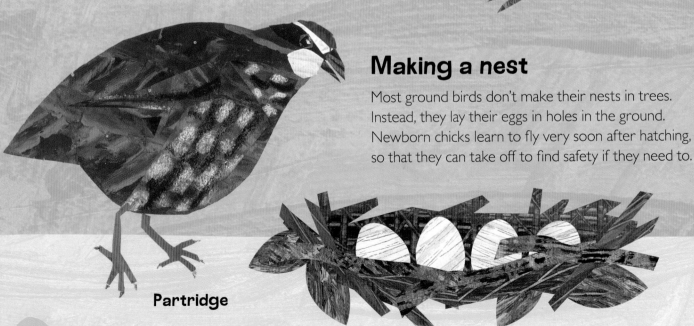

Making a nest

Most ground birds don't make their nests in trees. Instead, they lay their eggs in holes in the ground. Newborn chicks learn to fly very soon after hatching, so that they can take off to find safety if they need to.

Males and females

Most male ground birds are big and bold, with bright feathers to impress females. Females are usually much smaller and plainer. This helps them to blend in while protecting their chicks from predators.

Unlike most ground birds, male and female ptarmigans look almost the same.

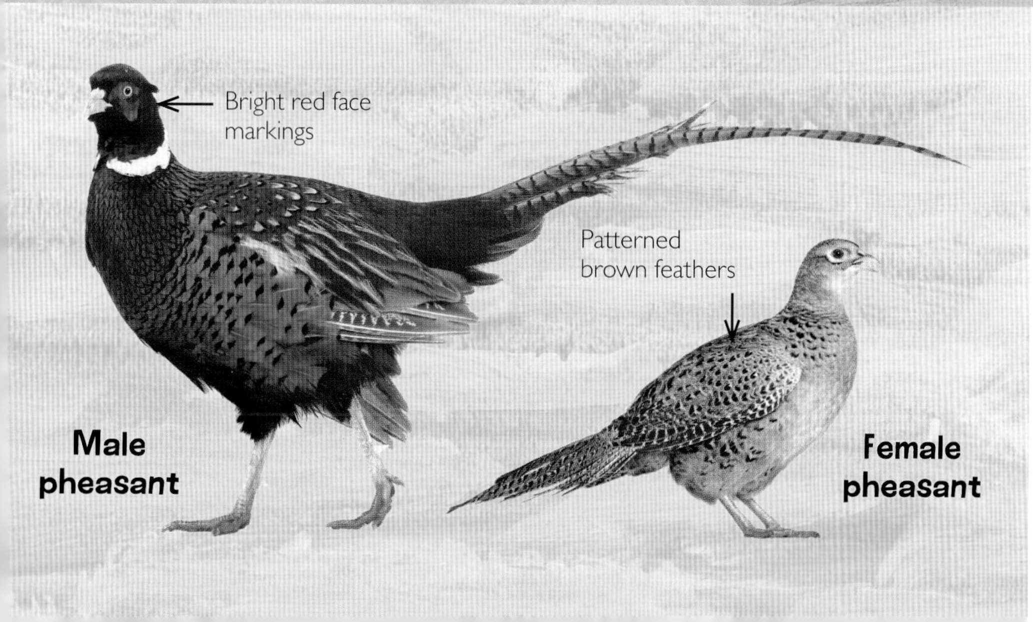

Game birds

Some ground birds are hunted by people for sport or for food. They are also called "game birds" because hunting them is a competitive sport in some parts of the world.

Extraordinary eagles

The most powerful birds of prey are eagles. They glide through the air, keeping their eagle eyes on the ground. When they spot possible prey, they dive down at high speed and make a grab with their deadly talons. The prey has no time to escape!

Birds of prey are also called raptors. Unlike owls, they mostly hunt in the daytime.

Fierce fliers

Birds of prey are awesome airborne hunters. These predators have keen eyesight, impressive speed, and sharp talons to grab prey on the move.

Stealing a meal

Many birds of prey, like these red kites, often steal food from other hunters. They swoop in on a predator, grab the fresh prey in their talons, then fly away with their stolen treasure!

Favorite foods

Some birds of prey will eat almost anything, dead or alive. Others are choosier and have developed different tactics to hunt down the prey they prefer.

Philippine eagle

This rain forest bird is strong enough to seize a monkey from a tree and carry it off in its gigantic talons.

Secretary bird

Snakes beware! This African bird uses its long, strong legs to stamp on snakes before eating them.

Egyptian vulture

This bird loves ostrich eggs. It cannot open the eggs with its beak, so it uses a stone to crack the shells.

Cleanup crew

Some birds of prey let other hunters do the dirty work. Vultures feast on the rotting remains of dead prey. These scavengers help to keep their environment clean and stop the spread of diseases.

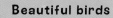

Nesting and hatching

Most birds build nests where they can lay their eggs in safety. When the time is right, C-R-A-C-K! The baby birds hatch. They need constant care until they are ready to leave the nest.

Hidey-hole

Woodpeckers build their nests in tree trunks. They peck away with their beaks to create a hollow inside the tree. This is a great place to hide eggs from prying predators.

Making a nest

Most birds build their nests in trees. These provide a safe place to hide eggs and raise chicks. Many nests are shaped like a bowl, with a hollow inside for the eggs.

The nest's rounded shape holds the eggs safely.

Grass, twigs, feathers, moss, and leaves are used to make the nest.

Bird eggs

The eggs laid by birds can be all kinds of colors, patterns, and sizes. Their waterproof, hard shells protect the developing chicks. Inside, the yolk provides the chicks with food to help them grow.

The ostrich lays the biggest egg of any bird. About 24 hens' eggs could fit inside one ostrich egg!

Ostrich egg

Hen egg

The bee hummingbird lays the smallest egg of any bird. Each egg is the size of a pea.

Bee hummingbird egg

Cuckoo tricksters

The cuckoo lays an egg in another bird's nest, then flies off. When it hatches, the cuckoo chick is cared for as though it were part of the other bird's family. This little reed warbler is feeding a chick that is already much bigger than she is.

Osprey

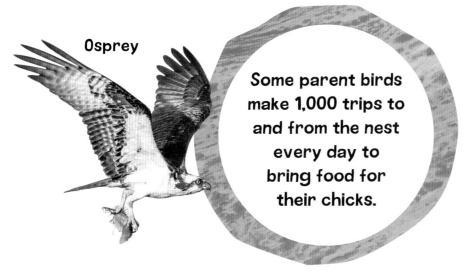

Some parent birds make 1,000 trips to and from the nest every day to bring food for their chicks.

Home ground

Some birds. such as this oystercatcher, lay their eggs on the ground. These eggs are usually patterned to blend in with their surroundings, so that predators cannot spot them easily.

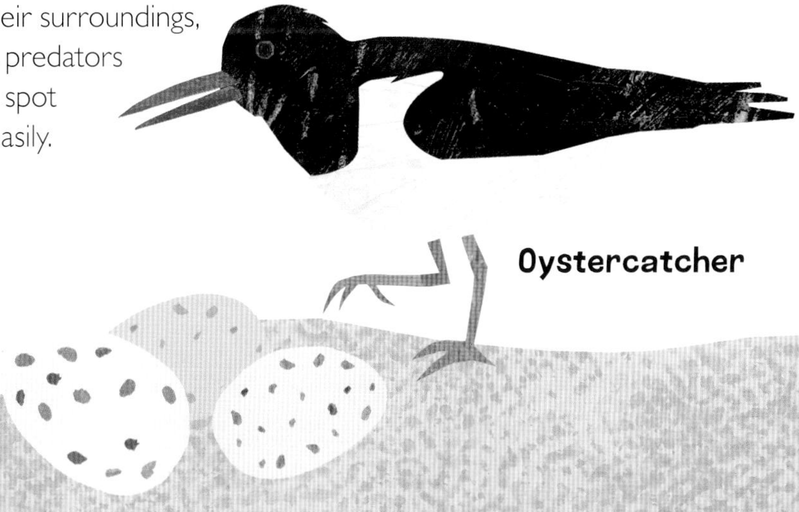

Oystercatcher

A chick's life

After the mother bird lays her eggs, she keeps them warm and safe while the chicks grow inside.

Hatching time

When they are ready to hatch, the chicks peck away at the eggshells until they break open. Hello, world!

Hungry babies

The helpless chicks rely on their parents to feed them. Bring on the worms, insects, or seeds!

Time to go!

Baby birds grow up fast. Within weeks, they are too big for their nest. Off they fly to start their new lives.

Freshwater birds

Many birds make their homes in lakes and rivers. Living by fresh water means there is always plenty to drink and a very big bathtub to keep feathers clean!

Ducking down

Sometimes all you can see of a duck is its bottom poking out of the water. This means the duck is feeding underwater, using its beak to grab insects and slippery water snails.

Built for swimming

Many freshwater birds have webbed feet to power them along and thick feathers to keep them warm. They find food underwater and nest in the reeds or at the water's edge.

Noisy geese

Honk! Honk! Listen for the honking sound geese make. Geese take flight by running across the surface of the water to gather enough speed to get airborne.

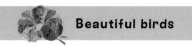

Elegant swans

These beautiful birds glide gracefully across the water. Swans stretch their long, flexible necks underwater to pull up plants to eat.

Long-legged waders

Some birds prefer paddling to swimming. They splash through shallow water and stick their big beaks under the surface to grab hold of food.

Spindly stork

The marabou stork is hard to miss, with its dangling neck pouch, giant beak, and long, skinny legs. It patrols African wetlands for fish, snakes, and frogs, but will feast on dead creatures, too.

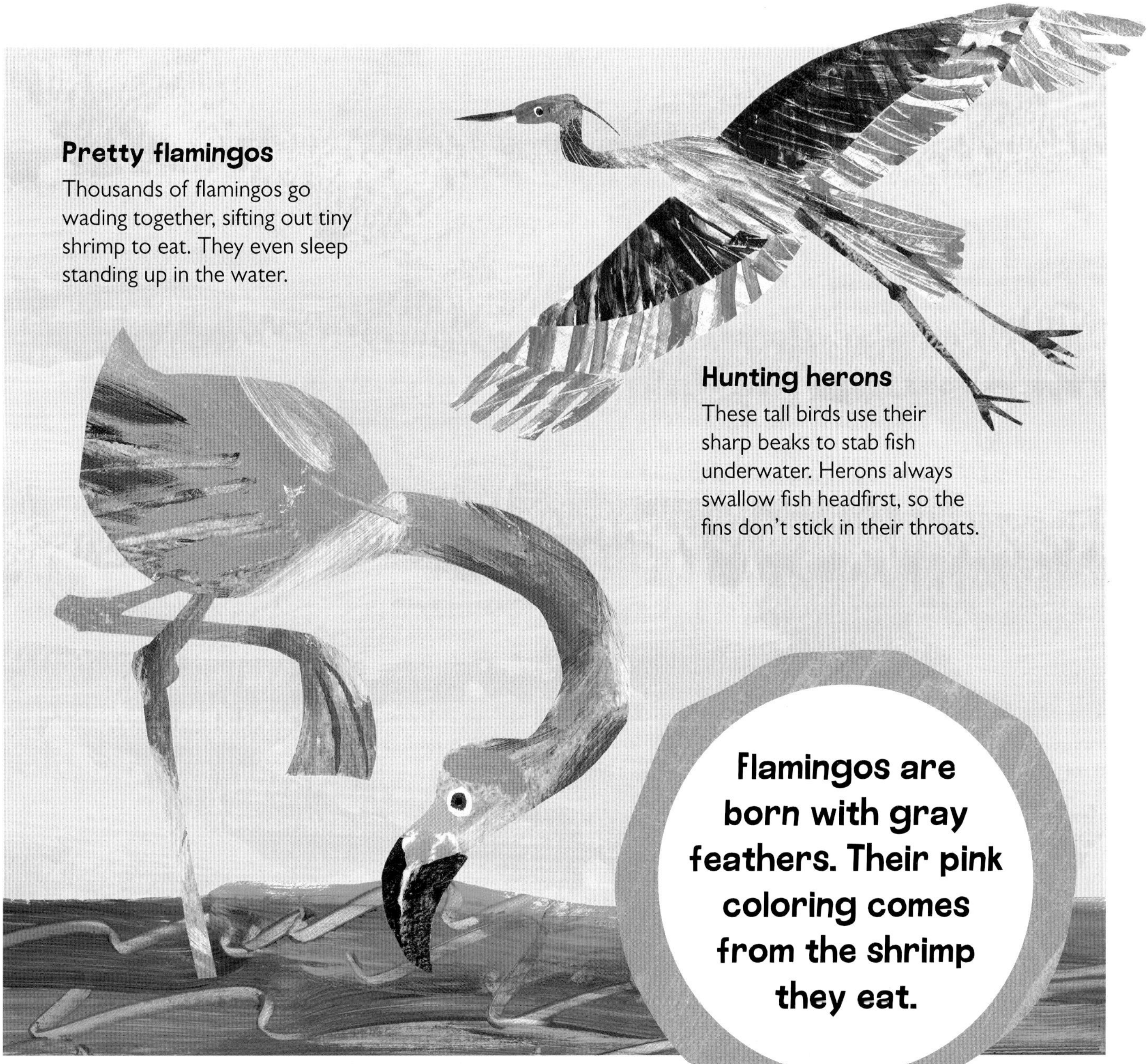

Pretty flamingos

Thousands of flamingos go wading together, sifting out tiny shrimp to eat. They even sleep standing up in the water.

Hunting herons

These tall birds use their sharp beaks to stab fish underwater. Herons always swallow fish headfirst, so the fins don't stick in their throats.

Flamingos are born with gray feathers. Their pink coloring comes from the shrimp they eat.

Seabirds

Our oceans and shorelines are home to a huge variety of seabirds. Some, such as the albatross, can live out at sea for years without ever touching down on land.

Clifftop colonies

Big groups of birds, called colonies, nest all along coastlines. Some birds live all year round on clifftops or ledges. Other birds, which usually live at sea, form temporary colonies when they come ashore to lay eggs and raise their chicks.

Colony of guillemots

Puffin

These little birds are very well adapted to life at sea. They have webbed feet to paddle through water, waterproof feathers to keep dry, and ridges on their beaks that can grip even the most slippery fish.

Short wings act like fins when the puffin swims.
Rough-edged beak holds fish tight.
Webbed feet

Gull

Hold onto your ice-cream cone! Gulls are the squawking scavengers of the seaside. They eat just about anything, including animal remains on the beach, garbage from trash cans, and even your seaside snacks.

Guano islands

There are tiny rocky islands in the middle of the ocean that are covered in bird waste, called guano. Some huge seabird colonies produce so much guano that the land is buried under layers of the white, stinky stuff.

On rocky islands with no trees, seabirds build nests from bird droppings!

Albatross

Meet the bird with the world's longest wingspan. The albatross can glide for hours without even flapping its wings. This expert flier can even fall asleep in midair.

Gannet

When a gannet spots a fish, it dives down headfirst. SPLASH! It breaks the water's surface at high speed and grabs its prey.

Pelican

The pelican uses its huge beak like a fishing net. The stretchy pouch attached to its beak can store three times more fish than the pelican's stomach.

Penguin parade

There are 18 types of penguin. Most, including the ones shown here, live in or around Antarctica. They are very well adapted to life in their frozen habitat. However, there are a few penguin types that live in the warmer seas of southern Africa and Australasia.

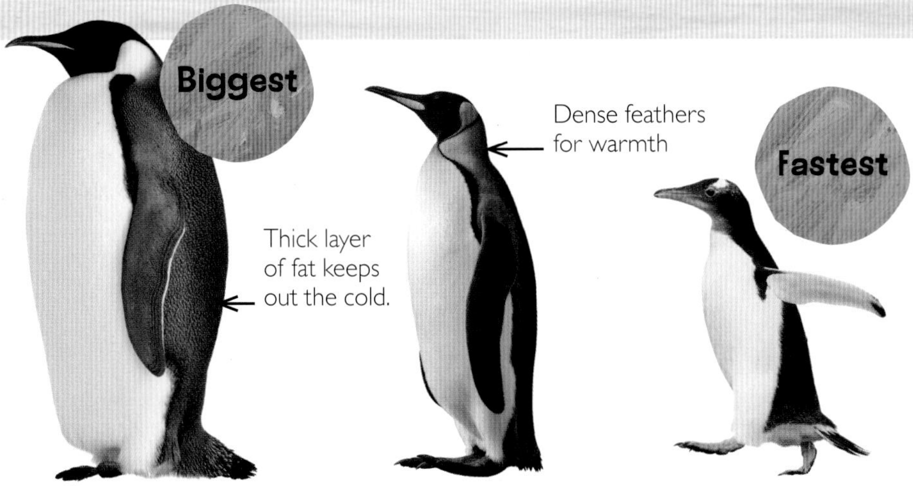

Emperor penguin **King penguin** **Gentoo penguin**

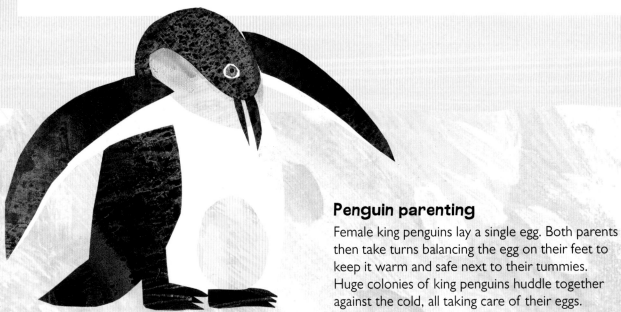

Penguin parenting

Female king penguins lay a single egg. Both parents then take turns balancing the egg on their feet to keep it warm and safe next to their tummies. Huge colonies of king penguins huddle together against the cold, all taking care of their eggs.

Antarctic birds

Antarctica is the coldest, driest, and windiest continent on Earth. Birds have to be tough and adapt to the challenging conditions here.

Smallest

Rockhopper penguin

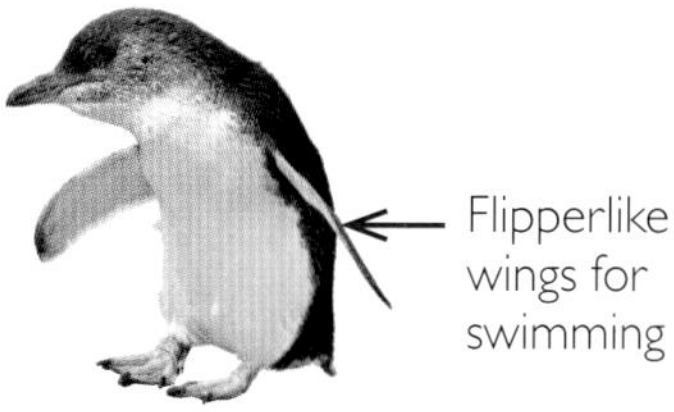

Little penguin

About 97 percent of Antarctica is covered in ice.

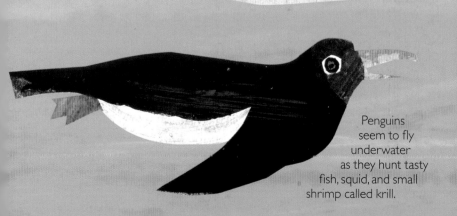

Ocean motion

Penguins cannot fly. They are clumsy on land, but graceful swimmers in the water. Their wings move like flippers, powering them along at high speed.

Penguins seem to fly underwater as they hunt tasty fish, squid, and small shrimp called krill.

Life on the ice

Penguins are not the only birds that have set up home on the ice. These three flying birds also live in the freezing cold of Antarctica.

Snow petrel

The pure-white snow petrel blends in with the snow and ice. This tough bird lives in Antarctica all year round.

Antarctic skua

Skuas hunt and scavenge whatever they can find, including fish, penguin eggs, and even newborn penguin chicks.

Snowy sheathbill

This bird shares the same coastlines as penguin colonies, feeding on eggs and other birds' leftovers.

Flightless birds

Some birds prefer to keep their feet firmly on the ground. Their bodies may be too big to take off, or they might just find running or swimming easier than flying.

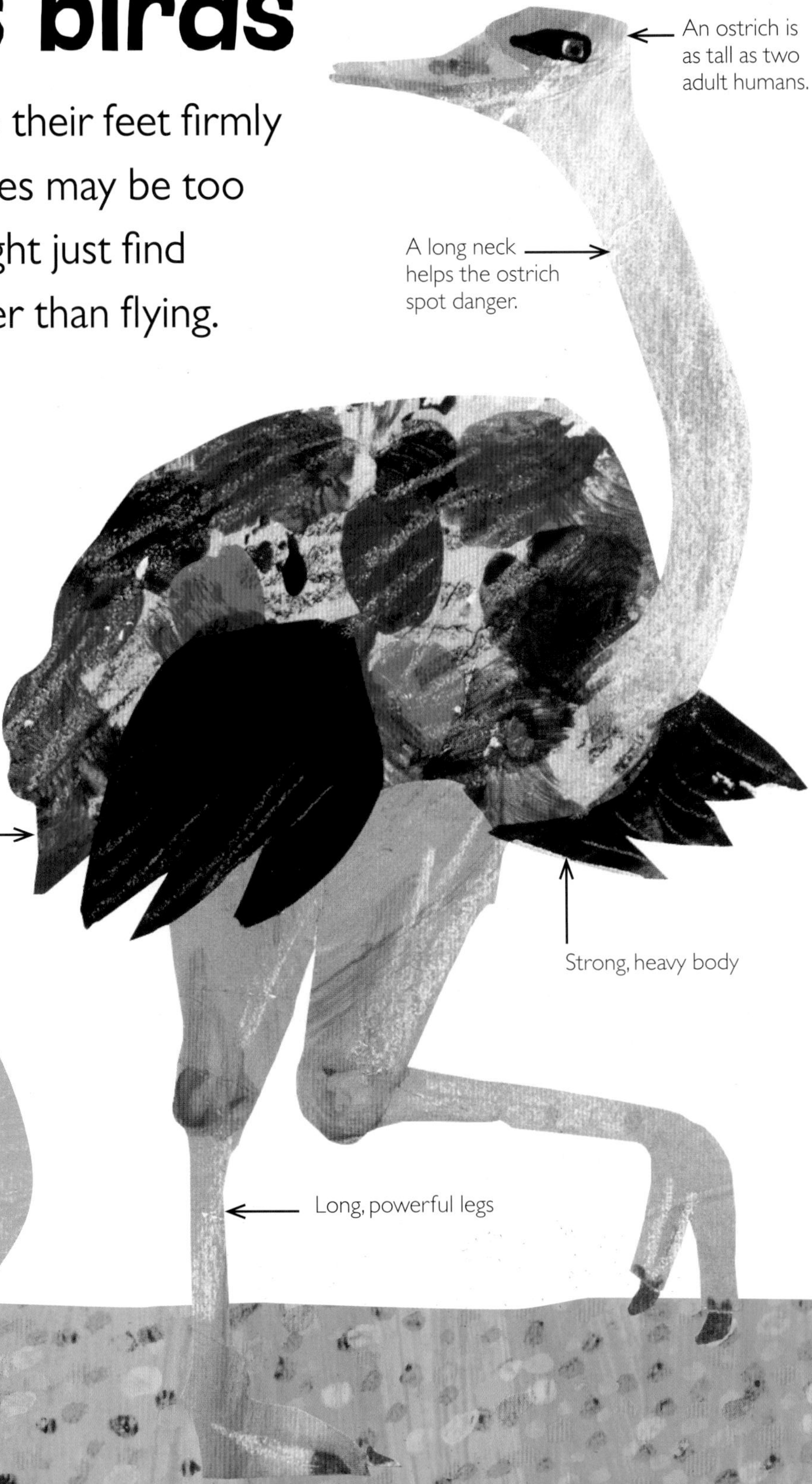
An ostrich is as tall as two adult humans.
A long neck helps the ostrich spot danger.
Soft, smooth feathers
Strong, heavy body
Long, powerful legs

Ostrich

The world's biggest bird is too heavy to fly. In the African savanna, the ostrich feasts on plants, lizards, and snakes and runs at high speed to escape hungry big cats and hyenas.

An ostrich can run faster than a racehorse!

In the water

Flightless birds that live in water use their wings like fins for swimming.

Flightless steamer duck

Instead of using their wings to fly, these ducks flap them in the water to help them swim faster. Male steamer ducks are very feisty and often have fierce fights.

Flightless cormorant

There are no predators on the islands where the flightless cormorant lives, so there is no need to fly away. This skillful swimmer has webbed feet and a hooked tip on its beak for catching fish and eels.

On the land

Flightless birds that live on the ground often have long, strong legs for chasing prey and running away from predators.

Kiwi

The world's smallest flightless bird is only the size of a chicken. The kiwi's tiny wings are hidden under its feathers. Nostrils at the end of its beak are used to sniff out insects in the soil.

Emu

One of the world's tallest birds, the emu strides over the Australian desert on its powerful legs. It covers huge distances in search of plants, insects, and fruit to eat.

Roadrunner

These birds can fly, but choose not to! Speedy roadrunners can take to the air in short bursts. However, they usually stay on land, where they can outrun predators, such as coyotes.

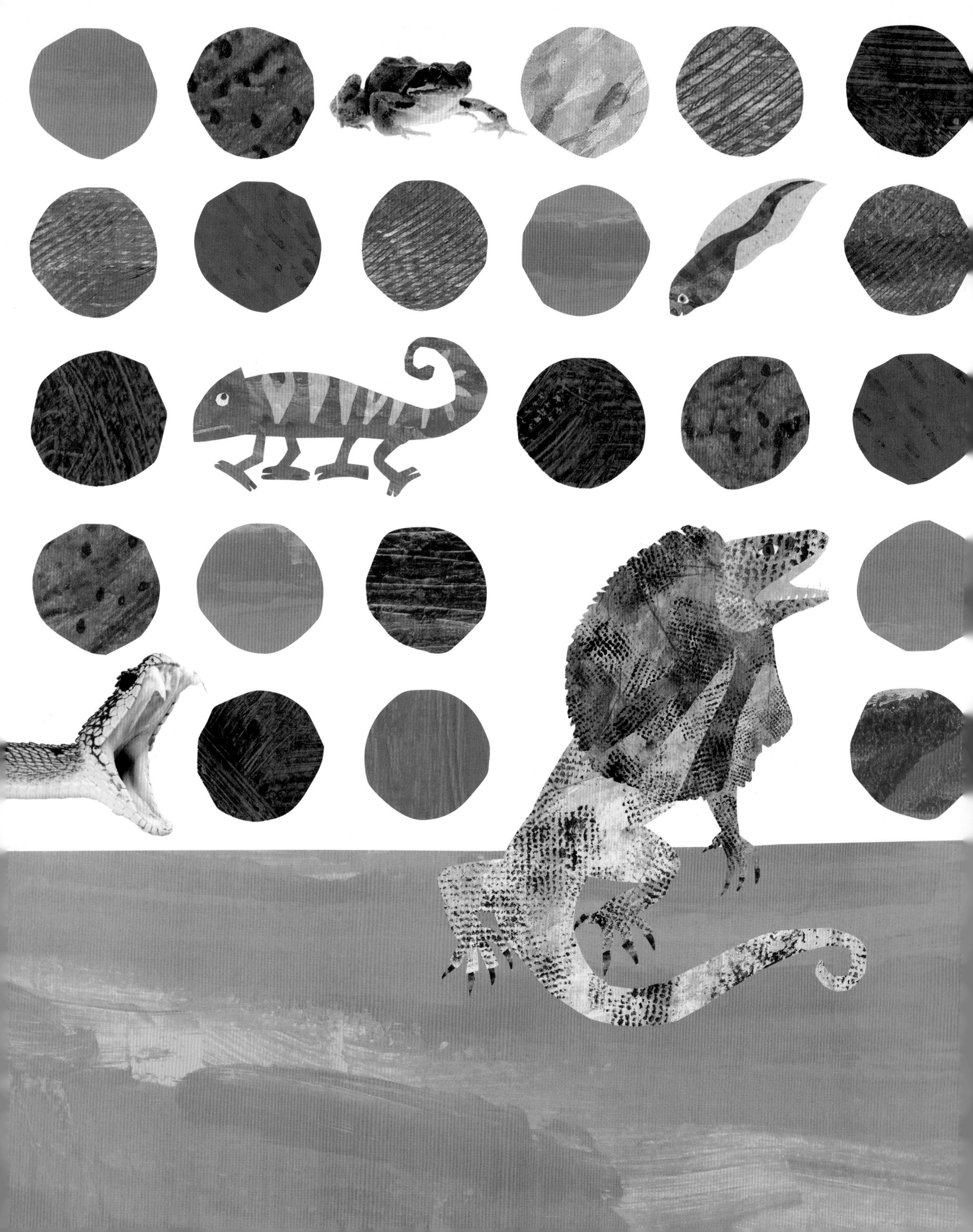

Remarkable reptiles and amphibians

Reptiles

The first reptiles lived on Earth millions of years ago and included dinosaurs. Today's reptiles are some of the planet's toughest animals, covered in protective scales or plates.

Green mamba

There are more than 10,000 different types of reptile.

Shedding skin

All reptiles regularly wriggle out of their old skin and grow a new one. Snakes lose their skin all at once.

Bush viper

Plumed basilisk

Reptile scales are made of keratin, which is the same material in your hair and nails and in bird feathers.

Cold blood

Reptiles are cold-blooded, which means that their body temperature matches the surrounding air or water. To warm up, reptiles come out in the open and bask in the sunshine. To cool off, they lie under rocks or stick to the shade.

Ball python

Mainly meat

Most reptiles are meat-eaters, on the prowl for insects, birds, frogs, or fish. After they eat an enormous dinner, reptiles can go without eating again for days, weeks, or months!

The ball python can survive on just one massive meal every year!

Prehistoric past

The very first reptiles were little, lizardlike animals. Over millions of years, they developed into many different dinosaurs. Modern reptiles, like their dinosaur ancestors, are covered in scales, and they live both on land and in water.

Herrerasaurus was one of the first dinosaurs to stomp the Earth.

Reptile babies

Almost all reptiles lay eggs. Some bury their eggs underground so predators cannot eat them. Unlike baby mammals, most newborn reptiles have to look after themselves as soon as they hatch. They look just like their parents, but smaller!

Sea turtles bury their eggs in the sand.

Crocodile

Armor plating

Reptiles have dry skin, covered in strong scales or sturdy plates. This layer of body armor stops predators from biting through their skin.

Hungry hunters

Crocodiles and alligators lie perfectly still in the water, looking like giant floating logs. Then, when an animal swims by or stops for a drink, they attack with a snap of their powerful jaws.

Crocodiles and alligators

Beware! Crocodiles and alligators are powerhouse predators with oversized jaws that can deliver the biggest bite on Earth.

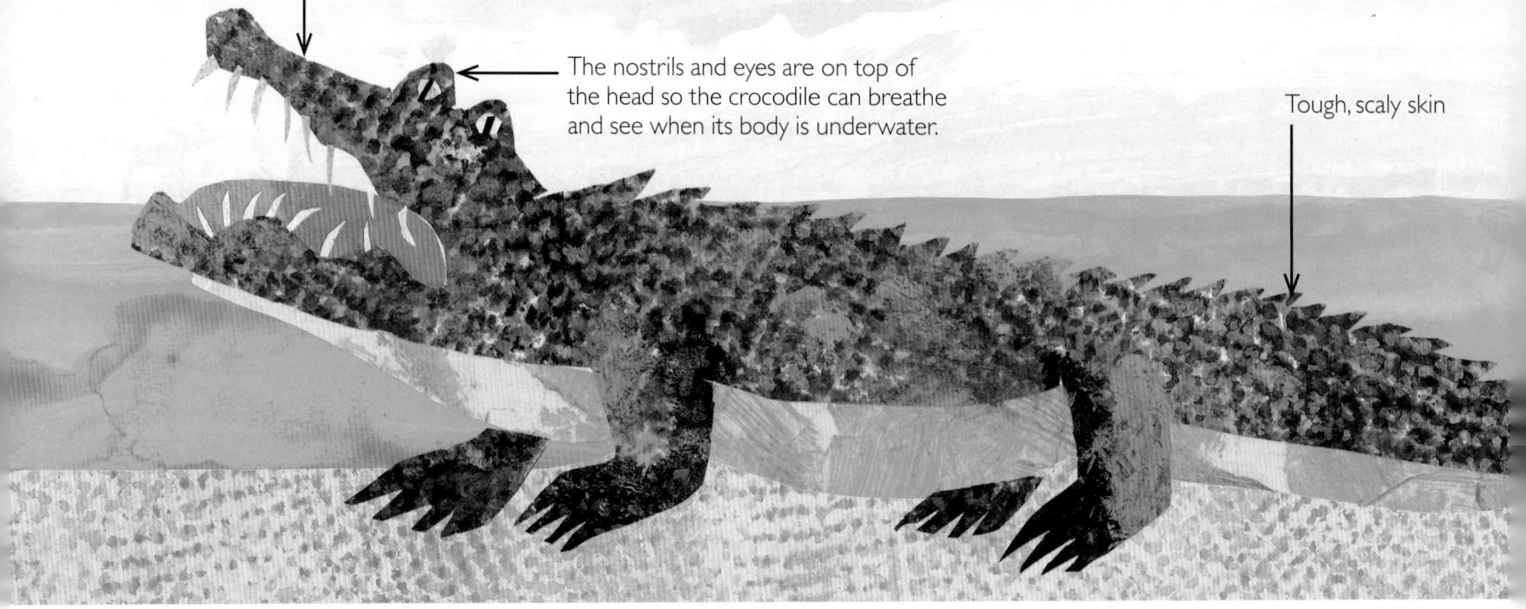

Giant jaws for seizing prey
The nostrils and eyes are on top of the head so the crocodile can breathe and see when its body is underwater.
Tough, scaly skin

Crocodiles can grow at least 40 new sets of terrifying teeth during their lives.

Family facts

Habitat
Freshwater lakes and rivers, and coastal areas

Location
Africa, Asia, Australia, North America, and South America

Diet
Anything meaty that makes the mistake of crossing their path

Family
The three members are crocodiles, alligators, and gharials.

Caring mothers
Female crocodiles dig a hole in a sandy riverbank to lay their eggs. They use their big bodies to keep the eggs warm until they hatch. Newly hatched babies are perfect mini versions of their mom.

Strong tail powers the body through water.

Lying in wait
Crocodiles and alligators look peaceful as they sunbathe and doze on riverbanks. However, these hungry hunters can spring into action instantly if they spot an animal that might make a meal.

Spot the difference
Alligators are usually smaller and darker than crocodiles. You can hardly see alligator teeth when their mouths close, but crocodiles show theirs in the famous crocodile smile!

Crocodile
Narrower, more pointed snout

Lizards

The smallest lizard of all is the nano-chameleon. It could sit on the tip of your finger!

There are more types of lizard than any other reptile. Most of them run and climb, but some can also swim, burrow, glide, stick to ceilings, and even walk on water!

Lizard life

Most lizards have scaly skin, four short legs, and a long tail. They spend a lot of time sunbathing, but can also move fast to chase prey and escape predators. They have big appetites, and some eat half their own body weight in insects every day.

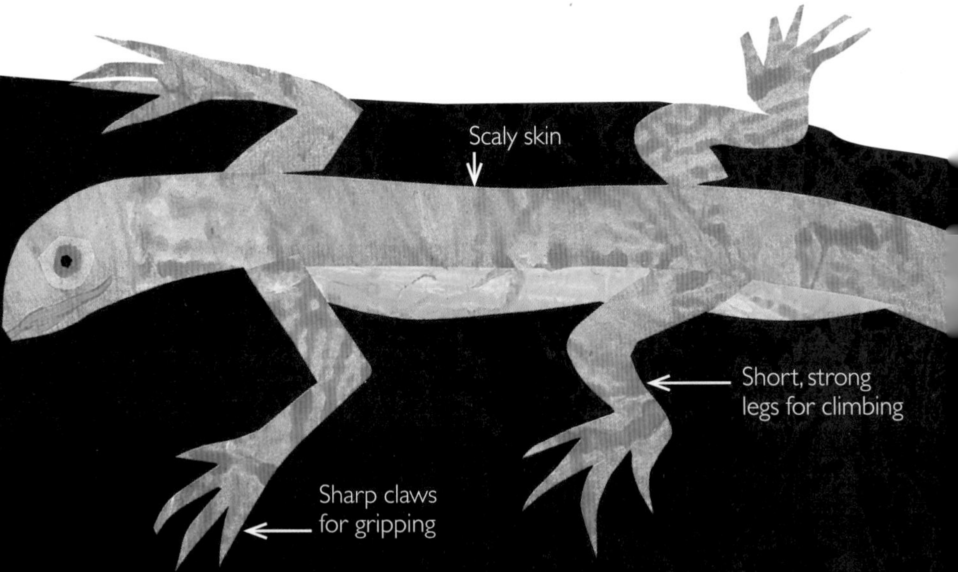

Ancient lizards

Tuataras lived alongside the dinosaurs millions of years ago, and they are still here today. These spiny-backed lizards live in burrows on islands off New Zealand.

Sticky feet

Geckos are among the smallest lizards. Their special skill is that they can climb steep walls and hang from ceilings without falling off. The gecko's tiny feet are packed with hairy spikes that stick to surfaces.

Slow worms

These European reptiles are unusual lizards because they don't have any legs. Instead, they slither along the ground like snakes. Slow worms live in burrows under logs or rocks and mainly eat insects, earthworms, and slugs.

Family facts

Habitat
Deserts, rain forests, woodland, grassland, and parkland

Diet
Small animals, insects, and sometimes plants

Location
Every continent, except Antarctica

Family
More than 6,000 types, including iguanas, geckos, and chameleons

Ocean lizard

Marine iguanas live on the Galápagos Islands off South America. They sunbathe on the rocks and dip into the ocean to find food. The seaweed they mainly eat turns their skin red and green.

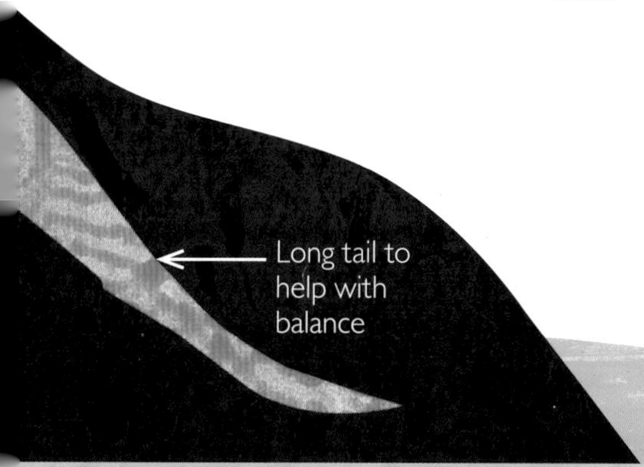

Forest glider

Known as the flying dragon, the Draco lizard has skin flaps on its legs that open out like wings. Although they can't fly like birds, these graceful reptiles glide easily between the trees.

Walking on water

Basilisk lizards are the only reptiles that can walk on water. They spread out their big feet and hop at high speed over the water's surface. This is the perfect way to escape from predators!

Komodo dragons

Although it doesn't breathe fire or fly like a storybook dragon, the Komodo dragon is the biggest, most fearsome lizard on the planet. Yikes!

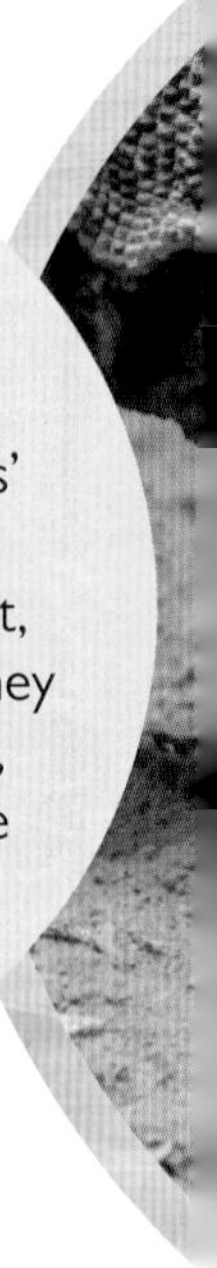

Dragon's dinner

Komodo dragons will eat almost anything, including birds' eggs, goats, buffalo, and even humans! They hide in the forest, waiting for prey to pass. Then they jump out and bite their victim, injecting venom to weaken the prey so it cannot run away.

Family facts

Habitat
Tropical rain forest and rocky coasts

Location
Indonesia, Asia

Diet
Meaty prey of all kinds

Family
The monitor lizard family has about 80 members, including Komodo dragons.

Komodo dragons

These gigantic reptiles have been on Earth for four million years. Today, Komodo dragons live on only a few remote Indonesian islands. They cool off in the ocean, lie low in burrows, and sniff out prey by flicking their forked tongues.

Dumeril's monitor lizard

Monitor family

The Komodo dragon is the largest member of the monitor lizard family. Meat-loving monitors live all over the world. They are fast walkers and strong swimmers. Their eyes are constantly open, looking for the next meal.

Fearless fighters

Komodo dragons have no predators to worry about. Their only threat is other Komodo dragons. Large dragons sometimes prey on weaker ones, and rival males often wrestle each other very fiercely over females.

Komodo dragons are the strongest, heaviest lizards of all.

Lizard defenses

Predators should think twice before they pounce on a lizard. These tough little reptiles are survival experts, using clever tactics and deadly weapons to avoid attack.

Gila monster

The North American Gila monster is one of the few lizards that are venomous. Its deadly bite is used for self-defense, ensuring that most predators steer clear.

Thorny devil

Living up to its name, this desert-dweller is totally covered in sharp spines. These spikes make it very hard for predators to grab or swallow the thorny devil.

Horned toad lizard

This desert reptile has a shocking response for attackers; it blasts jets of foul-tasting blood from its eyes. This terrifying tactic ensures that most predators don't hang around for long.

Western green lizard

Some lizards have a surprising escape strategy. If a predator grabs the Western green lizard's tail, part of the tail breaks off, giving the reptile time to run for cover.

Blue-tongued skink

If predators come too close, this lizard pretends it is poisonous by flashing its bright-blue tongue. Most attackers back off immediately, but, if not, the skink can also deliver a nasty bite.

Frilled lizard

When threatened, the frilled lizard opens the giant skin flaps on its neck to look four times bigger. But that's not all; this small but fearless lizard also hisses loudly and thrashes its tail to scare predators away.

Frilled lizards can run upright on their two back legs when escaping danger.

Chameleons

Chameleons are among Earth's most colorful creatures. They change color depending on the light and temperature, or sometimes they just match their color to their mood!

Slow movers

Chameleons prefer to stay still for most of the day. They climb trees and hide in the leafy shade. Their gripping claws and flexible tails help them to stay balanced on the branches.

Curly tail helps with balance.

Rainbow reptiles

Chameleons change color when they are scared or angry. Most chameleons change from brown to green, and back again, but some can change to almost any color of the rainbow.

The brighter its colors, the angrier the chameleon!

Family facts

Habitat
Rain forests and deserts

Location
Africa, Asia, and Europe

Diet
Insects, including crickets and flies

Sharp claws for gripping
Each eye moves separately so the chameleon can see in different directions.

The tongue unrolls to catch passing prey.

Sticky tongue

Chameleons have a superlong, stretchy tongue with a sticky tip. When a chameleon spots prey, its tongue shoots out at lightning speed. Snap! As soon as the insect is caught in the sticky trap, the chameleon reels its tongue back in and swallows the prey.

Nearly half of all types of chameleon live on the African island of Madagascar.

Littlest lizards

Dwarf chameleons are the world's smallest reptiles, and tiniest of all is this nano-chameleon. It was discovered in 2021, living in the rain forests of Madagascar.

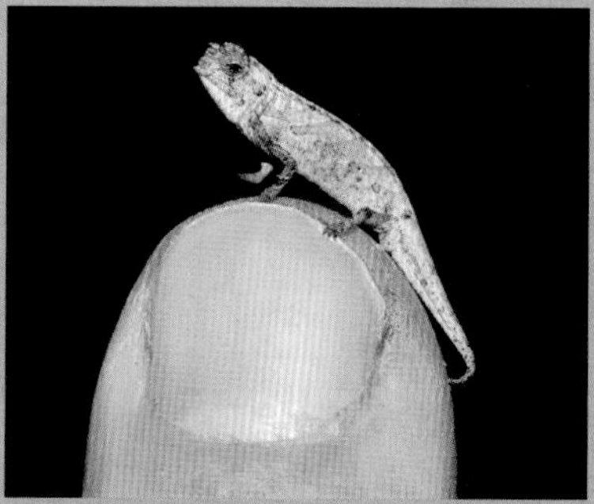

Tortoises

Slowly, but surely, tortoises shuffle along looking for tasty plants. Their heavy shells make moving around hard work, but they also provide protection from danger.

Tortoises have a super sense of smell to sniff out tasty food.

Plant-eaters

Most reptiles eat meat, but not tortoises. They are far too slow to chase prey. Instead, they clip off lush leaves and chewy twigs with their sharp-edged, toothless beaks.

Life on land

Tortoises are different from turtles because they only live on land. But they still love to wallow in a muddy puddle.

Family facts

Habitat
Forests, grasslands, and deserts

Location
Africa, Asia, Europe, North America, and South America

Diet
Grass, fruit, leaves, and the occasional insect or worm

Shell shield

The tortoise's shell is made of solid plates, called scutes, joined together. If a hungry rat or raven comes close, the tortoise pulls its head and legs completely under the shell and stays still. Unable to get at any edible parts, the predator soon gives up.

Island giant

The Galápagos tortoise wins the prize for the world's biggest tortoise. This gentle giant is as long as a two-seater sofa. It is found in the Galápagos Islands off South America and can live for up to 200 years.

There were tortoises living on Earth even before the dinosaurs.

Shades and shapes

Tortoise shells can be different colors. The lighter the color, the hotter the habitat. Tortoises in the Sahara Desert have the palest shells of all. Most tortoise shells are dome-shaped, which makes them harder for a predator to bite. However, the shell of this pancake tortoise is as flat as… a pancake!

Turtles

Very few reptiles live in the ocean, but turtles are very much at home in the water. These savvy swimmers rely on their shells for protection against ocean predators.

Family facts

Habitat
Mainly oceans, but also freshwater lakes and rivers

Location
Oceans of every continent, except Antarctica

Diet
Insects, fish, or ocean plants and seaweed

Some turtles are kept clean by tiny fish, which nibble off any dirt and dead skin.

Streamlined swimmers

Most turtles have flatter shells than tortoises, to create a streamlined shape for swimming. They use their flippers to propel themselves through the water.

What's in a name?

Some turtles have names that give us clues about their appearance or lifestyle.

Snapping turtle

This turtle cannot pull its head and legs under its shell for safety. Instead, it uses its powerful jaws to snap at predators and scare them away.

A turtle's life

After they are born, male sea turtles spend their whole lives in the sea. Adult females return to the shore every year to lay their eggs.

1. Eggs

A female sea turtle goes back to the beach where she was born. She digs a hole, lays her eggs, then goes back to the sea.

2. Hatching

After about six weeks, the eggs hatch and baby turtles crawl out onto the sand.

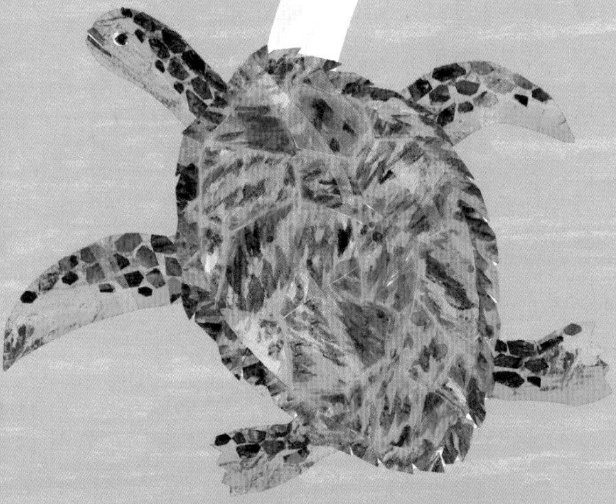

3. Baby turtles

The hatchlings rush down the beach, trying to avoid hungry crabs and seagulls. Once they reach the sea, they swim off and eventually grow into adults.

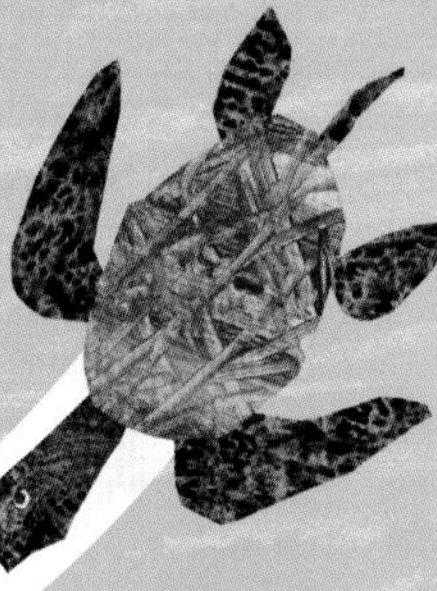

4. Adults

After about 10 years, turtles are fully grown and ready to find a mate, lay eggs, and start the circle of life all over again.

Green turtle

This turtle gets its name from the layer of greenish fat under its shell, which comes from the green marine plants that it eats.

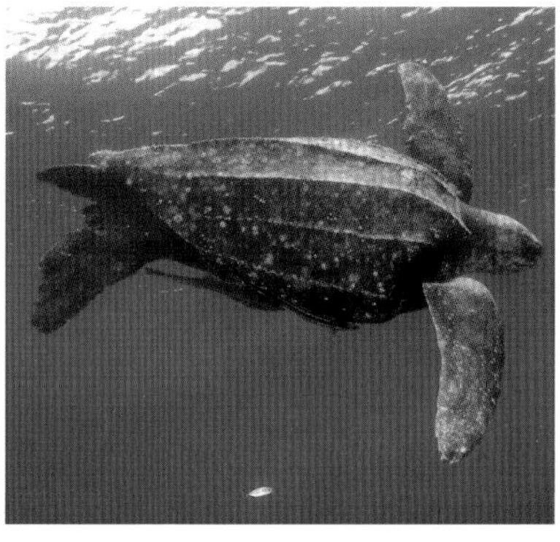

Leatherback turtle

This turtle's shell is soft, like leather. Although this gives less protection than a hard shell, the turtle's large size and high-speed swimming help it to escape most predators.

Venomous snakes

There are about 600 types of venomous snake. When they hunt, they first deliver a toxic bite, then open their mouths wide to swallow prey in one gulp.

Snake senses

Snakes don't have ears or noses. Instead, they sense vibrations in the ground through their skin, and they smell by "tasting" the air with their sensitive, forked tongues. Venomous snakes have sharp fangs to inject venom into their prey.

King cobra

The king cobra is the world's largest venomous snake. Before it strikes, it rears up angrily, then delivers a bite with enough powerful venom to take down an elephant.

Inland taipan

Australia's inland taipan has the strongest venom of any snake. There is enough venom in one bite to kill 100 people.

Sea krait

This underwater predator is extremely venomous. It catches eels by ambushing them from a hiding place in a coral reef. Before the eel can wriggle free, this ferocious hunter bites down hard, then gobbles its prey whole.

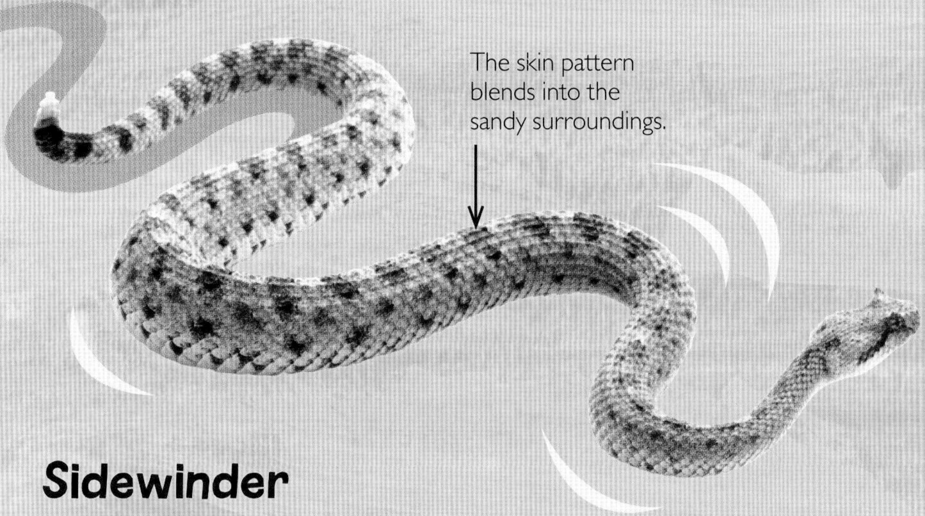

The skin pattern blends into the sandy surroundings.

Sidewinder

This desert rattlesnake gets its name from the way it slithers sideways across the sand. It is so hard to spot that prey is caught by surprise before it can escape.

Even if it is chopped off, a rattlesnake head can still deliver a deadly bite!

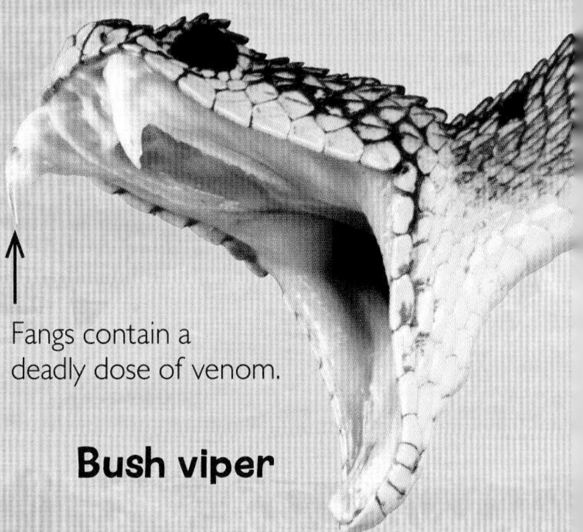

Fangs contain a deadly dose of venom.

Bush viper

Fixed fangs

Many venomous snakes have long fangs that fold up inside their mouths. However, coral snakes have smaller fangs that are always in position, ready to bite.

Coral snake

Milk snake

Copycat snake

The milk snake does a great impression of the venomous coral snake, but is actually completely harmless. The skin pattern fools predators into thinking the snake is too dangerous to attack.

What's for dinner?

Almost any animal can become a meal for a constrictor. These hungry carnivores wrap themselves around creatures small and large, from mice and squirrels to turtles and deer.

Boa constrictor

Squeeze and swallow

Constrictor snakes are often enormous and always powerful. After they have crushed their prey, these snakes open their mouths as wide as possible, so that they can swallow the prey whole.

Corn snake swallowing prey.

Squeezing snakes

Some snakes are not venomous, but they are still deadly predators. Constrictor snakes coil their bodies around their prey, then squeeze really tightly, so that the victim cannot breathe.

Reticulated python

Pythons are among the world's longest snakes, and the reticulated python is the longest of all. It usually hunts at night. Supersensitive areas, called pits, around its mouth pick up the heat given off by prey in the darkness.

Some pythons can even swallow alligators!

Rainbow boa

With its multicolored, scaly skin, the rainbow boa shimmers in the forest sunlight. This massive rain-forest reptile ambushes rodents and birds on the forest floor or targets amphibians at the water's edge.

Green anaconda

This gigantic South American constrictor holds the record as the world's heaviest snake. A slinky swimmer, it hunts by lurking silently under the water, waiting for alligators or other animals to come within striking distance.

Female green anacondas can be up to five times longer than males.

Indigo snake

Some snakes are neither venomous nor constrictors. This indigo snake is fierce and strong enough to simply grab hold of prey with its mouth and gobble it down instantly.

Laying eggs

Most reptiles hatch from eggs. Females lay their eggs in places where they will be safe until the babies are ready to emerge.

The hawksbill turtle lays up to 240 eggs at a time. That's more than any other reptile!

Reptile eggs

Crocodiles and tortoises lay eggs with hard shells. Turtle, snake, and lizard eggs have softer, leathery shells that are easier to break open. Here are some examples.

Snakes

Some female snakes leave their eggs as soon as they lay them. Others stay around to guard the eggs, then leave when the eggs hatch. The babies have to survive on their own from the moment they are born.

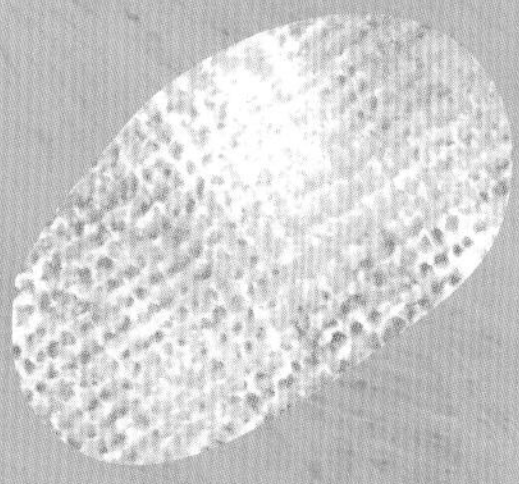

The king cobra lays up to 40 oval-shaped eggs.

Sea turtles

Female turtles lay eggs on the beach at night, then go back to the sea. When the babies hatch, they dig themselves out of the sand and start their short but dangerous journey toward the safety of the sea.

The loggerhead turtle lays about 130 round eggs.

Baby slowworms

The slowworm is an unusual reptile because the female lays her eggs inside her own body! The eggs hatch inside the mother, then the babies are born alive, in the same way as baby mammals.

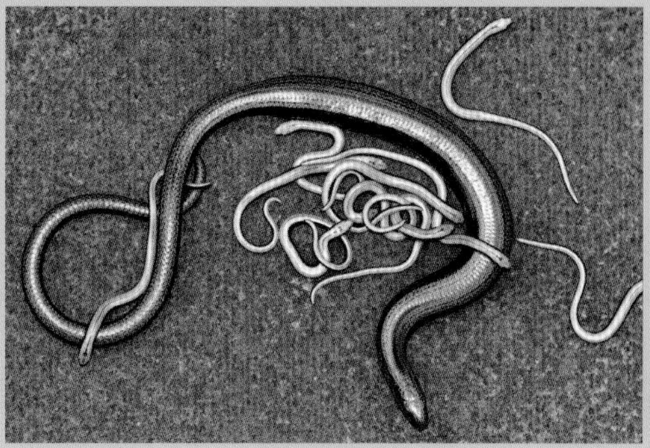

Tortoises

Most female tortoises lay their eggs in the spring. This gives the hatchlings time to grow and put on weight before hibernating in winter. Baby tortoises hatch with their hard shells already on their backs.

The African spurred tortoise lays up to 30 hard, round eggs.

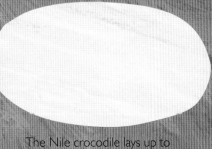

Crocodiles

If a crocodile's eggs are kept at a temperature of 90°F (32°C), the hatchlings will be male. If the eggs get colder or hotter, they will be female. The mother pops her babies in her mouth to keep them safe.

The Nile crocodile lays up to 80 large, oval-shaped eggs.

Lizards

Some lizards lay their eggs in holes or under the ground to keep them safe. Females cover their eggs with leaves or sand to hide them. They choose moist, damp places to prevent the eggs from drying out.

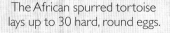

The Southern angle-headed dragon lays up to eight oval-shaped eggs.

Amphibians

Amphibians are born in water, but when they are fully grown, they can live both in the water and on land. Their skin is supersmooth, with no scales or hair.

Frogs, toads, salamanders, and newts are all types of amphibian.

Breathe easy

Amphibians start their lives in water, where they breathe through their skin. Their thin skin allows them to take in air more easily. As they develop, many amphibians grow lungs so they can breathe when they are on land.

Moist skin

Amphibians must keep their smooth skin wet to breathe properly. They usually stay near water, like this toad, so they can make sure their skin never dries out.

Total transformations

Most amphibians look completely different as babies and as full-grown adults. It's hard to imagine that a tiny, swimming tadpole will turn into a croaky, jumping frog!

Frog tadpole

Adult frog

Land and water

The word "amphibian" means "double life" in Greek. This is because amphibians have the choice of living on land or in water. Most live in places where they can easily reach both.

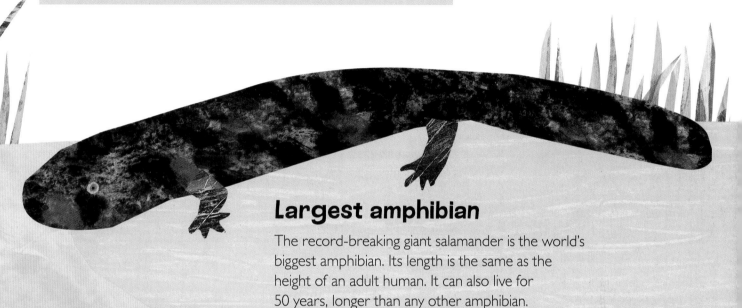

Largest amphibian

The record-breaking giant salamander is the world's biggest amphibian. Its length is the same as the height of an adult human. It can also live for 50 years, longer than any other amphibian.

Axolotls

Unlike other amphibians, these unusual salamanders never change out of their baby stage. Instead, they just grow bigger and bigger. If they get injured, axolotls grow new body parts. They can even grow a new brain if they need to.

Eastern newt

Cold-blooded

Amphibians are cold-blooded, which means they cannot control their own body temperature, as mammals do. Instead, they warm up or cool down by sunbathing or heading for the shade.

Circle of life

Amphibians start their lives in the water, then their bodies change to allow them to live on land, too. This total transformation is called metamorphosis.

Toad spawn

Toads go through a circle of life similar to a frog's. One difference is that female toads lay eggs in long lines, rather than in one big blob.

A frog's life

A frog starts life as a tiny, fishlike tadpole. It then goes through different stages before it becomes a hopping, croaking adult!

1. Frog spawn

The female frog lays a clump of eggs, called frog spawn, in the water. The eggs are surrounded by jelly to protect them. Some of the frog spawn is eaten by fish or insects.

6. Going home

In spring, a female frog goes back to the pond where she was born to lay her eggs. Then the cycle begins again.

5. Adult frog

After about four months, the frog is fully grown. Its muscular body is adapted for both swimming in water and jumping on land. Ribbit!

2. Tadpole

About two weeks later, the frog spawn hatches into tiny creatures with long tails, called tadpoles. They wriggle free from the jelly and start to swim.

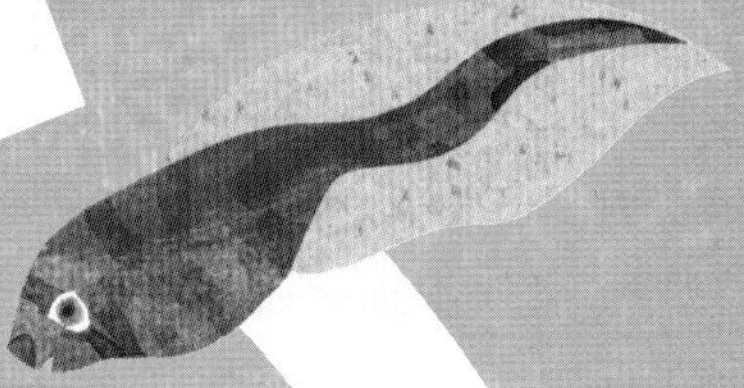

3. Growing legs

The tadpole eats water plants and grows bigger. Its tail gets smaller and tiny buds appear, which will grow into legs.

The tail is now just a stump.

4. Froglet

The tadpole becomes a young frog called a froglet. It has developed lungs for breathing air, grown four little legs, and now has webbed feet.

Unusual egg-layers

These frogs and toads are different because they don't lay their eggs in water, as most of their relatives do.

Midwife toad

After the female lays the eggs, the male takes care of them. He attaches the eggs to his legs until they hatch.

Green tree frog

This frog lays eggs in a treetop nest of foam made from its body slime. The foam keeps the eggs from drying out.

Red-eyed tree frog

These frogs lay their eggs on tree leaves. The rain-forest air is humid enough to keep the eggs moist.

Frogs and toads

Frogs and toads are among the most common types of amphibian on Earth. They are just as comfortable leaping around on land as they are taking a dip in water.

Frog faces

Frogs have bulgy eyes and big heads. They have a wide mouth to catch prey and a loud croak to attract females.

Family facts

Habitat
Forests, wetlands, and gardens with ponds

Location
Every continent, except Antarctica

Diet
Insects

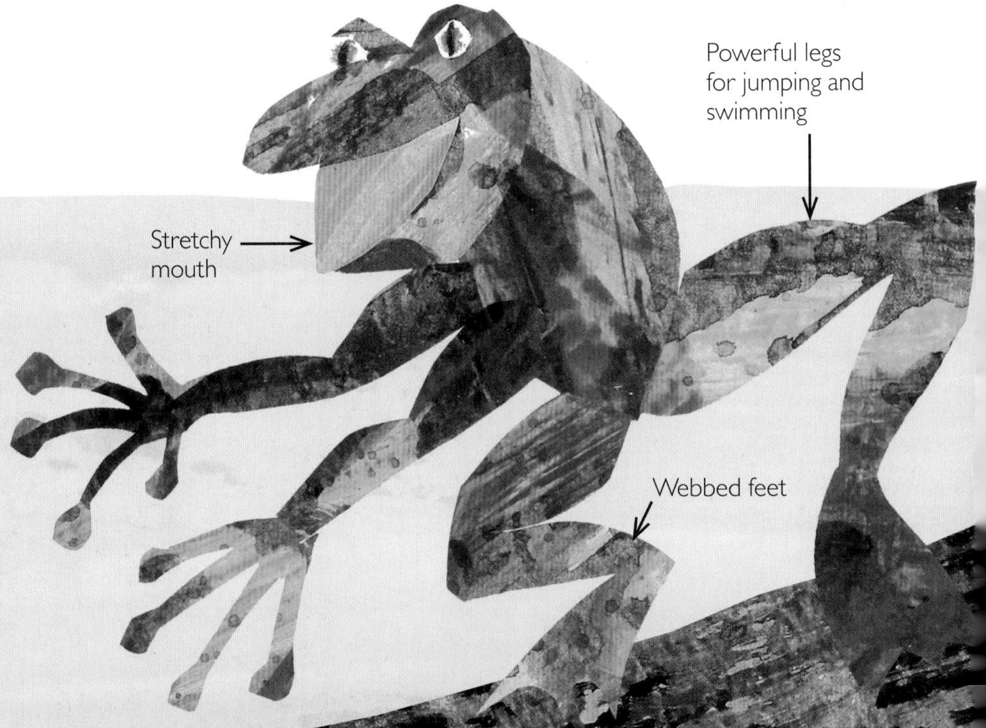

World of frogs

There are about 5,000 different types of frog, living in all kinds of habitats.

Tree frog

Tree frogs have tiny suction cups on their toes so they can cling tightly to twigs and plant stems. They live in trees and only return to water to lay their eggs.

Toxic toads

Toads are usually bigger than frogs, with stubbier legs and drier skin. If they are attacked, toads puff up their bodies to look more threatening. They also release poison from their skin, so that any predator who takes a bite will get a toxic mouthful.

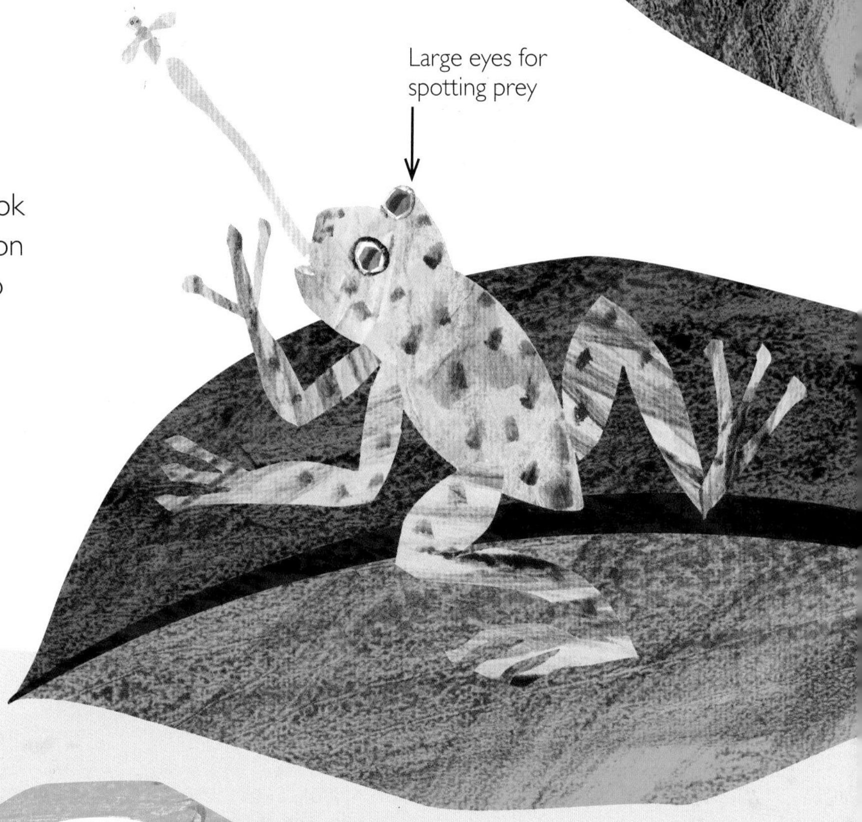

Common toad

Some frogs can make their skin turn lighter or darker to suit their surroundings.

Catching prey

Frogs and toads hunt live insects, but they don't chew their prey. Instead, they open their mouths wide, flick out a sticky tongue to catch a passing insect, then gulp the prey down whole.

Chilean four-eyed frog

This frog's two extra "eyes" are actually big spots on its back. These markings trick predators into thinking that the frog is bigger and more threatening.

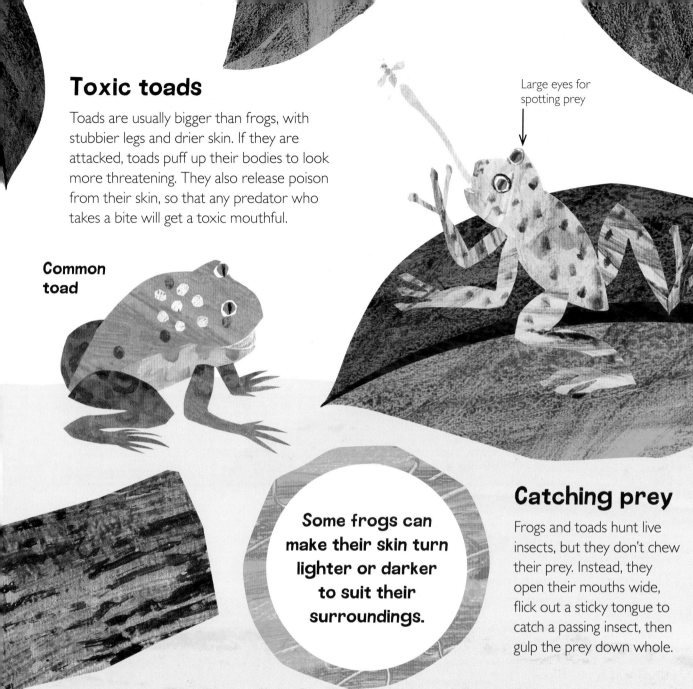

Wood frog

This Alaskan frog has a special way of avoiding freezing to death when it hibernates in winter. Its heart stops beating until the summer, when the frog thaws out and comes back to life.

On the hunt

Newts and salamanders have thin skin, slender bodies, and long tails. They hunt by sniffing out fresh worms and insects. Then they stick out their long tongues to snag the prey.

Water babies

Newts and salamanders lay their eggs in water. Newly hatched babies look like frog tadpoles. However, as they grow, the babies develop four legs, but keep their tails.

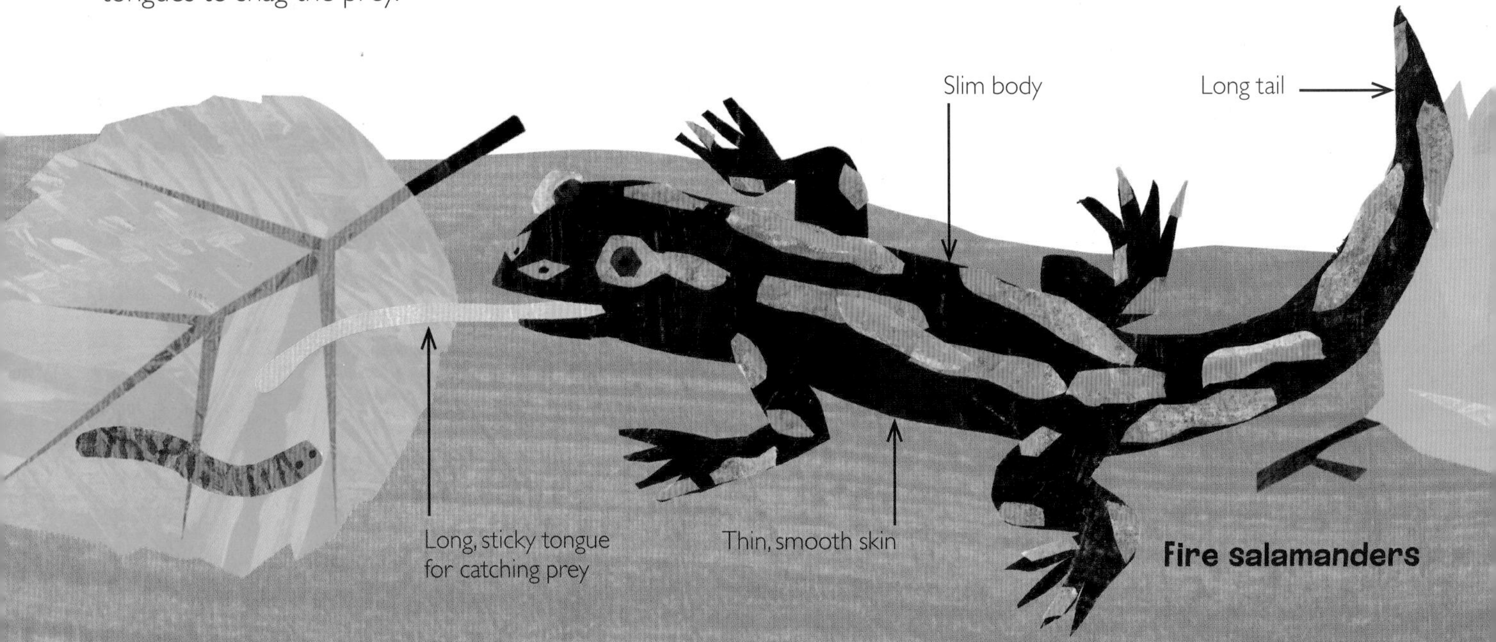

Fire salamanders

Newts and salamanders

Although newts and salamanders look like lizards, they are amphibians, like frogs and toads. Newts stay mainly in the water, while salamanders prefer damp places on land.

Family facts

Habitat
In and around freshwater rivers, lakes, and ponds

Location
Every continent, except Antarctica

Diet
Meat, such as insects and worms

Self-defense

Newts and salamanders use different tactics to keep safe. Many have brightly colored skin, which sends a warning to predators that they are poisonous to eat.

Spanish ribbed newt

When it senses danger, this spotted newt pokes its sharp, toxin-covered ribs outside of its body!

Fire salamander

This colorful creature sprays jets of poison from pores in its skin.

Brand new bodies

Both newts and salamanders can grow new body parts to replace damaged ones. If they lose a leg or tail, the missing part grows back again within weeks.

Caecilians

These long, legless amphibians do a good impression of worms. Caecilians (say "sess-illy-anns") make underground burrows, using their heads to push the soil away. They use their short fangs to chomp wriggly worms.

Spot the difference

One way to tell newts and salamanders apart is by looking at their skin. Salamanders mostly have shiny, smooth skin. Newt skin is covered in tiny bumps.

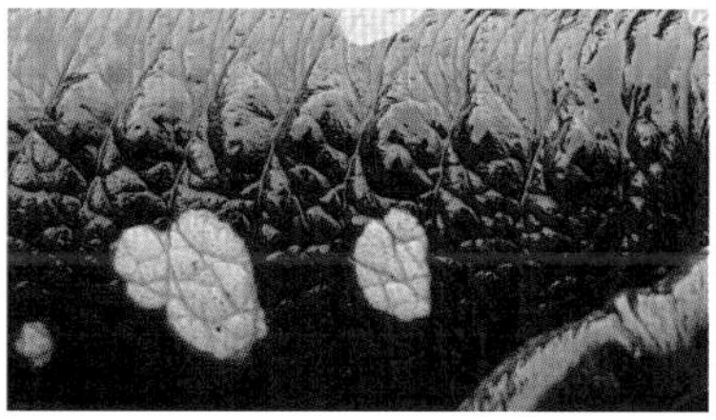

Salamander skin

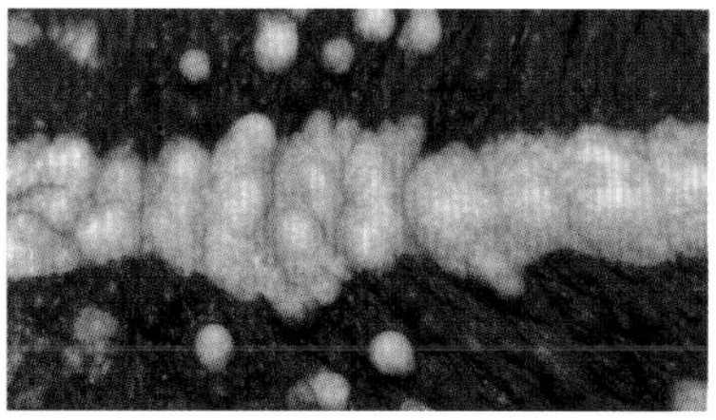

Newt skin

Fantastic fish

Fish

Fish first appeared in Earth's oceans and rivers about 400 million years ago. Today's fish come in an awesome range of shapes, sizes, and colors.

There are more than 33,000 different types of fish.

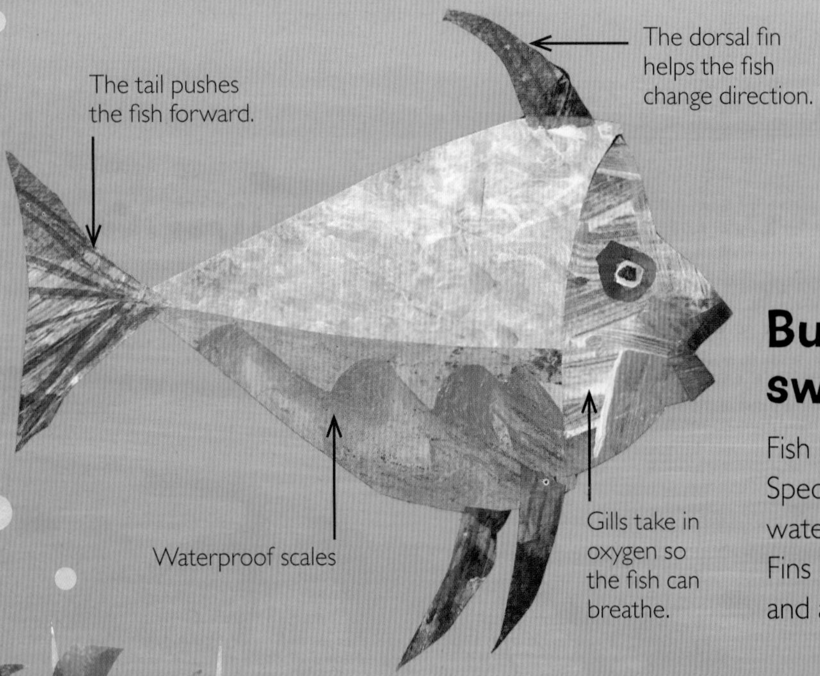

The dorsal fin helps the fish change direction.
The tail pushes the fish forward.
Waterproof scales
Gills take in oxygen so the fish can breathe.

Built for swimming

Fish bodies are well suited to swimming. Special slits called gills take in oxygen from the water. Scales help the fish move more easily. Fins help it to steer and stay the right way up, and a swishing tail powers the fish along.

Biggest fish

The whale shark is the biggest fish in the ocean; it is even longer than a double-decker bus. The European catfish is the largest freshwater fish. It lives in lakes and rivers and is almost as long as two adult humans.

Whale shark

European catfish

Back to school

Fish often move around in groups called schools. This is for safety, since predators find it hard to pick out a single fish in a crowd of hundreds or thousands.

Stone fish

Barracuda

Salty or fresh

Almost all fish live either in salty seawater or fresh water, but not both. A goldfish couldn't survive in the ocean, and a swordfish can't live in a river. Fish are cold-blooded, which means that their bodies are the same temperature as the water around them.

Trumpet fish

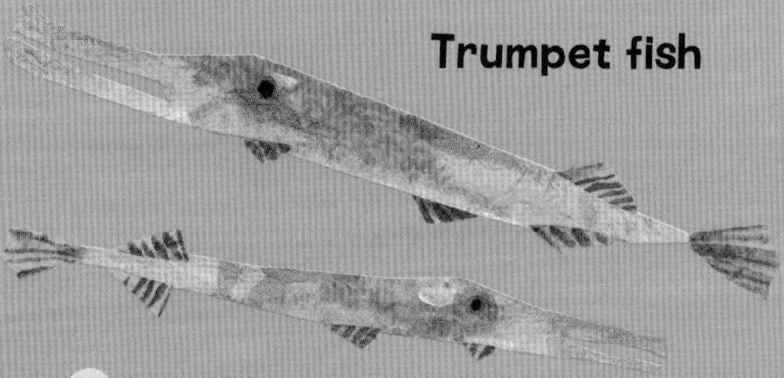

Funky fish

These three fish are decidedly different from any others!

X-ray fish

This little pond fish has see-through skin, which means that its skeleton is visible, just like human bones on an X-ray.

Handfish

The Australian handfish walks on the ocean floor on its four fins. It is a poor swimmer and finds walking much easier.

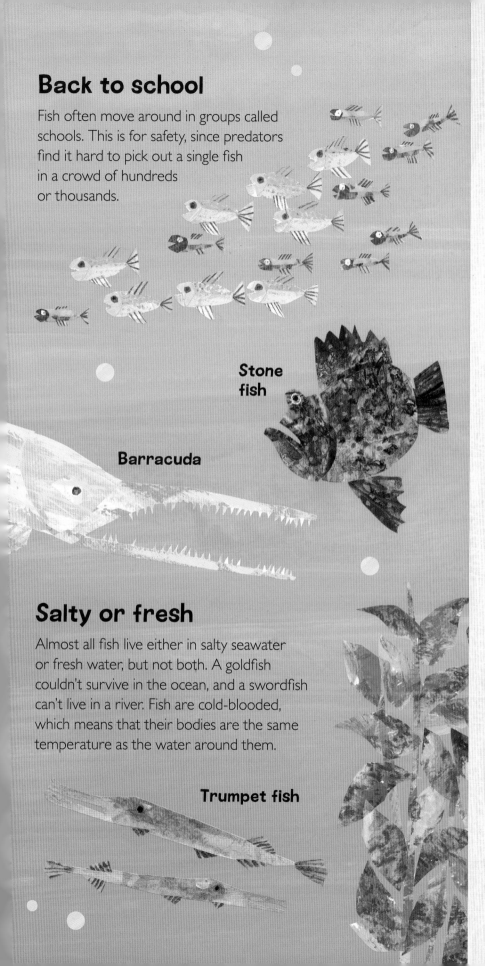

Sockeye salmon

Salmon are very unusual fish because they can survive both in fresh water and in the salty ocean.

Bony fish

Like humans, all bony fish have skeletons made of bone. They make up by far the biggest group of fish.

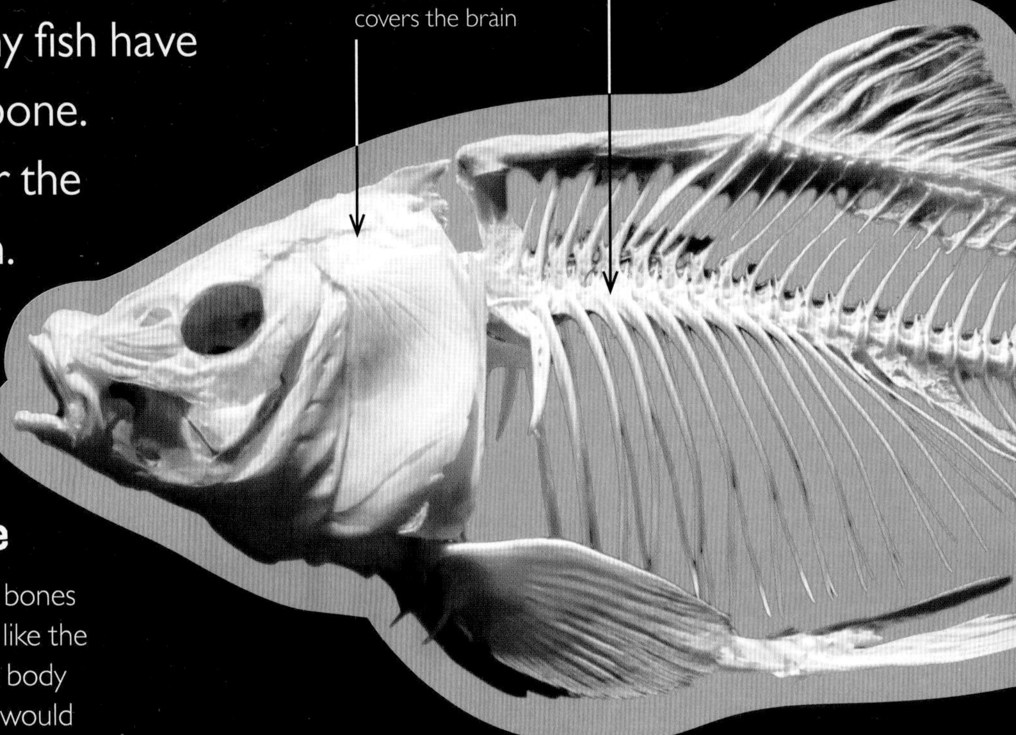
Hard skull covers the brain
The spine is also called the backbone.

Protective frame

The skeleton is a framework of bones that protects important organs like the heart and brain. It also gives the body its structure; without it, the fish would just be a shapeless blob!

Tuna

Bendy bodies

Although fish bones are strong, they are light and slightly flexible, which allows the fish to swim more easily. Bony fins keep their shape, helping the fish steer better. The tailbone adds power as the fish flicks its tail to move forward.

Bony fish make up 95 percent of all the fish in the world.

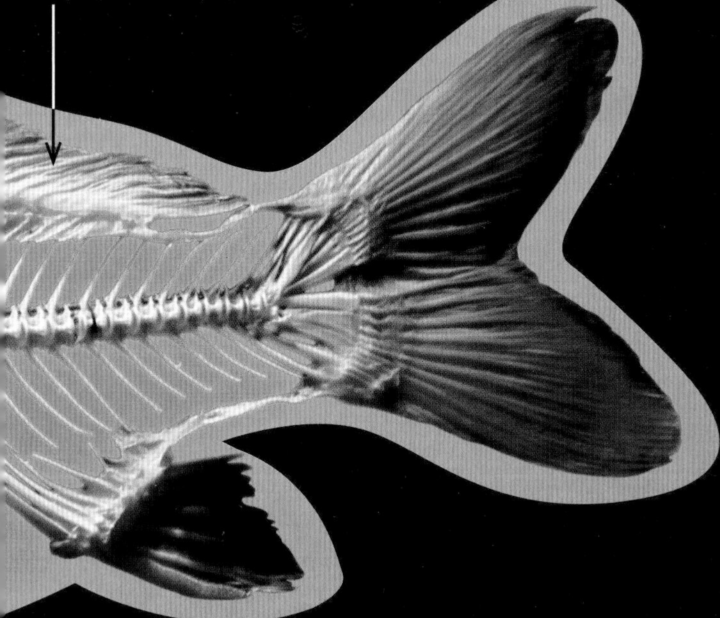

The dorsal fin is held up by thin, bony spines.

Smooth skin has no scales.

Heaviest fish

The ocean sunfish is the heaviest of all bony fish. It has a huge, round, tailless body and weighs more than a family car.

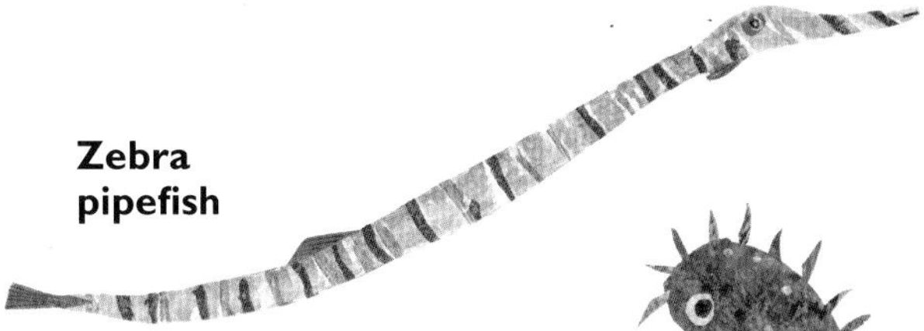

Zebra pipefish

Leaf fish

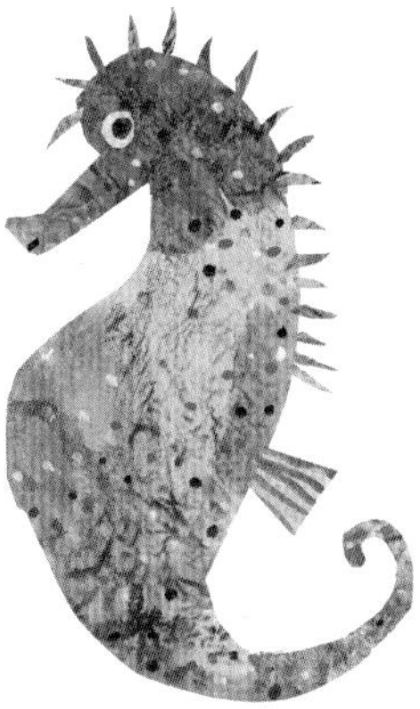

Seahorse

Gigantic group

Bony fish come in a huge range of shapes and sizes. They live all over the world, both in salty oceans and in freshwater lakes and rivers. Some live for only a few months, while others live well past their 100th birthday.

Yellow wrasse

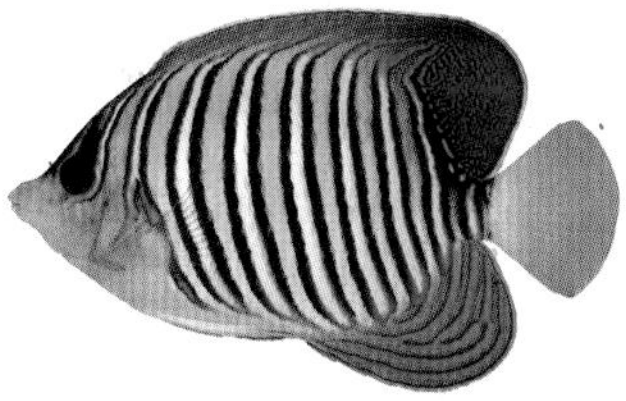

Angelfish

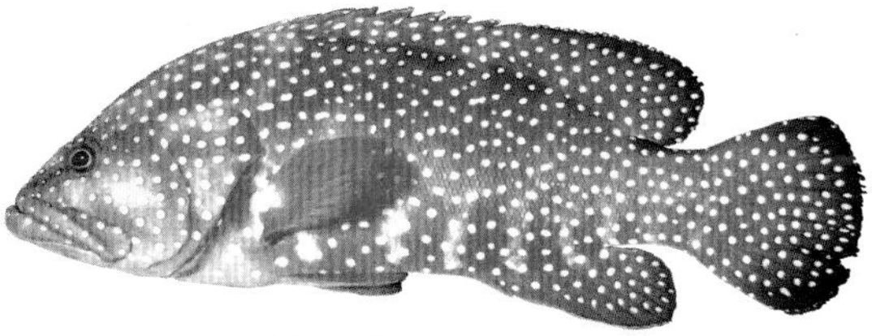

Coral trout

Cod

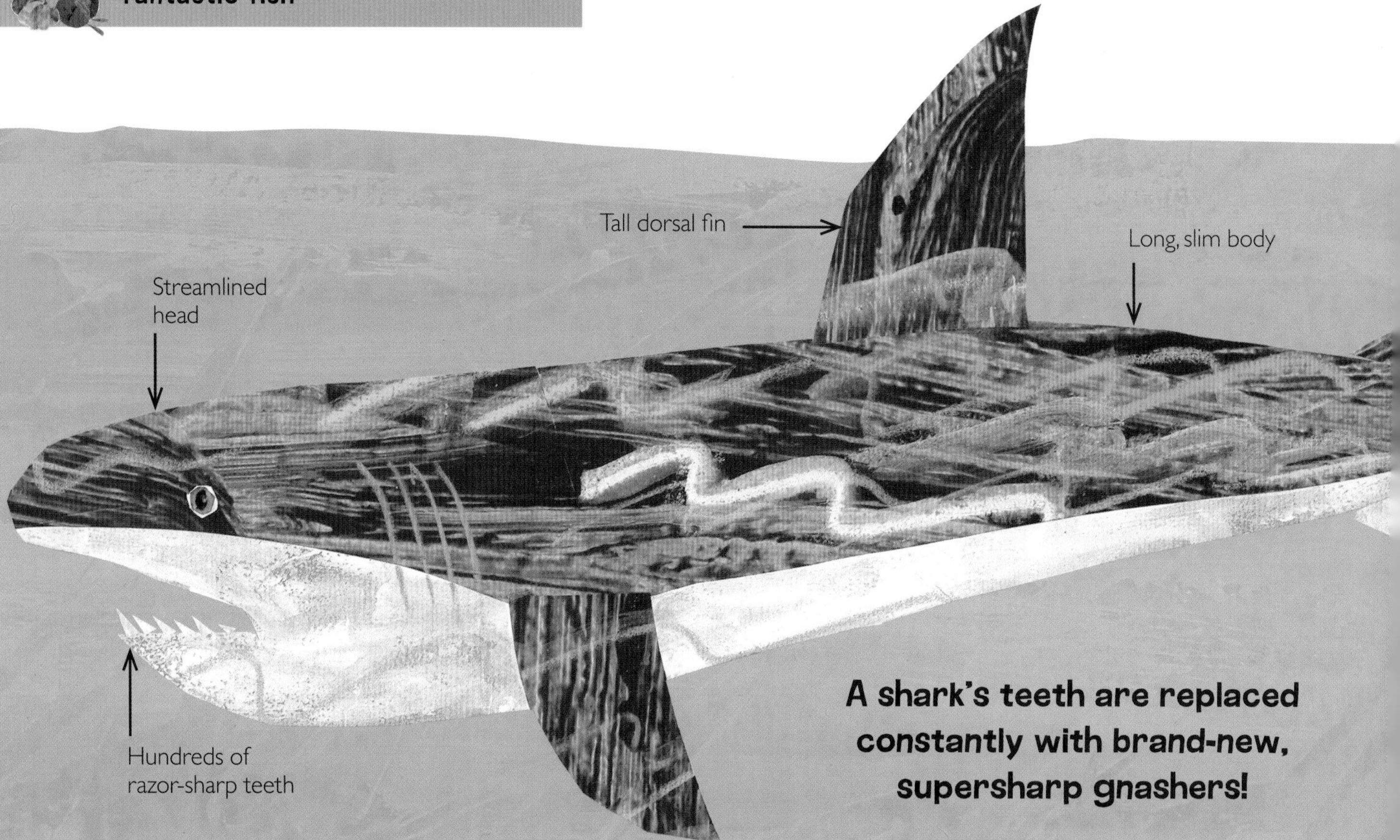

A shark's teeth are replaced constantly with brand-new, supersharp gnashers!

Great white shark

The world's biggest toothed shark has excellent eyesight, incredible hearing, and a strong sense of smell. This hunter is an apex predator and the only threats it faces come from humans.

Sharks

Sharks have ruled the oceans for 400 million years. They are still among Earth's biggest, most fearsome hunters.

Shark shapes

There are more than 500 different types of shark. While many are no bigger than this book, the basking shark is the size of a truck.

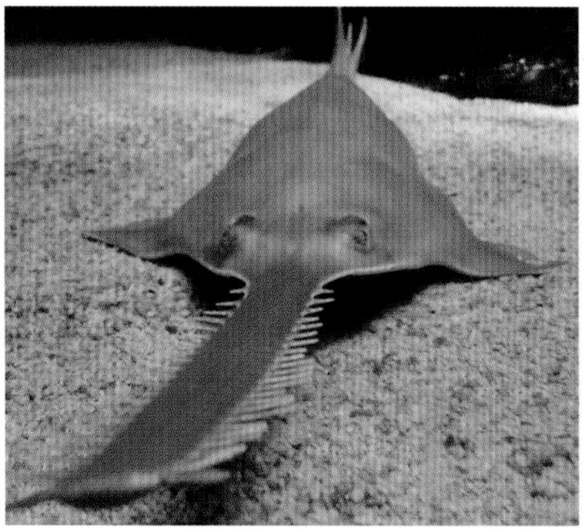

Saw shark

This shark has a long, thin nose with sharp teeth running down each side. The saw shark uses this nose like a sword to swipe and slash through schools of small fish.

Ancient shark

Megalodon was a supersized shark from prehistoric times. It was three times bigger than its descendant, the great white shark.

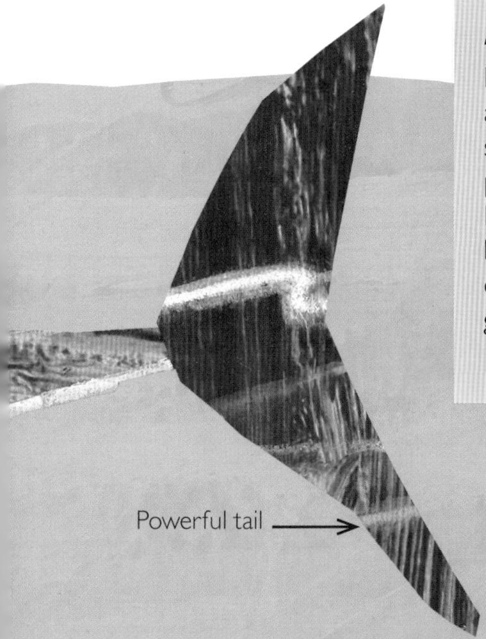

Living with sharks

Some fish actually choose to live right alongside deadly sharks. Remoras hitch a ride through the water by clinging to a shark's skin. Along the way, they eat any scraps of tasty meat that fall from the shark's mouth.

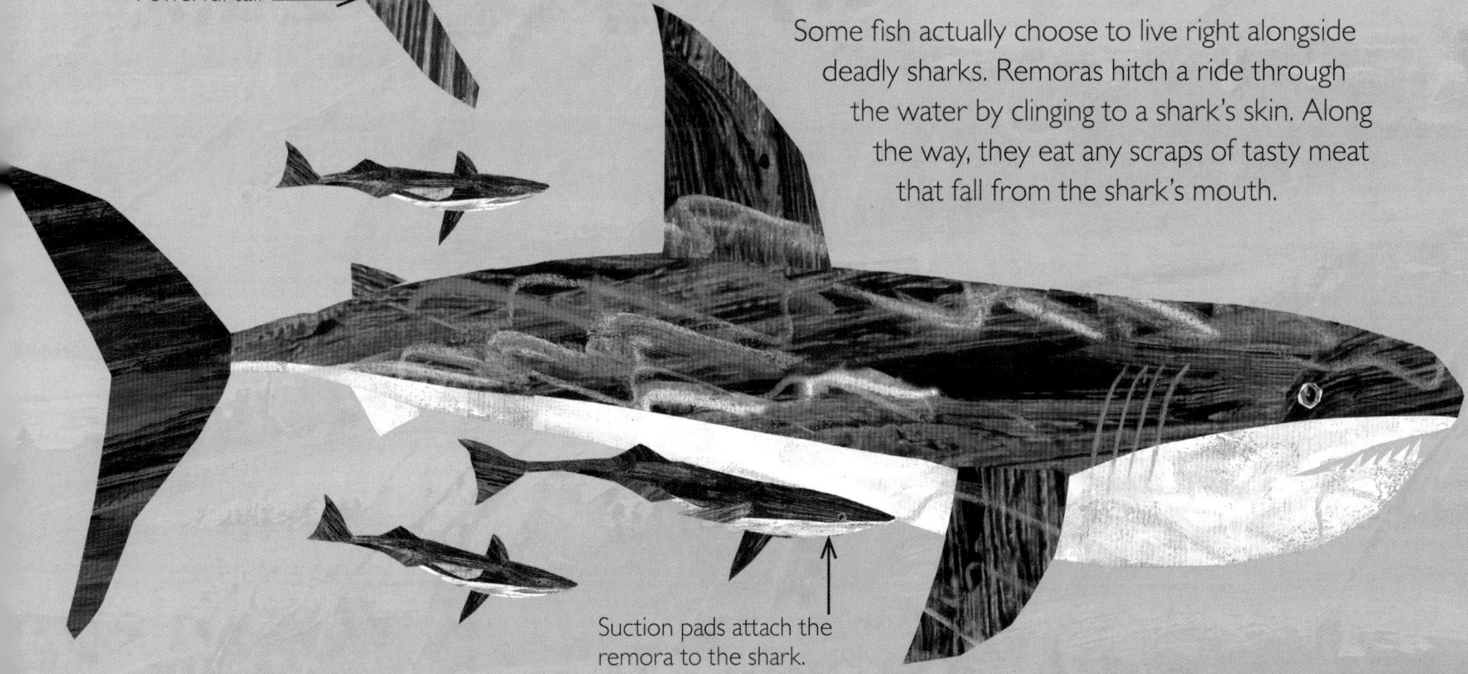

Suction pads attach the remora to the shark.

Leopard shark

With leopardlike, spotted skin, this shark lives in shallow seas and river estuaries. The spots help it to hunt under the sun-dappled surface of the water without being seen.

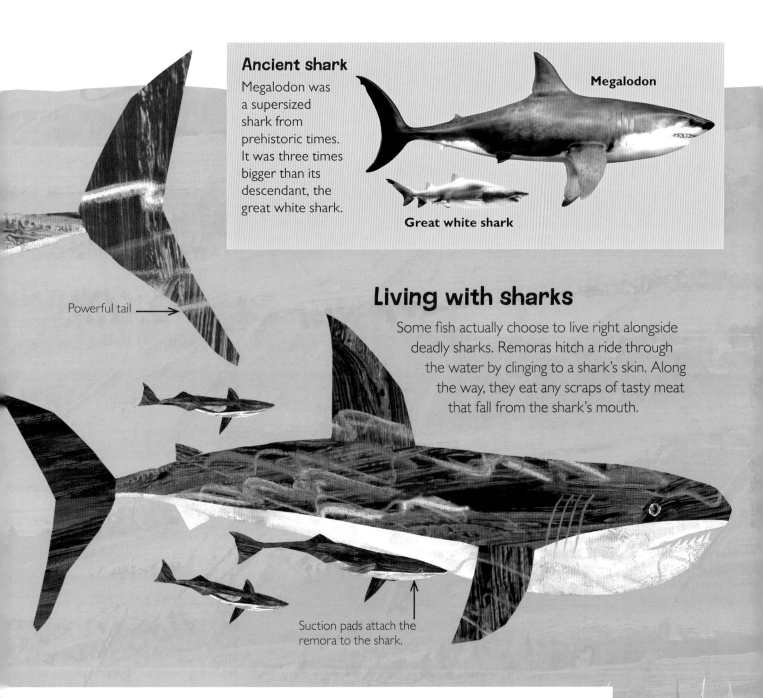

Basking shark

Massive basking sharks eat zooplankton, which are the ocean's tiniest creatures. These sharks swim with their mouths open, trapping the food in bony bristles called gill rakers.

Rays and skates

The giant manta ray has the biggest brain of any fish.

Rays and skates are flat fish that use their huge, winglike fins to fly through the oceans like underwater airplanes.

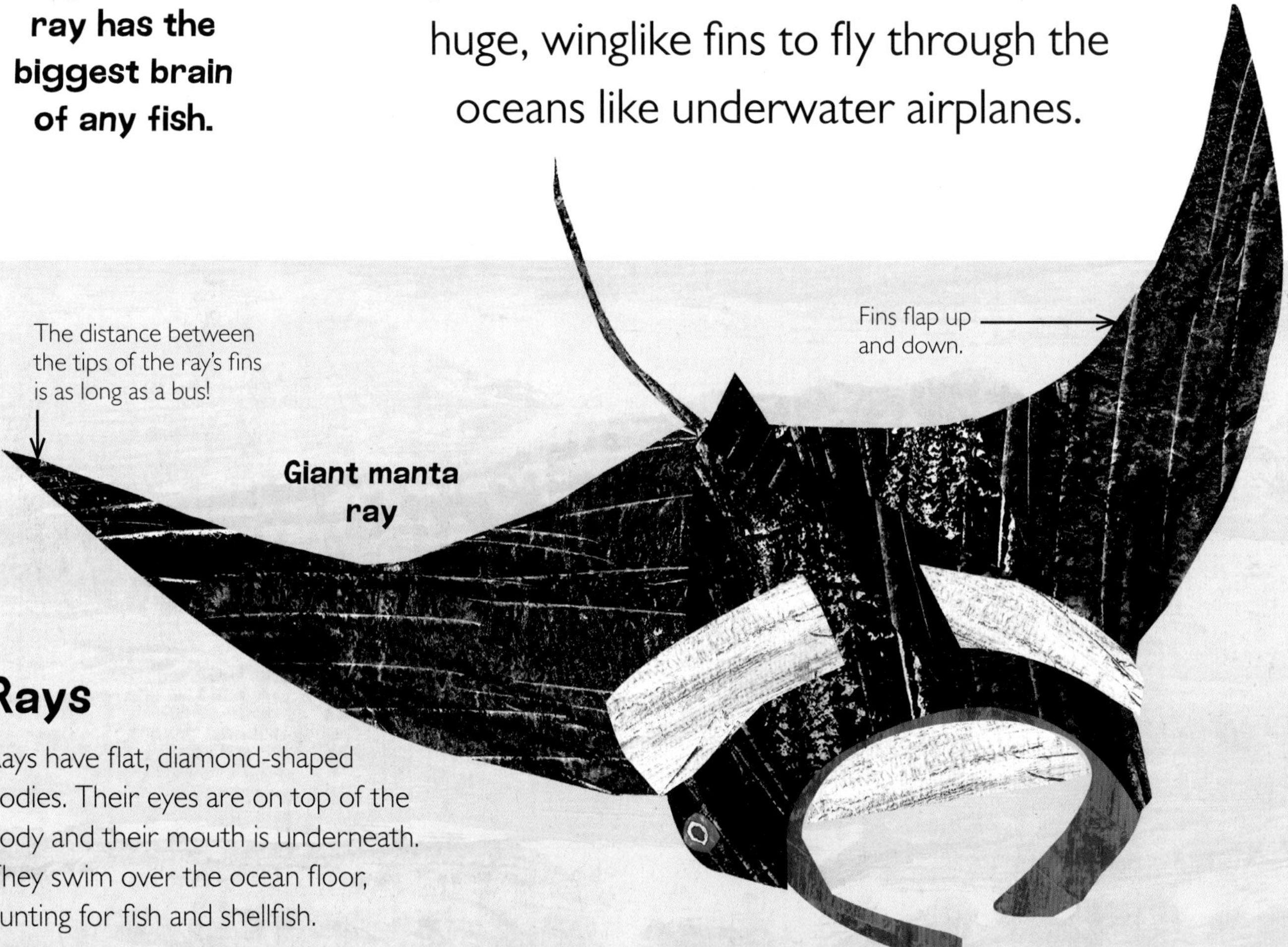

The distance between the tips of the ray's fins is as long as a bus!
Giant manta ray
Fins flap up and down.

Rays

Rays have flat, diamond-shaped bodies. Their eyes are on top of the body and their mouth is underneath. They swim over the ocean floor, hunting for fish and shellfish.

Manta rays

The biggest member of the ray family gets its name from "manto," the Spanish word for a cloak. Despite its size, it can leap right out of the water when trying to avoid predators.

Stingrays

Some smaller rays are armed with venomous stings. A razor-sharp spine on the end of the stingray's tail injects predators that come too close with a nasty dose of venom.

Bendy bodies

If you squeeze the tip of your nose, it feels squishy and flexible. Instead of bone, it is made of cartilage. The bodies of rays and skates are also made of cartilage, making them more flexible than bony fish.

There are about 500 types of ray and 150 types of skate.

Skates

These fish look similar to rays, with flat bodies and big, wing-shaped fins for swimming. Skates have sharp thorns along their backs and tails to pierce predators.

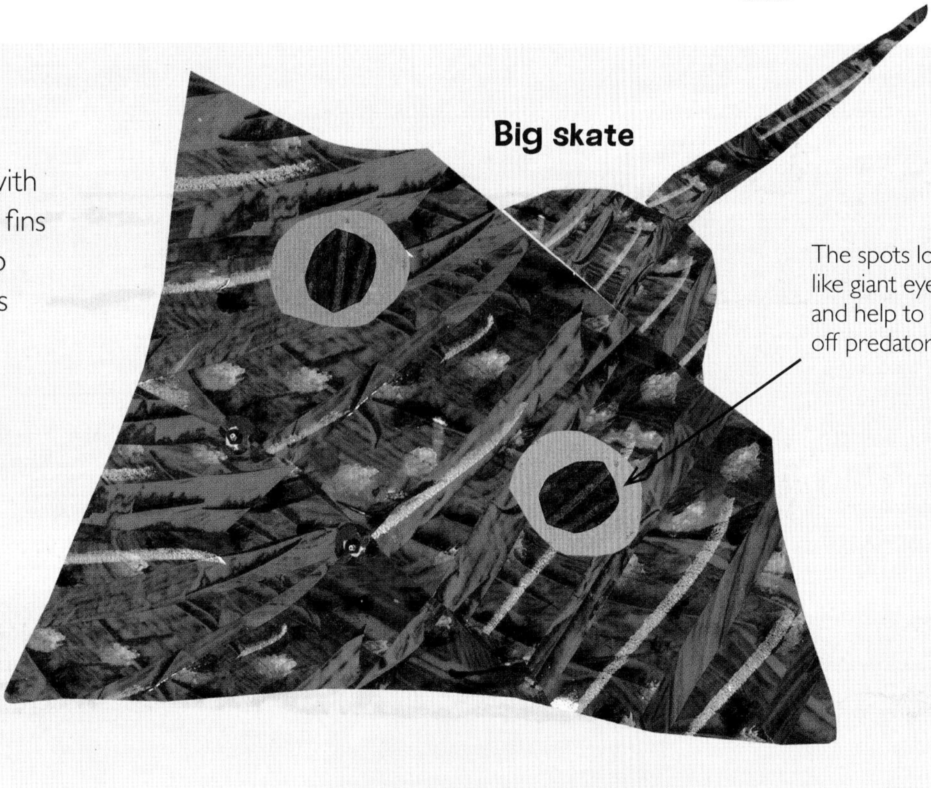

Big skate
The spots look like giant eyes and help to put off predators.

The big skate is about the same length as a tiger.

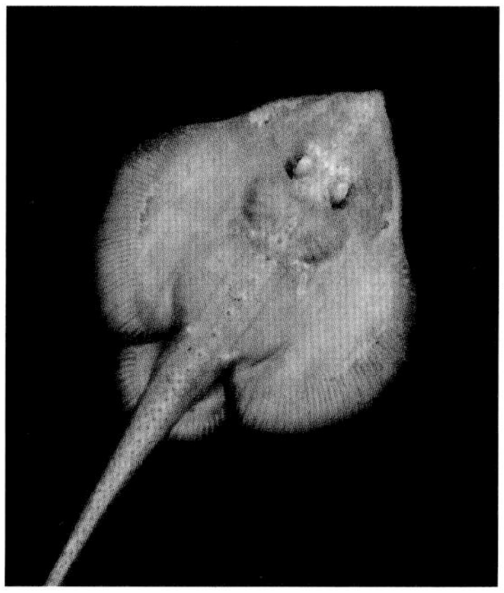

Deep-sea skates

The midnight zone of the ocean is dark and cold, with extreme pressure. Deep-sea skates survive in this harsh habitat by feeding on the tiniest marine life.

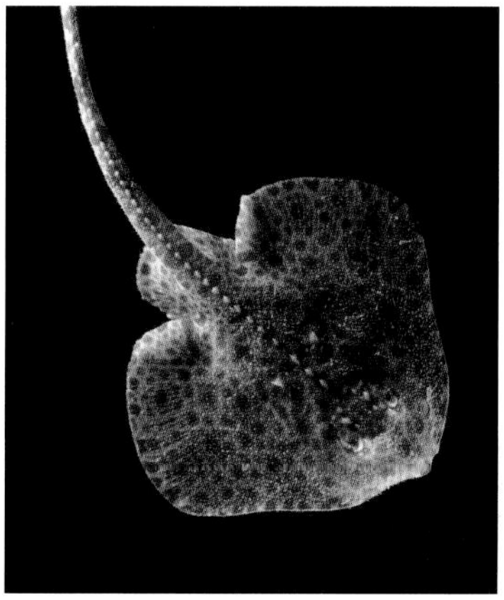

Arctic skates

These tough fish live in the freezing waters of the Arctic and Antarctic. They use their thorny tails for defense and their sharp teeth to munch on small fish and shellfish.

Slinky slurpers

Jawless fish cannot open and close their mouths. They eat by clamping their suckerlike mouths onto prey animals, then scraping away their flesh with sharp teeth and a tough tongue.

Lampreys

Lampreys are eel-shaped, with long, slinky, slimy bodies. Like sharks and flat fish, their bodies are made of flexible cartilage, not bone. Unlike most fish, they don't have scales.

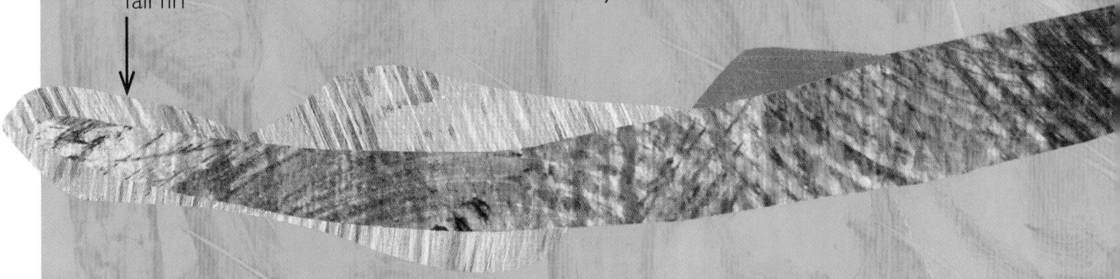
Tail fin

Slime-fest!

Hagfish hunt on the seabed for prey. Huge amounts of slime ooze from their bodies to cover their victims and stop them from breathing. If they find dead meat, hagfish still cover it with slime to make sure no other animals try to join the feast.

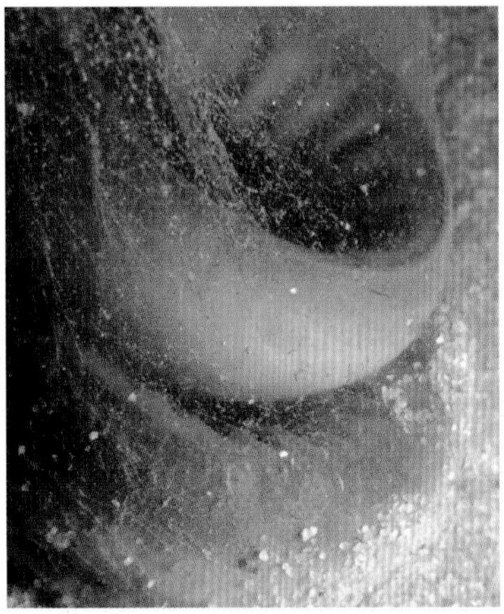

Tentacles around the mouth feel for prey.

In the US, Hagfish Day is held every year to celebrate the beauty of all animals.

Jawless fish

Millions of years ago, the first fish on Earth did not have jaws. Some of them have survived as the bloodsucking, slime-shooting vampires of today's underwater world.

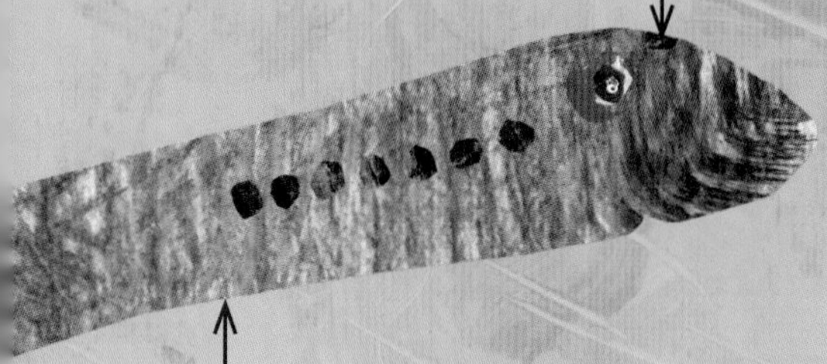

Nostril on top of the head detects prey.
Long body is coated in slime.

Bloodsuckers

Lampreys feed on the blood of other living creatures. Their massive round mouths, which are lined with tiny teeth, work like vacuum cleaners, gripping hold of a bony fish's body and sucking up the blood.

Hagfish

Like lampreys, hagfish have no bones. Their bodies are so flexible that they can tie themselves into a perfect knot. They do this to get a better hold on prey or to slip free of predators.

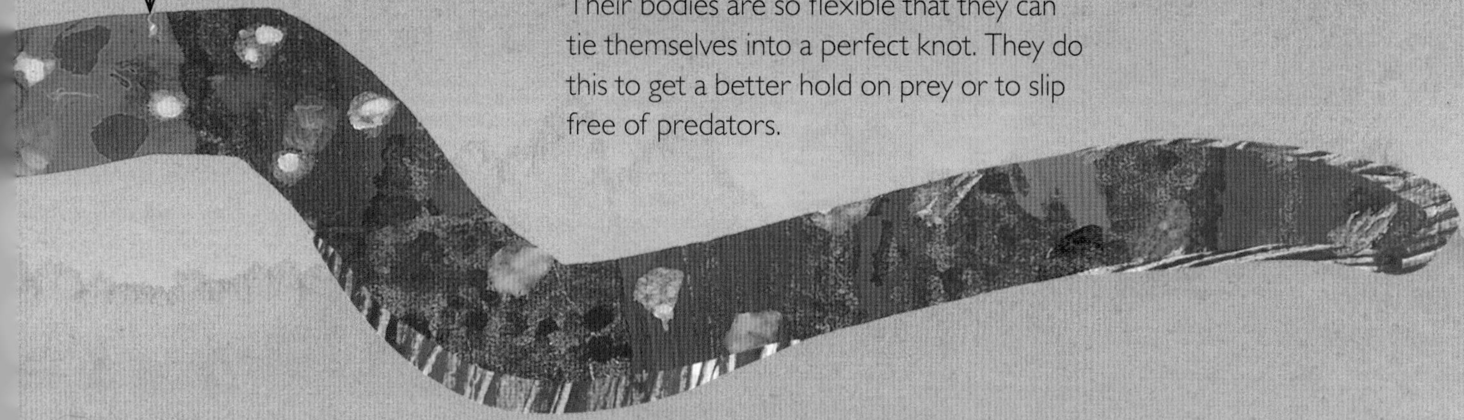

Slime oozes from tiny pores in the skin.

There are about 100 types of jawless fish and all are either in the lamprey or hagfish families.

Living fossils

When scientists discovered a 300-million-year-old fossilized hagfish, it looked just the same as today's hagfish. These fish have never had to change because their slimy hunting method is so successful.

Super hunters

The ocean is full of deadly predators with big appetites. Some target their prey with amazing accuracy, while others simply tear in with their terrifying teeth.

Not all types of piranha are ferocious meat-munchers. Some are vegetarians.

Piranhas

These small, South American fish have supersharp teeth to strip the flesh off fish in seconds. Red-bellied piranhas are especially ferocious. They hunt in groups, attacking anything that comes their way. Often, they leave only a skeleton behind.

Red-bellied piranha

Atlantic wolffish

This huge-mouthed predator has a long, slinky body and two fearsome front fangs, like the canines of a wolf. It uses these sharp teeth and its bony mouth to pierce and crush the shells of crabs, lobsters, and sea urchins.

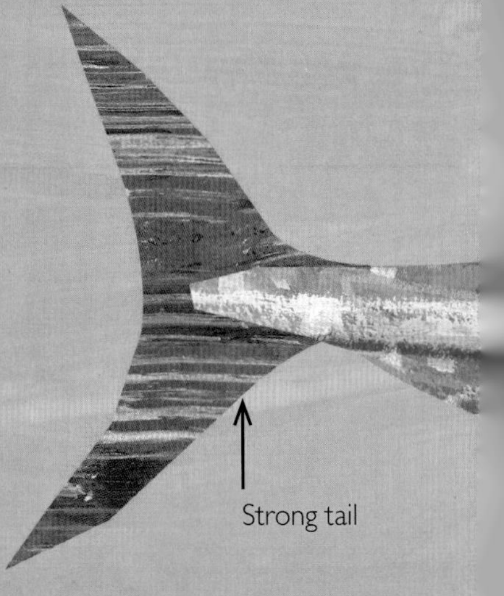

Goliath tigerfish

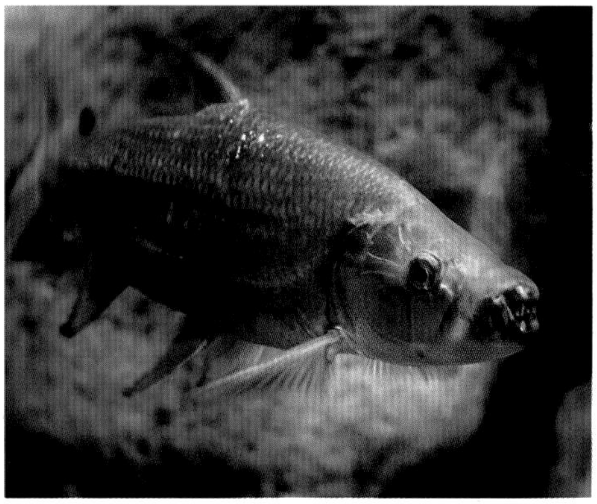

These giant predators live in the rivers and lakes of Africa. They hunt in groups, cornering their prey and attacking with daggerlike teeth. Goliath tigerfish are fearless enough to attack crocodiles and even humans.

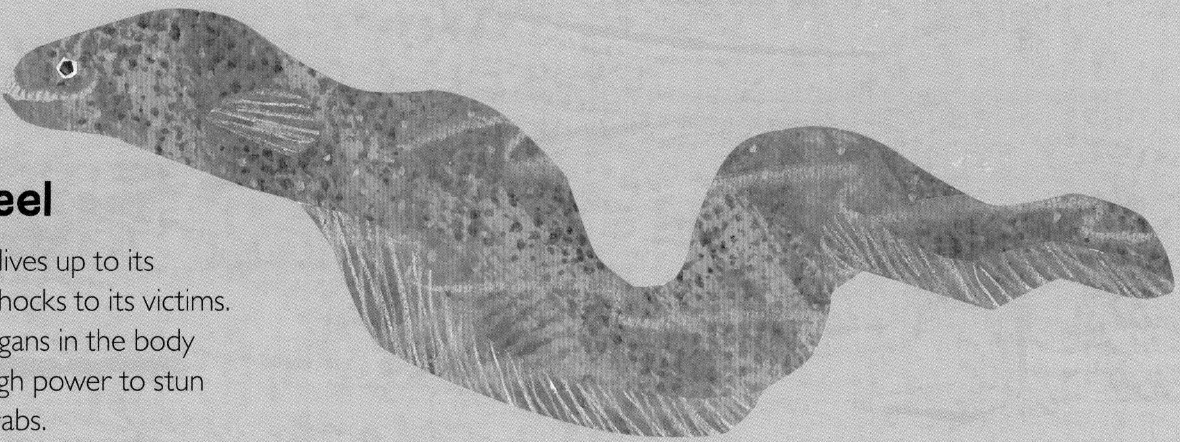

Electric eel

The electric eel lives up to its name by giving shocks to its victims. Three special organs in the body can create enough power to stun or kill fish and crabs.

Swordfish

The swordfish swims at high speed through the ocean, searching for prey. One swipe of its long, sharp, swordlike nose is enough to stun small fish, so the swordfish can swoop in and eat its fill.

Survival skills

Most fish that live in the deep sea have soft skeletons to keep them from being crushed by the weight of the water above. Some have enormous eyes to see in the darkness. Others produce their own light to trap prey or attract partners.

Creatures of the deep

It is a struggle to survive in the darkest depths of the ocean. Only a few fish can cope with the intense pressure, freezing cold, and permanent gloom.

Anglerfish

When you're hunting in the dark, one solution is to have a built-in light of your own! The anglerfish dangles a glowing light just like a fishing rod to tempt prey fish to come closer.

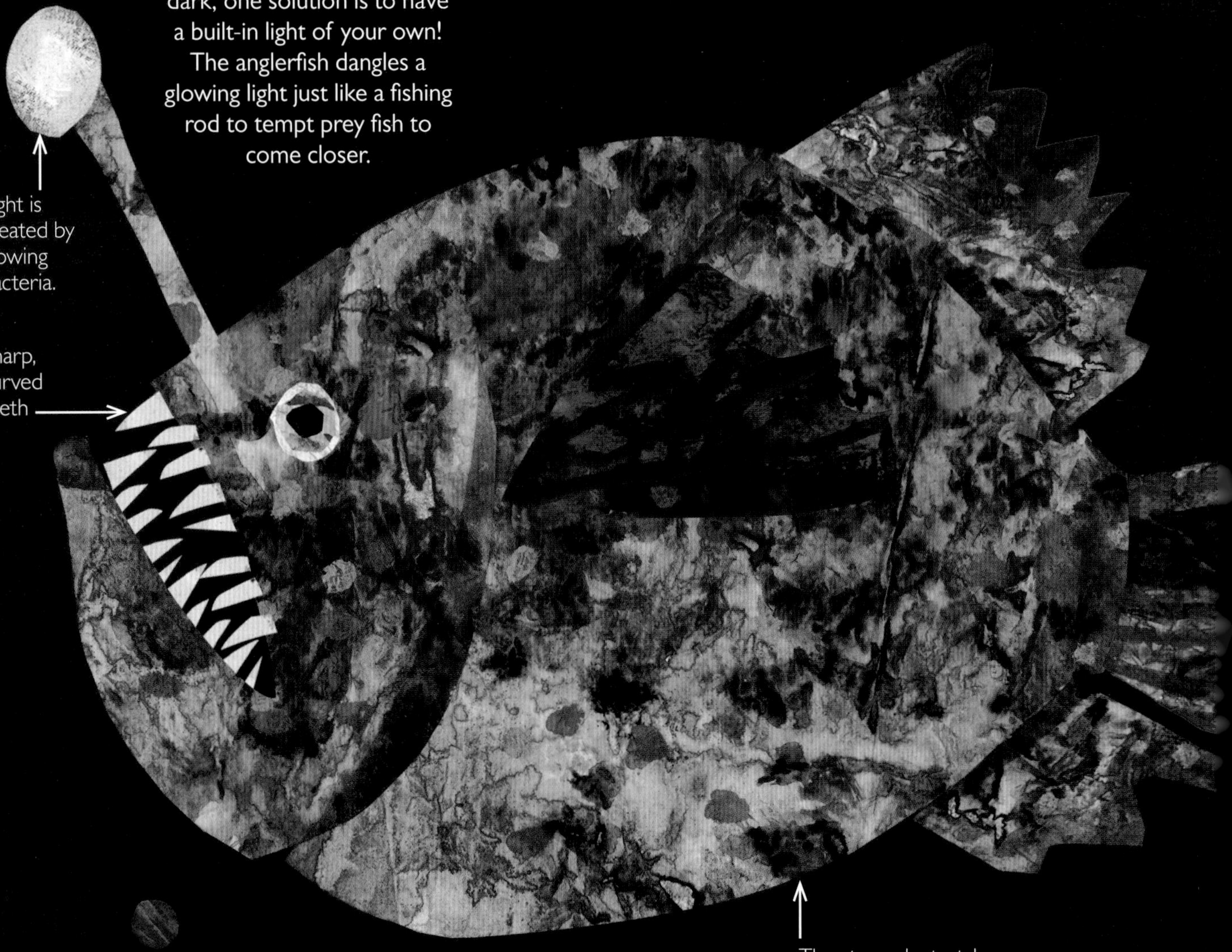

Light is created by glowing bacteria.
Sharp, curved teeth
The stomach stretches to fit prey inside.

Fang tooth

This fearsome fish lurks in deep oceans before heading into shallower waters to hunt. It grips prey with its huge fangs, giving small fish and squid no chance to wriggle free.

The fang tooth swims with its mouth open. Its front teeth are so long that its mouth can never be closed fully.

Goblin shark

This shark has a superlong snout and sharp teeth lining its massive jaws. The snout detects prey in the darkness, while the jaw juts forward so the teeth can easily bite into fish and squid.

Hatchet fish

The row of lights under the hatchet fish's belly are bright enough to help it blend in with the sunlit water above. These fish can also swim up to the surface and jump right out of the water!

Special organs produce faint light.

Mudskippers

Almost all the world's fish live in water, but there are exceptions to the rule. Meet the fish that can live out of water…

Living on land

Mudskippers live in swampy habitats and can breathe both in and out of the water. They use their fins to jump, climb, or drag themselves over the ground as they hunt small shellfish, insects, and worms.

Mudskippers can breathe through their gills and their skin.
Bulging eyes can see in all directions.

Mudskippers can stay on land for 90 percent of their lives.

Land-loving fish

Mudskippers aren't the only fish that can survive out of water. Here are three more amazing fish that are able to pop out of the water and spend time on dry land.

Walking catfish

Like a slithery snake, this Asian catfish can wriggle along the ground for hours at a time as it travels between different sources of water. It uses the whiskers around its mouth to feel for prey.

Move it!

Mudskippers get their name from the way they seem to "skip" across the squishy mud.

Mangrove rivulus

When rivers run dry in its swampy habitat, this tiny fish can survive on land for months. It finds a soggy hollow log and moves in until it can return home to the river.

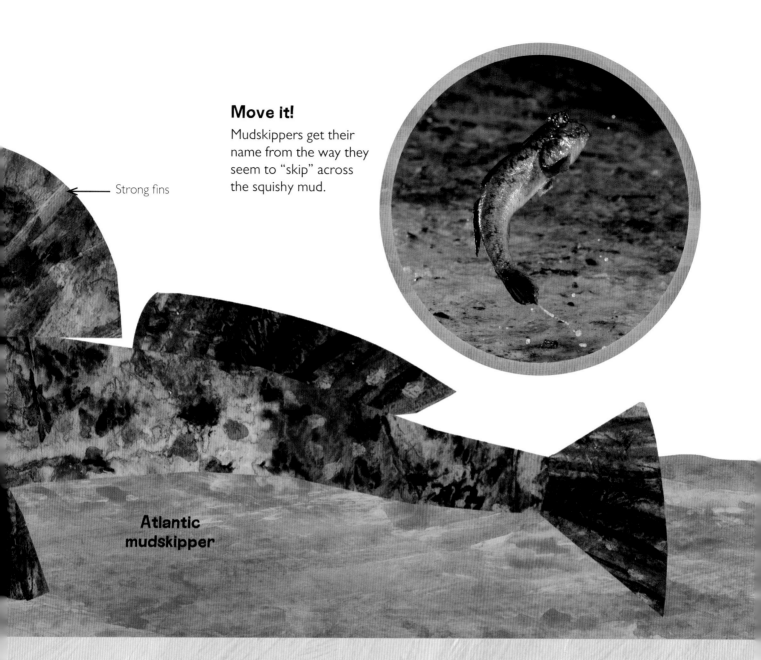

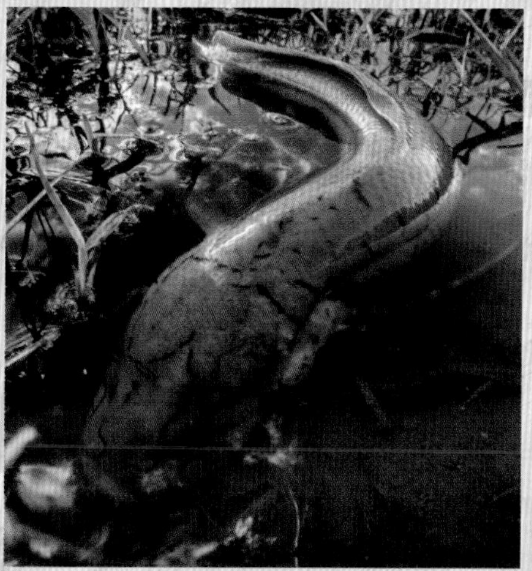

Lungfish

This fish lives in Africa, where droughts can last a long time. In dry weather, the lungfish curls up in a muddy puddle and sleeps until the rains come again. It can last an incredible five years without eating or drinking.

On the defense

The ocean can be a dangerous place, full of hungry hunters. Fish use cunning tactics to fight back or stay hidden. None of them wants to end up as another animal's dinner.

Clown fish

Sea anemones help clown fish to hide. Their floating tentacles contain venom, but clown fish have a protective coating so they don't get stung. When predators get too close, the fish swim inside the anemones and take cover.

Twinspot wrasse

The two large spots on this fish's body look like giant eyes. The wrasse wriggles into the sand, so only the spots are showing. Passing predators see the big eyes and assume that the little fish is too big to eat!

It takes just one or two seconds for the porcupine fish to inflate its body fully.

Its spines lie flat when the porcupine fish is calm.

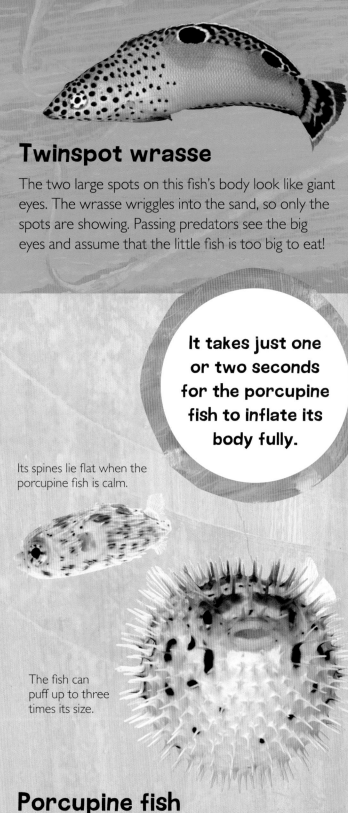

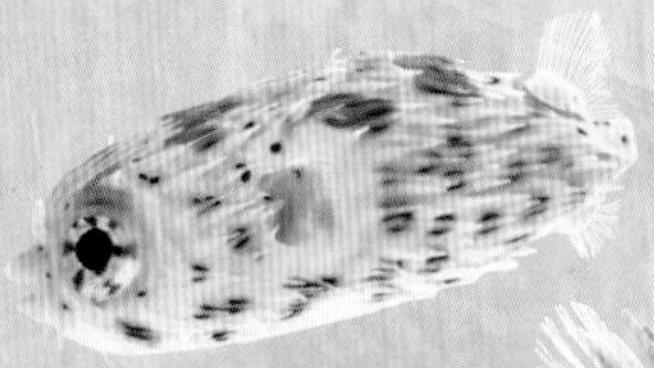

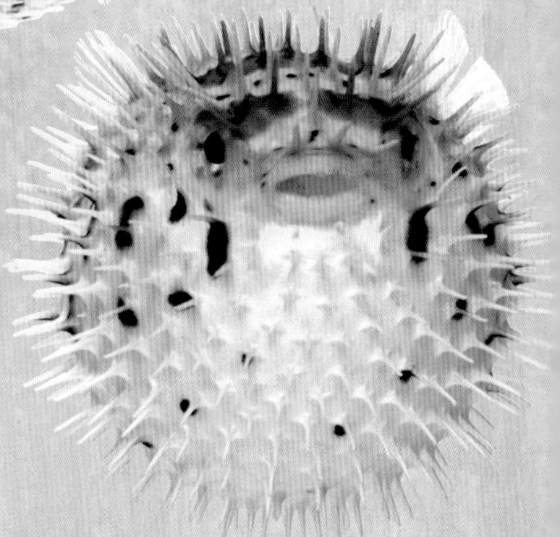

The fish can puff up to three times its size.

Porcupine fish

This tropical fish is covered in sharp spines. If a predator comes close, it sucks in water and puffs up into a big, prickly ball. Predators can't wrap their jaws around the fish without getting injured.

Lionfish

The striped lionfish is one of the ocean's deadliest fish. Its trailing spines look beautiful, but they are packed with venom that can kill predators in an instant.

Cuttlefish

This marine magician can instantly change the color, pattern, and texture of its skin. The transformations match the cuttlefish's surroundings, so predators are fooled into thinking it is just part of the scenery.

Blue-spotted stingray

The brilliant blue spots of this stingray are a colorful "keep away" sign. If predators ignore the warning and get too close, the fish produces poison from its tail stinger. Ouch!

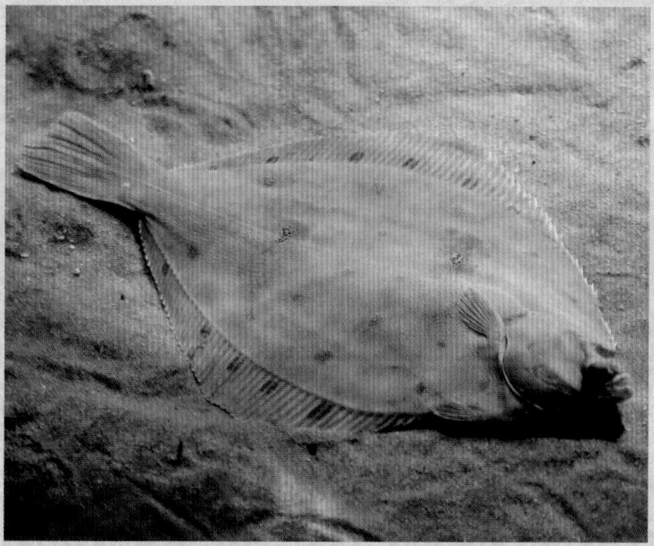

Plaice

These fish avoid danger by nestling their flat bodies into the sand on the seabed. Predators swim over them without noticing the tasty prey hiding below.

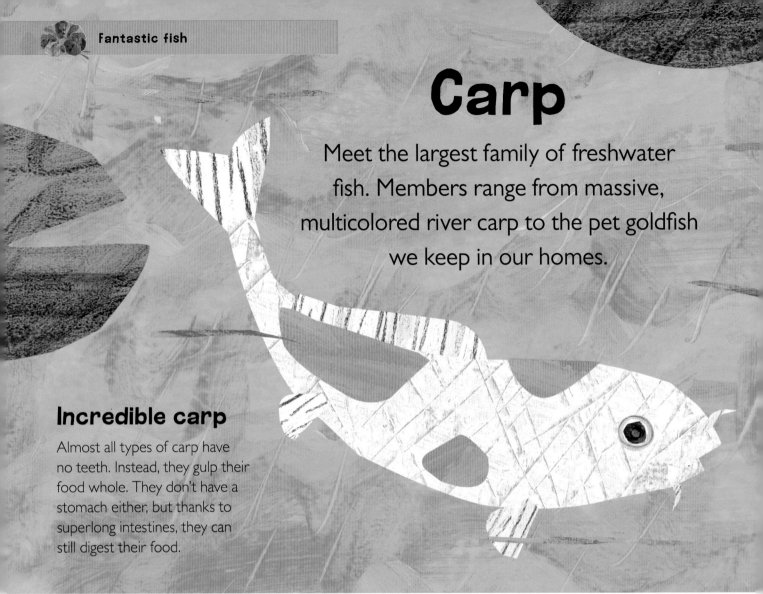

Carp

Meet the largest family of freshwater fish. Members range from massive, multicolored river carp to the pet goldfish we keep in our homes.

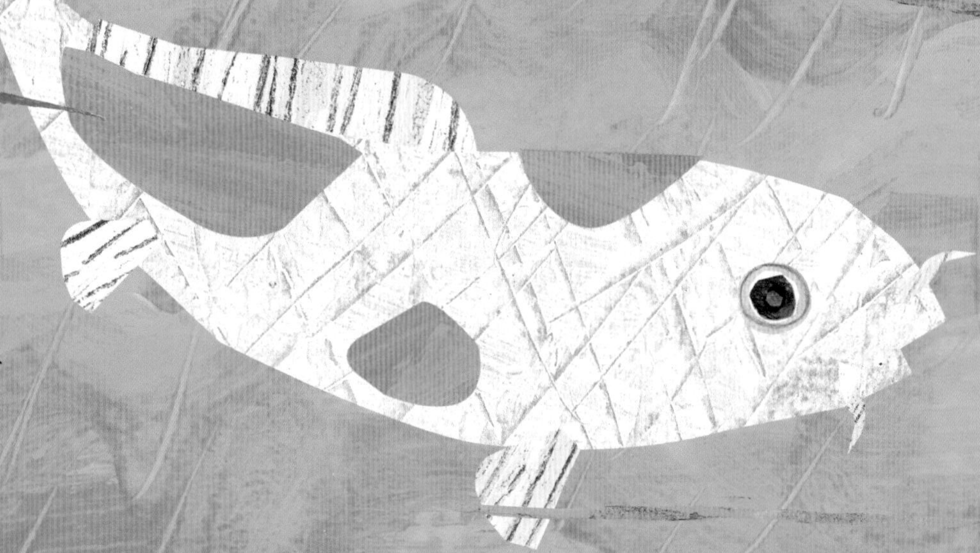

Incredible carp

Almost all types of carp have no teeth. Instead, they gulp their food whole. They don't have a stomach either, but thanks to superlong intestines, they can still digest their food.

Family facts

Habitat
Freshwater rivers, lakes, and ponds, and home aquariums

Location
Europe and Asia

Diet
Insects, plankton, and water plants

Family
About 2,000 types including carp, bream, tench, barbel, and goldfish

Goldfish

These small carp make good pets, as they are tough and easy to care for. Despite their name, goldfish come in many colors, including black, blue, green, red, and gold, of course.

Goldfish can live for more than 200 years.

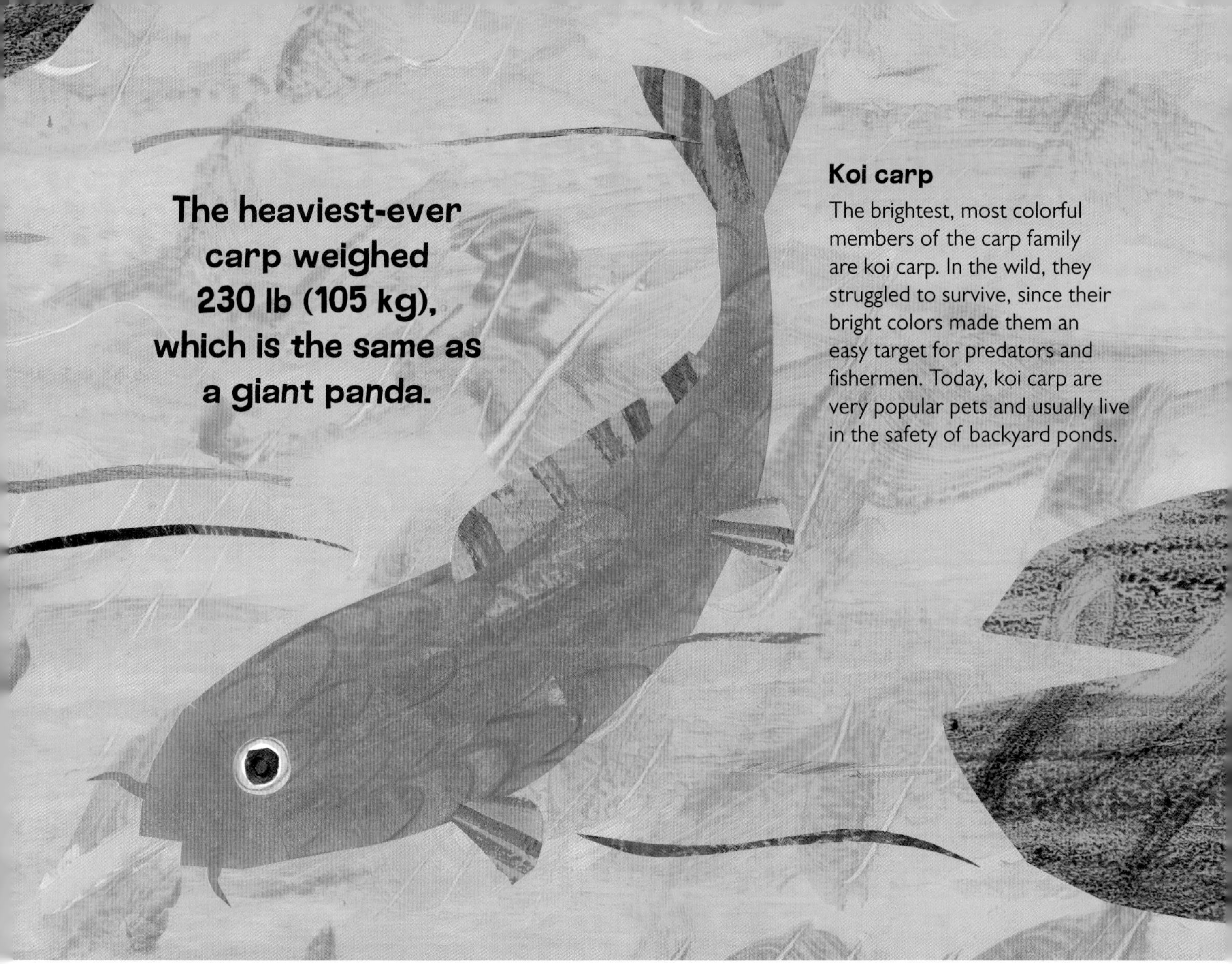

The heaviest-ever carp weighed 230 lb (105 kg), which is the same as a giant panda.

Koi carp

The brightest, most colorful members of the carp family are koi carp. In the wild, they struggled to survive, since their bright colors made them an easy target for predators and fishermen. Today, koi carp are very popular pets and usually live in the safety of backyard ponds.

Barbels

These small fish are named after their dangling mouth parts, called barbels, which means “beards” in Latin. Unlike most carp, barbels have rows of sharp teeth. They are fierce hunters and often attack fish twice their size.

Minnows

Teeny-tiny minnows are silvery swimmers that are constantly on the move, scouring the water for plants and creatures to eat. They aren’t fussy eaters and will target almost anything they find, including the eggs of other fish.

Black marlin

Top three

The world's three fastest fish are all members of the same family of long-nosed ocean hunters. Which one comes out on top?

Sailfish

Fast fish

The world's fastest fish whiz through the water at incredible speed. Human champion swimmers would be completely outclassed in a race with these ocean athletes.

Striped marlin

Gold medal

The winner is the black marlin! Powering through warm, tropical seas, it reaches speeds of 80 mph (129 kph)—faster than the speed limit on the highway.

Silver medal

The sailfish races into second place. Reaching speeds of 60 mph (110 kph), this ocean hunter can swim 10 times its own body length every single second.

Bronze medal

The striped marlin finishes in third place and bags the bronze. A close relative of the black marlin, it chases prey at 50 mph (80 kph) and uses its long bill to knock out victims.

Swift sharks

In addition to the marlin family, the shark group also has lots of superspeedy members.

Thresher shark

This high-speed hunter swims at top speed, swatting schools of sardines with its huge tail. It is also the highest-jumping fish and can leap the height of two adult humans out of the water.

Mako shark

The fastest shark of all is the mako. Slim and slinky, it travels at about half the speed of the black marlin when chasing dolphins, fish, or squid.

Tropical fish

The world's warmest waters are home to some of the brightest, most beautiful fish. All-day sunshine, vast coral reefs, and crystal-clear waters combine to create a dazzling home, full of light and color.

Parrotfish

This fish has a sturdy beak, like the rain-forest bird it is named after. The parrotfish bites off crunchy coral to get to the plants, called algae, growing from it.

Spectacular show

Tropical fish are the most colorful on the planet. Their colors and patterns give camouflage among the multicolored corals on the seabed. Being gloriously gorgeous also helps these fish get noticed by potential mates.

Crimson soldierfish

Golden butterfly fish

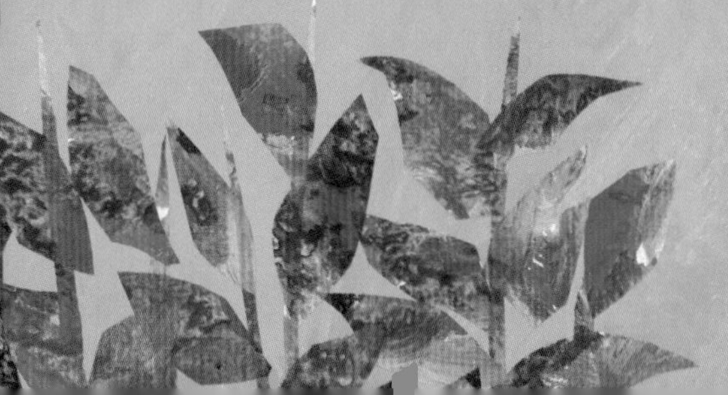

Striped cleaner wrasse

These little fish set up cleaning stations where they pick off the dead skin and bugs from fish and turtles that swim past. Not only does this keep the larger animals clean, but the wrasse also enjoy the snacks.

Great Barrier Reef

The world's biggest structure made up of living things is the Great Barrier Reef, off the coast of Australia. This enormous underwater bed of coral is a paradise for tropical fish. The reef is so big it can be seen from space.

Forceps fish

A long snout helps the forceps fish suck up little creatures hiding in the cracks and crevices of coral reefs. The black eyespots on their fins fool predators into thinking they are bigger, scarier fish.

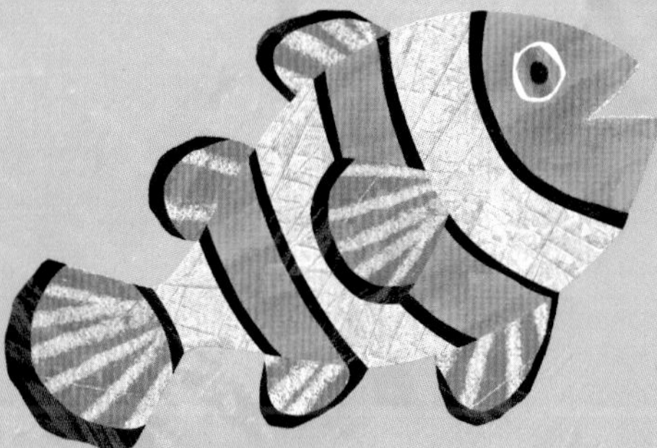

Clown fish

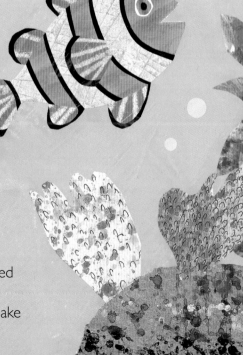

Blue chromis

Coral reefs

Tropical fish often live near coral reefs, where there is plenty of food and places to hide. Coral reefs are created from the hard outer skeletons of single corals, called polyps. Millions of these polyps join together to make the colorful, rocky reef.

Fishy fathers

For almost all animals, mothers have the babies and care for them until they can survive on their own. However, the seahorse is unique, because it is the father who gives birth.

Male seahorses give birth to up to 2,000 babies at a time.

Seahorse parenthood

The female seahorse lays her eggs inside pouches on the male's body. He warms and protects the eggs for weeks until they hatch inside the pouches. Then the male releases the baby seahorses into the water. After that, he returns to the female to pick up another batch of eggs and does it all over again.

Proud parents

Seahorses are not the only father fish that take on the task of caring for and defending their babies...

Bullhead fish

When the female bullhead lays her eggs, her male mate becomes their bodyguard. For the next month, he keeps predators away and uses his fins to fan the eggs regularly with fresh water.

Stickleback

Parenting duties are left to male sticklebacks. They build a nest for the eggs, then defend them against attack. The fathers keep the newly hatched sticklebacks close until the babies can swim properly.

Tilapia

This father fish takes no chances with his eggs. Once the female lays them, the male pops them all into his mouth for safekeeping until they hatch. He only takes the eggs out occasionally to rinse them in fresh water.

Food links

Fish are at the very heart of this network of ocean food and feeders. At the bottom are microscopic animals and plants. Right at the top are the biggest hunters, called apex predators.

Orcas

These giant dolphins are speedy, fierce hunters. They are apex predators and they eat seals, whales, and even other dolphins.

Ocean food web

Fish are an important source of food for hungry marine life. This food web shows who eats what, from tiny plants and shellfish, to fish of all sizes, to huge mammals.

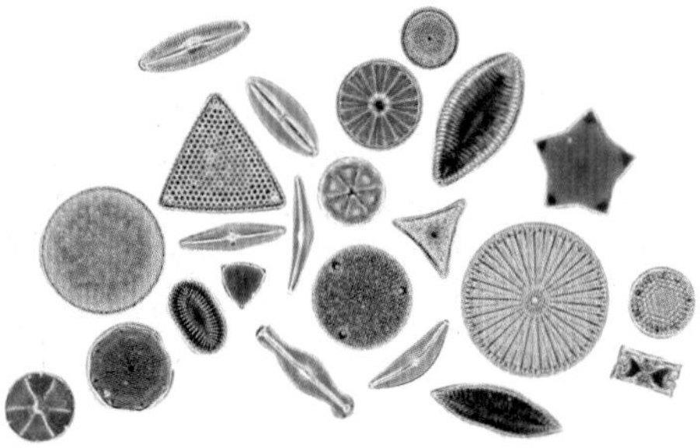

Phytoplankton

These extremely tiny marine plants are too small to see, but they are a vital food source for many marine animals.

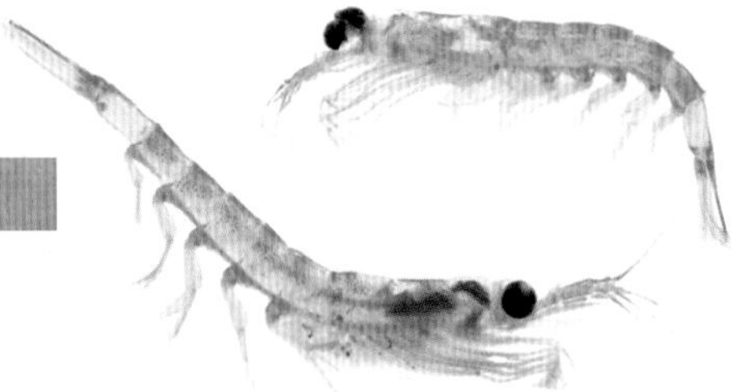

Zooplankton

These very small marine animals eat phytoplankton. They include krill, which are tiny, shrimplike creatures.

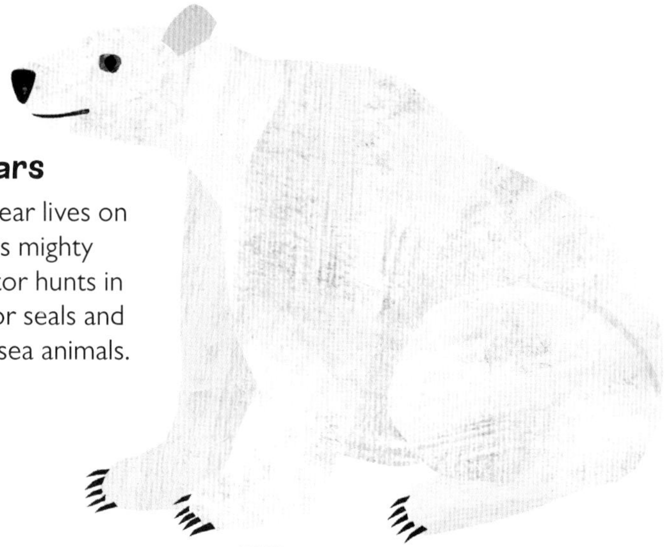

Polar bears

The polar bear lives on land, but this mighty apex predator hunts in the water for seals and other large sea animals.

Seabirds

Seagulls, terns, and other seabirds compete with seals to catch larger fish.

Seals

Seals are one of the main predators of large ocean fish.

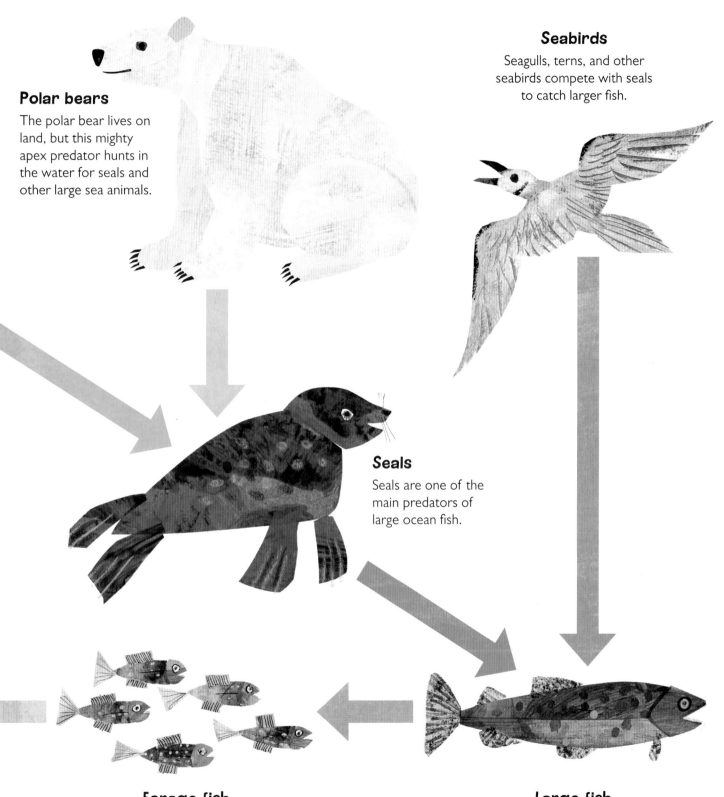

Forage fish

The smallest fish are forage fish, which include sardines and herrings. They are the main predators of zooplankton.

Large fish

This group includes fish such as salmon and trout. They mainly eat forage fish.

Incredible invertebrates

Invertebrates

Invertebrates make up most of the world's animals. Their bodies look very different from ours. We are shaped by the skeleton inside our bodies and our long backbone, but invertebrates don't have either.

Hard or soft

Some invertebrates have a soft, flexible body. Others have a tough outer shell to hide beneath, but most invertebrates have a skeleton on the outside, which covers their whole body.

A worm has a squishy body.

A snail has a shell.

An ant has a skeleton on the outside.

Huge family

Invertebrates come in all shapes and sizes, from tiny beetles on land to giant squid in the ocean. They live in just about every kind of habitat on Earth.

97 percent of animals on Earth are invertebrates. The word means "without a backbone."

Slug

High-fliers

Flying invertebrates include winged insects, such as bees, butterflies, flies, ladybugs, and wasps.

Butterfly

Ladybug

Creepy-crawlies

Instead of flying, some invertebrates, such as spiders and wood lice, prefer to crawl and scuttle along the ground. They have lots of legs to help them move quickly.

Spider

Wood louse

Slithering sliders

Snails, worms, and slugs are also part of the invertebrate gang. These animals have no legs, so they slip, slide, or wriggle along.

Worm

Ocean-dwellers

Many invertebrates live in the sea. Like their relatives on land, they come in many shapes and sizes, from squishy jellyfish to hard-shelled lobsters.

Octopus

Jellyfish

Lobster

Crab

Ants and termites

You won't have to look hard to find an ant. There are trillions and trillions of ants and termites in the world, which is more than any other insect.

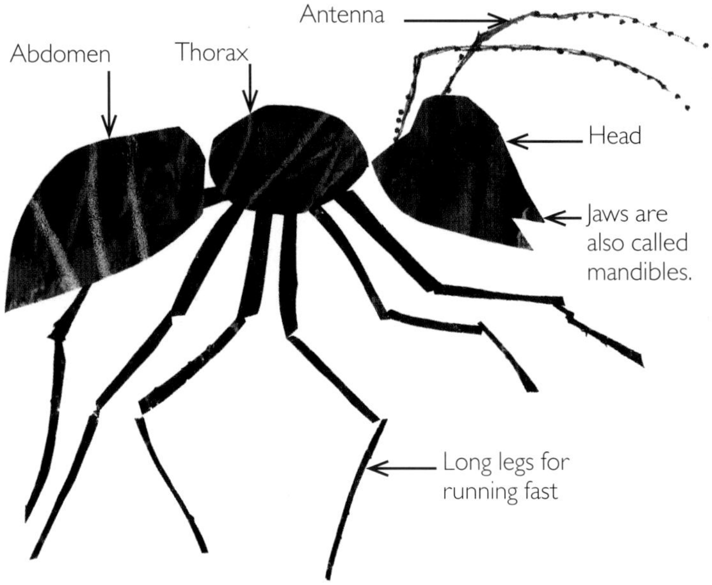

Anty-bodies

Like all insects, ants have six legs and a body made up of three joined parts. They have antennae to feel for food or predators. They lift and carry things in their strong jaws. Ants live in a big group, called a colony, where they all have different jobs to do.

The strongest ants can carry 5,000 times their own weight!

Leaf-cutter ants

These busy ants are strong enough to carry 50 times their own body weight. They cut leaves and carry them back to the nest. Then they grow their favorite fungus food on huge, underground beds of leaves.

Anteater

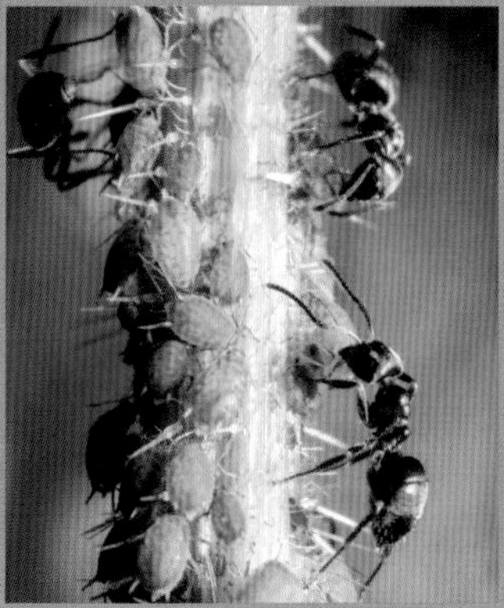

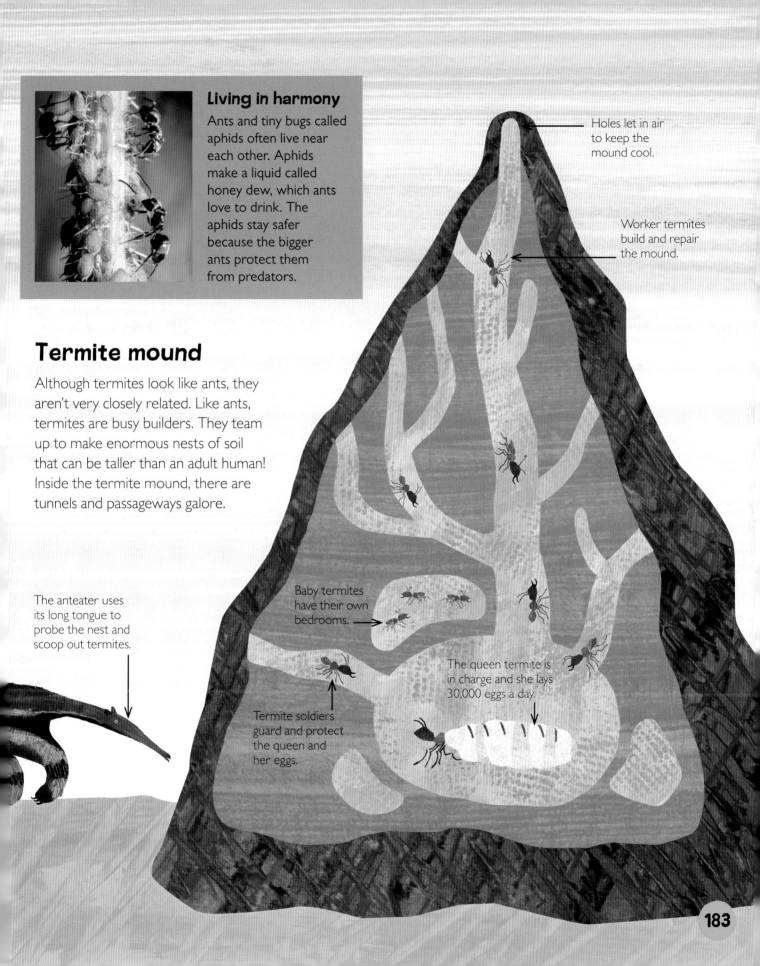

Living in harmony

Ants and tiny bugs called aphids often live near each other. Aphids make a liquid called honey dew, which ants love to drink. The aphids stay safer because the bigger ants protect them from predators.

Termite mound

Although termites look like ants, they aren't very closely related. Like ants, termites are busy builders. They team up to make enormous nests of soil that can be taller than an adult human! Inside the termite mound, there are tunnels and passageways galore.

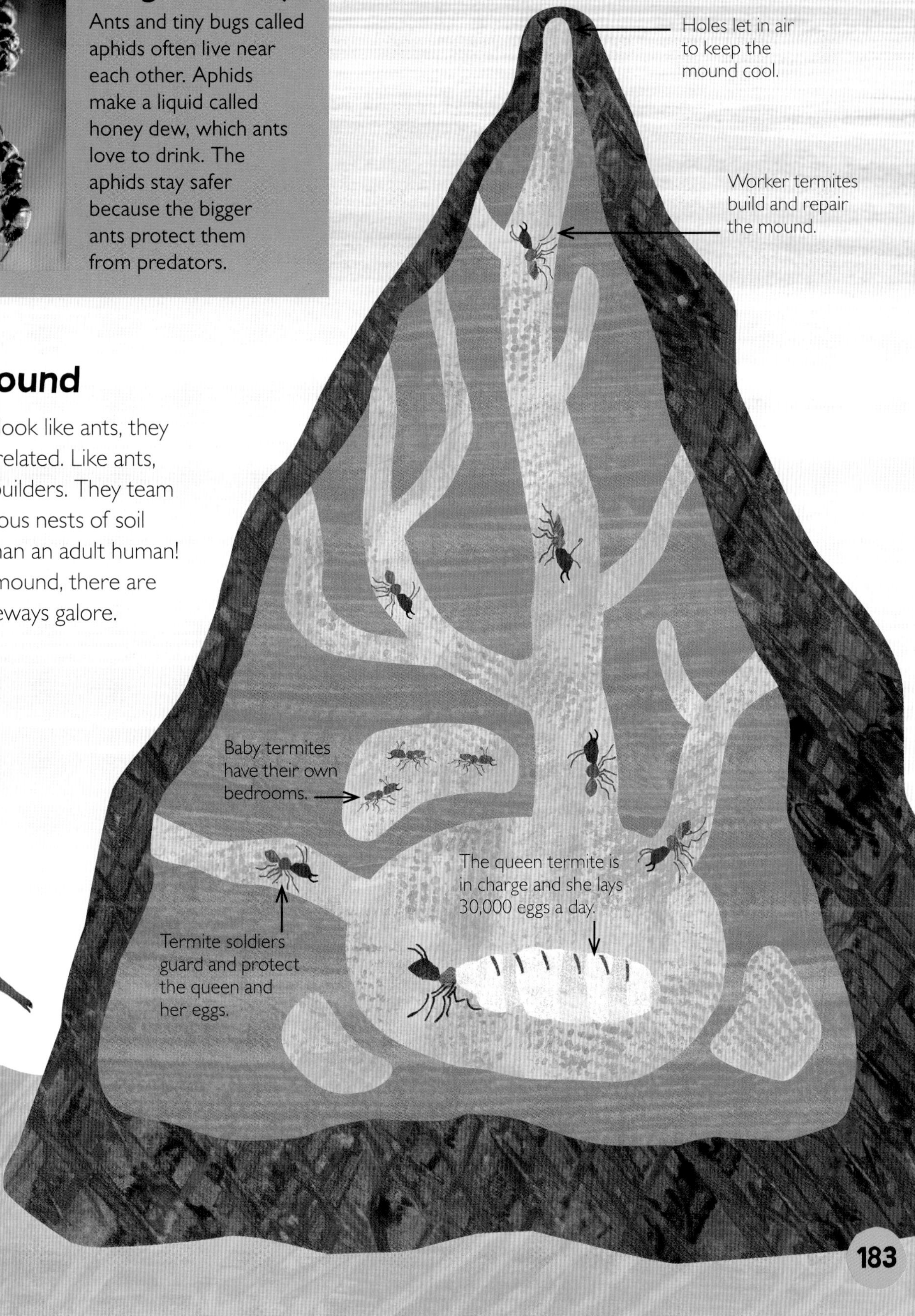

Holes let in air to keep the mound cool.
Worker termites build and repair the mound.
Baby termites have their own bedrooms.
The queen termite is in charge and she lays 30,000 eggs a day.
Termite soldiers guard and protect the queen and her eggs.

The anteater uses its long tongue to probe the nest and scoop out termites.

Flying insects

During spring and summer, flying insects fill the skies, on the lookout for sweet treats or unsuspecting prey. Most are harmless, but some have a sting in their tails.

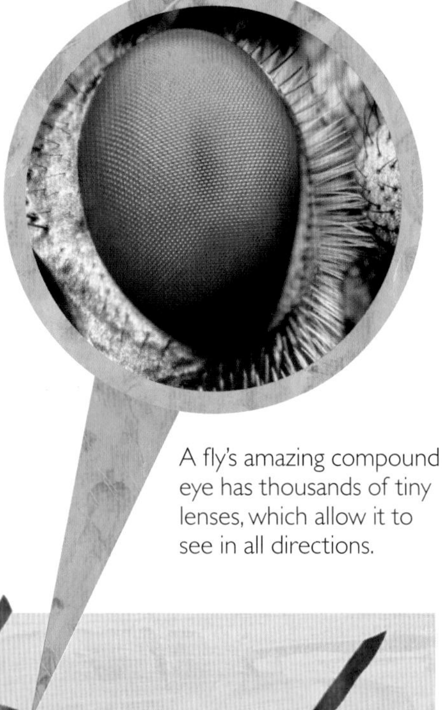

A fly's amazing compound eye has thousands of tiny lenses, which allow it to see in all directions.

Houseflies

If houseflies land on human food, they can spread diseases via their sticky feet. However, they also do good by eating up rotting food and dead creatures. Their bodies are made of three linked parts: the head, the thorax, and the abdomen.

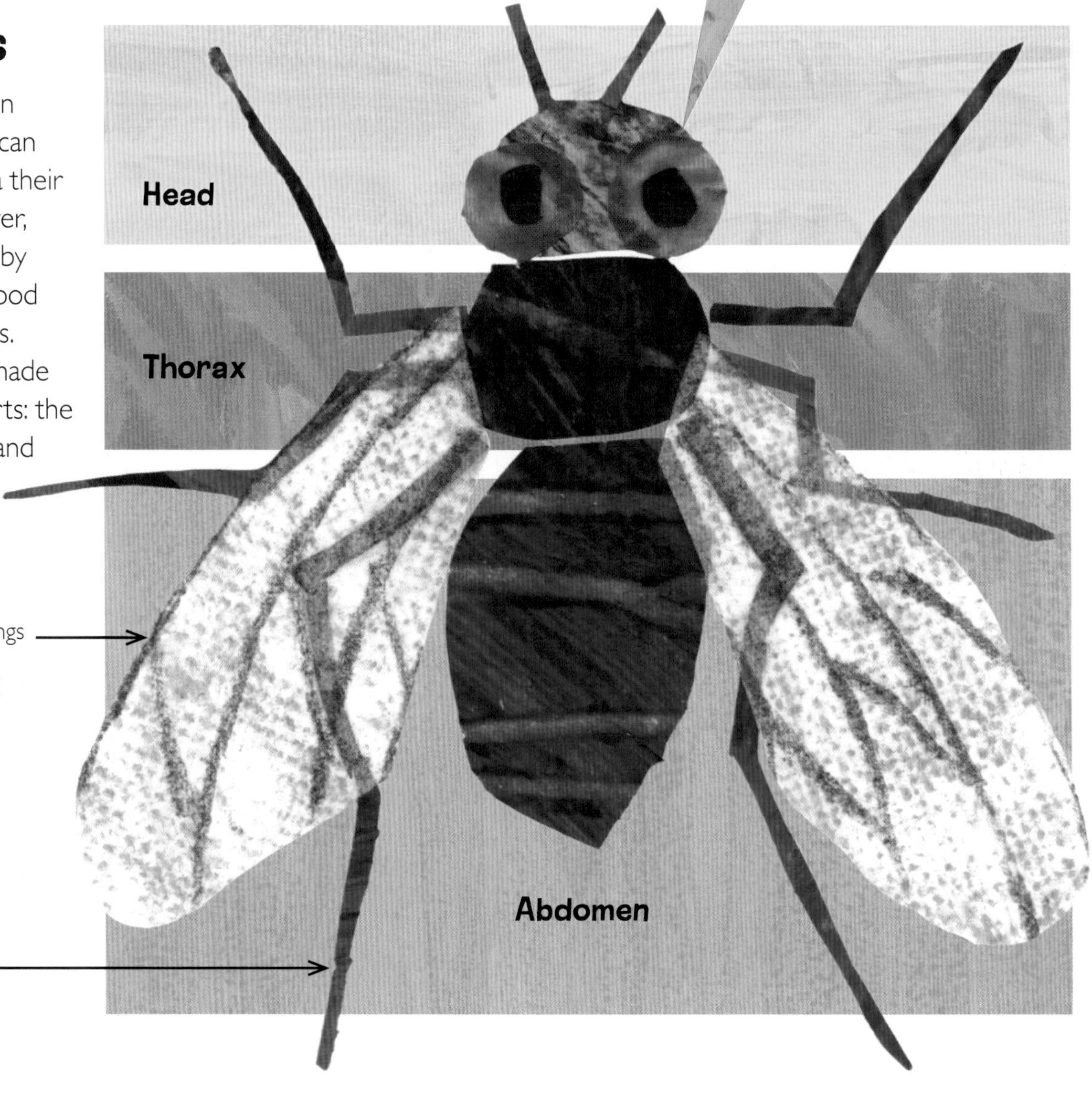

A housefly's wings can beat 200 times a second!

Flies have taste buds on their legs and feet.

Wasps

These high-speed fliers produce painful venom to kill insect prey or harm predators. Unlike bees, wasps can sting again and again without hurting themselves.

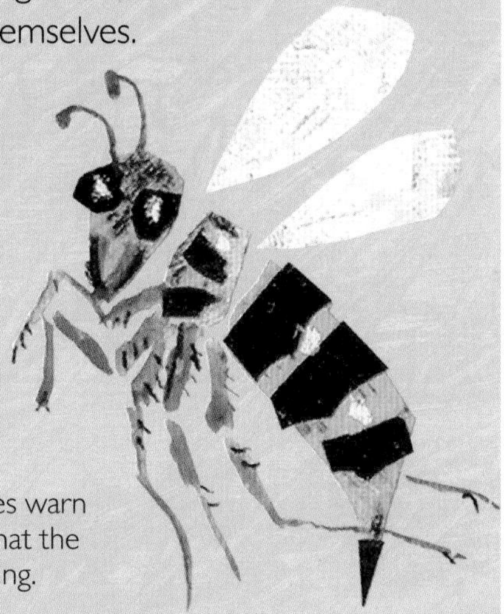

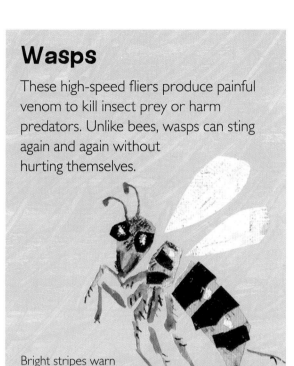

Bright stripes warn predators that the wasp can sting.

Fireflies

Some flying insects get busy at night. Fireflies use chemicals inside them to make their bodies glow in the darkness. These homemade lights attract mates and confuse predators.

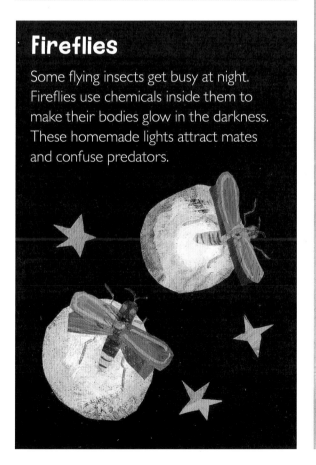

Beetles

These shiny, often colorful insects have two sets of wings: a hard pair on top can close to protect the soft flying wings underneath.

There are more than 350,000 types of beetle!

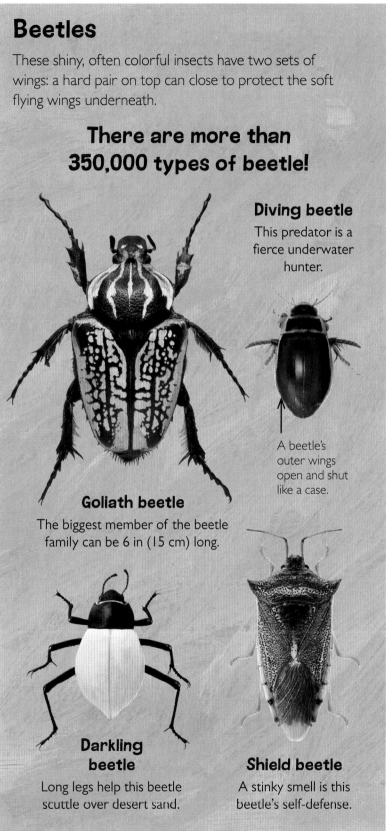

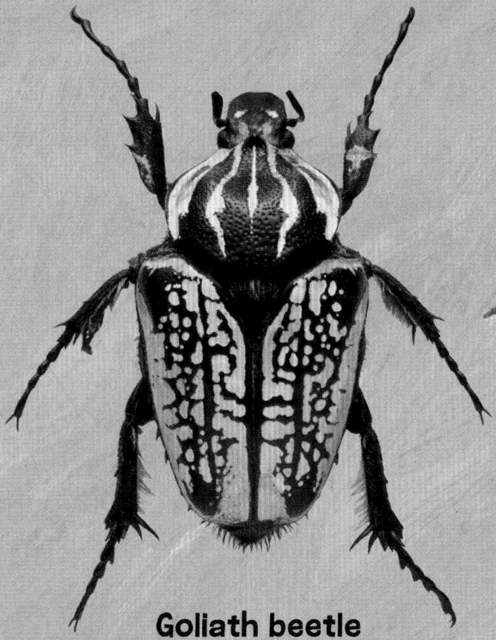

Goliath beetle

The biggest member of the beetle family can be 6 in (15 cm) long.

Diving beetle

This predator is a fierce underwater hunter.

A beetle's outer wings open and shut like a case.

Darkling beetle

Long legs help this beetle scuttle over desert sand.

Shield beetle

A stinky smell is this beetle's self-defense.

Butterflies and moths

Beautiful butterflies flutter in the summer sunshine, while moths fly mostly at dusk. They have all gone through total transformations to reach adulthood.

Spot the difference

Butterflies and moths have similarly shaped bodies. Butterflies are often brightly colored, but most moths are plainer, with camouflaged colors. Butterflies sleep with their wings shut, while moths keep their wings open when they rest.

Red admiral butterfly

In *The Very Hungry Caterpillar*, the caterpillar forms a cocoon instead of a chrysalis. (Almost always, cocoons are made by moths, not butterflies.) Eric Carle has called his caterpillar "very unusual." When he was a small boy, his father would say, "Eric, come out of your cocoon." And, so, for *The Very Hungry Caterpillar*, poetry won over science!

Metamorphosis

Butterflies and moths look completely different when they are fully grown, compared to when they were young. Their bodies go through four stages of development: egg, larva, pupa, and adult. This complete transformation is called metamorphosis.

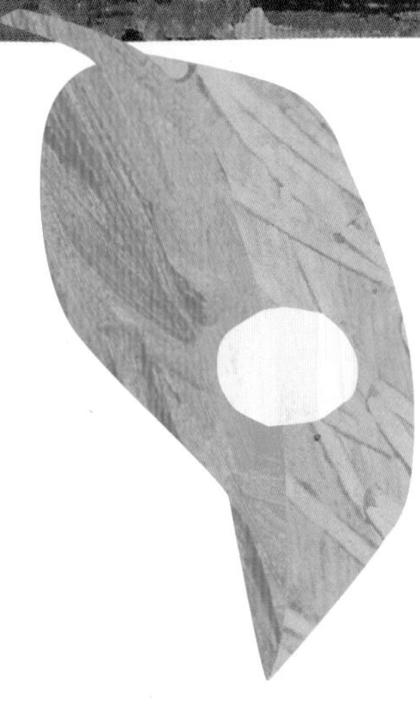

1. Egg

An adult female butterfly lays her eggs on a leaf.

2. Caterpillar

Each egg hatches into a little larva, called a caterpillar. The baby caterpillar begins eating the leaf it hatched on.

Purple emperor butterfly

Hawk moth

Mottled green moth

Butterflies and moths are the only insects that have wings covered in tiny scales.

Giant peacock moth

Swallowtail butterfly

3. Growing bigger

The very hungry caterpillar, whom we know and love, munches leaves nonstop. It grows very quickly and sheds its skin several times as its body grows... and grows!

4. Chrysalis

A tough shell, called a chrysalis (or pupa), grows around the caterpillar. In the next weeks or months, the caterpillar inside gradually changes.

5. Butterfly

Finally, the chrysalis breaks open. The caterpillar is gone… and in its place is a beautiful adult butterfly.

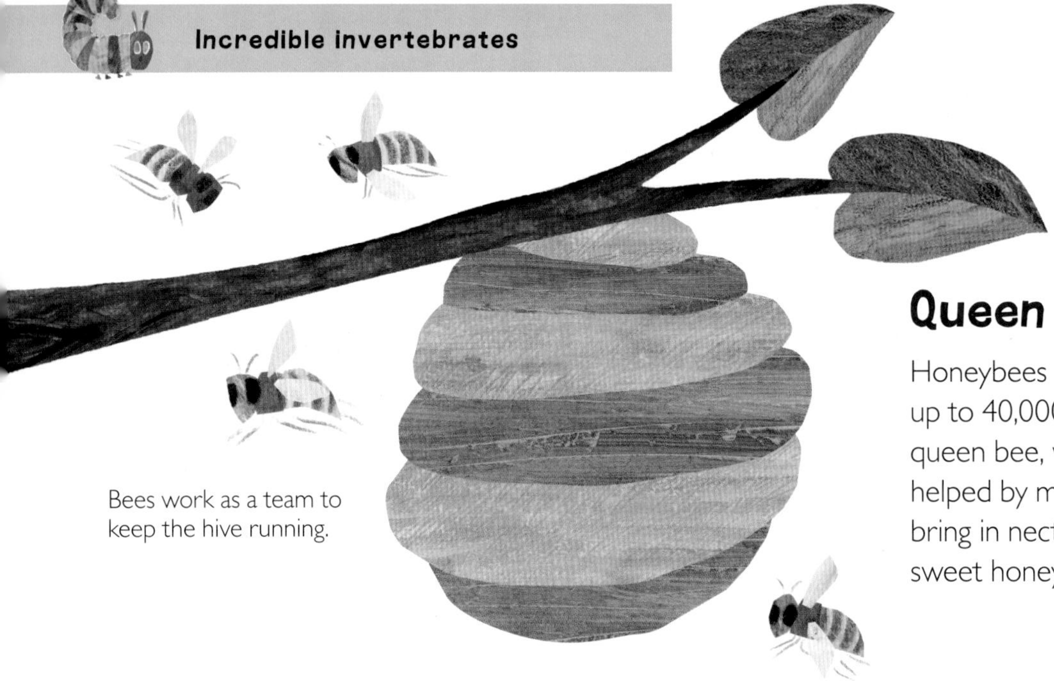

Bees work as a team to keep the hive running.

Queen bee

Honeybees live in hives that can contain up to 40,000 bees. The hive is run by the queen bee, who lays all the eggs. She is helped by male drones, while worker bees bring in nectar. The nectar is turned into sweet honey to feed the hive.

Brilliant bees

Bees are essential to our planet. They help to keep habitats healthy and colorful and play an important part in keeping the circle of life turning.

Bees from just one hive can pollinate 300 million flowers every single day.

Pollen carriers

When a bee lands on a flower, its feet get covered in pollen, a yellow powder made by the flower. As the bee flies around, it transfers this pollen to other flowers, which causes new flowers to grow and make fruit. This is called pollination.

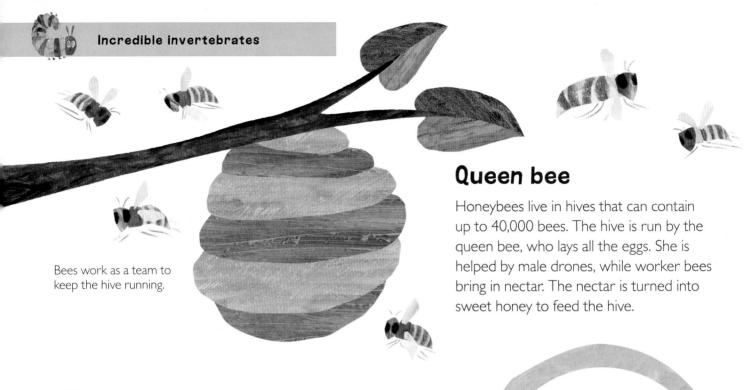

Hairy feet are coated in pollen.

Honeycomb hive

Inside the hive, worker bees produce beeswax from their bodies. The wax is used to make hexagon-shaped cells, which are joined together to make a honeycomb. The bees use honeycombs to store food: pollen for the baby bees and honey for the adults.

Bees are friends of farmers, too. They pollinate about one-third of all our fruits and vegetables.

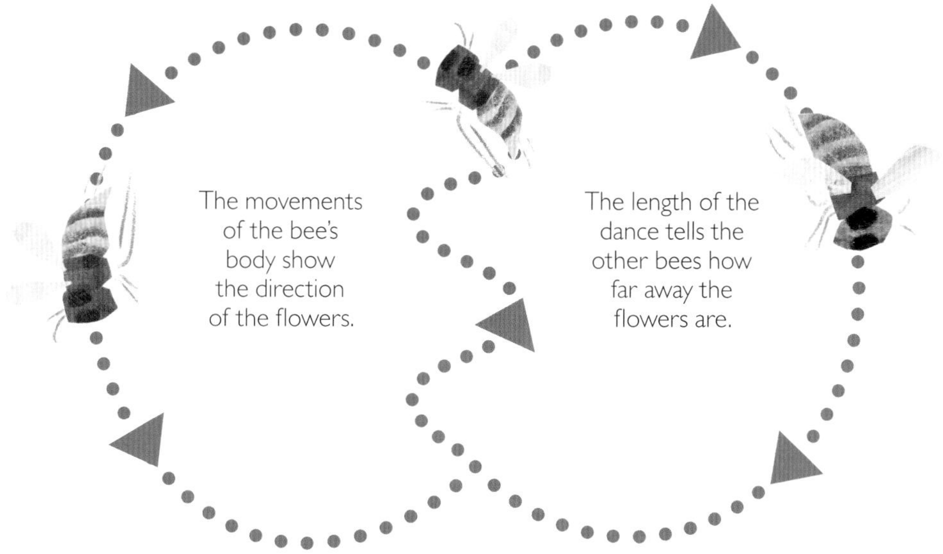

The movements of the bee's body show the direction of the flowers.
The length of the dance tells the other bees how far away the flowers are.

Dancing bees

Multitalented bees are also excellent dancers. When a bee finds a new source of nectar, it goes back to the hive and performs a complicated "waggle dance" to let the other bees know exactly where to find the flowers.

When the bee lands on the next flower, it leaves pollen from other flowers behind.

Honey history

Beekeepers collect leftover honey for people to eat. Yum! Honey has been eaten for 15,000 years. In ancient Egypt, pharaoh kings had jars of honey buried with them in their tombs. If it is stored properly, honey will last forever without going bad.

Spiders and scorpions

Some people think spiders and scorpions are scary, but these eight-legged predators are amazingly talented and most are harmless to humans.

Arachnids

Spiders and scorpions belong to the group called arachnids. They have a body divided into two segments and no wings. Instead of a skeleton inside their bodies, arachnids have an outer casing, called an exoskeleton.

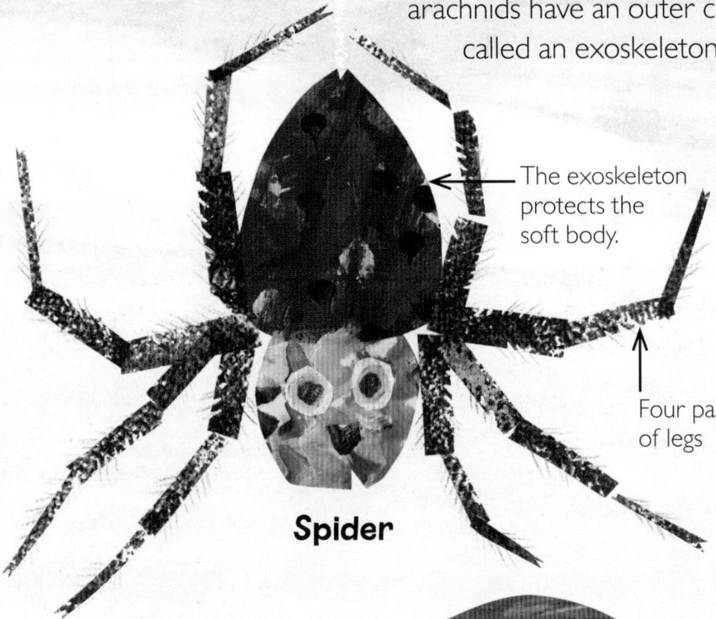

The spider spins strands of strong silk.
The exoskeleton protects the soft body.
Four pairs of legs
Spider

Silky trap

Spiders create silk inside their bodies. Then they weave the silk into a web to trap prey. The spider waits patiently for insects to fly into the sticky web and get themselves tangled up. Then it is time to move in and devour the prey.

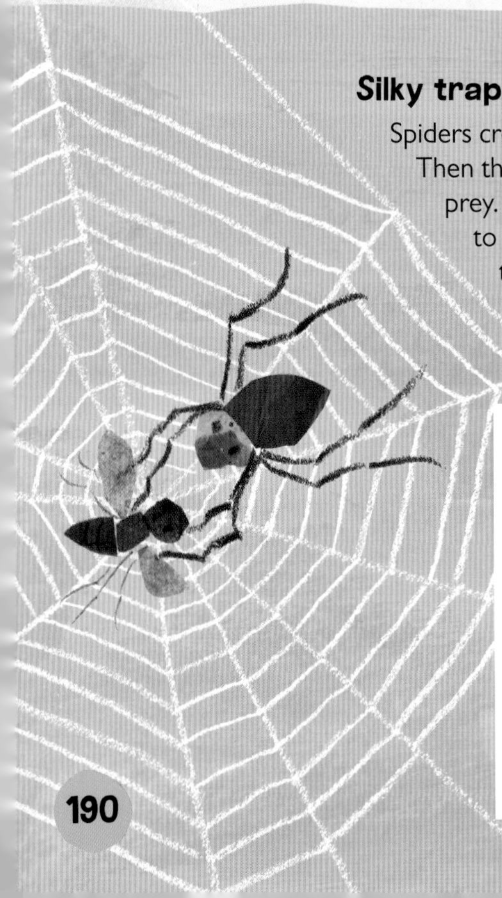

In addition to eight legs, most spiders have eight eyes, too!

Spider selection

There are about 40,000 types of spider. Here are three of the most amazing.

Jumping spider

This athletic hero uses its silk to hang from one thing, then leap onto another. It also swings at high speed from its silk threads to pounce on insect prey.

Bringing up babies

Newborn scorpions, called scorplings, do not have exoskeletons yet, so they are soft and easy to attack. Mothers carry the babies safely on their backs and lash out at potential predators with their stinging tails.

Bloodsucking tick

Tiny ticks are arachnids with big appetites. They bite into animals and suck their blood. A well-fed tick can swell up to more than 10 times its normal size.

Scorpions

At night, these predators emerge to hunt for food. Their powerful pincers pin down prey, then the venomous sting in the tail delivers the killer blow. Scorpions can chomp their way through their own weight in insects every night.

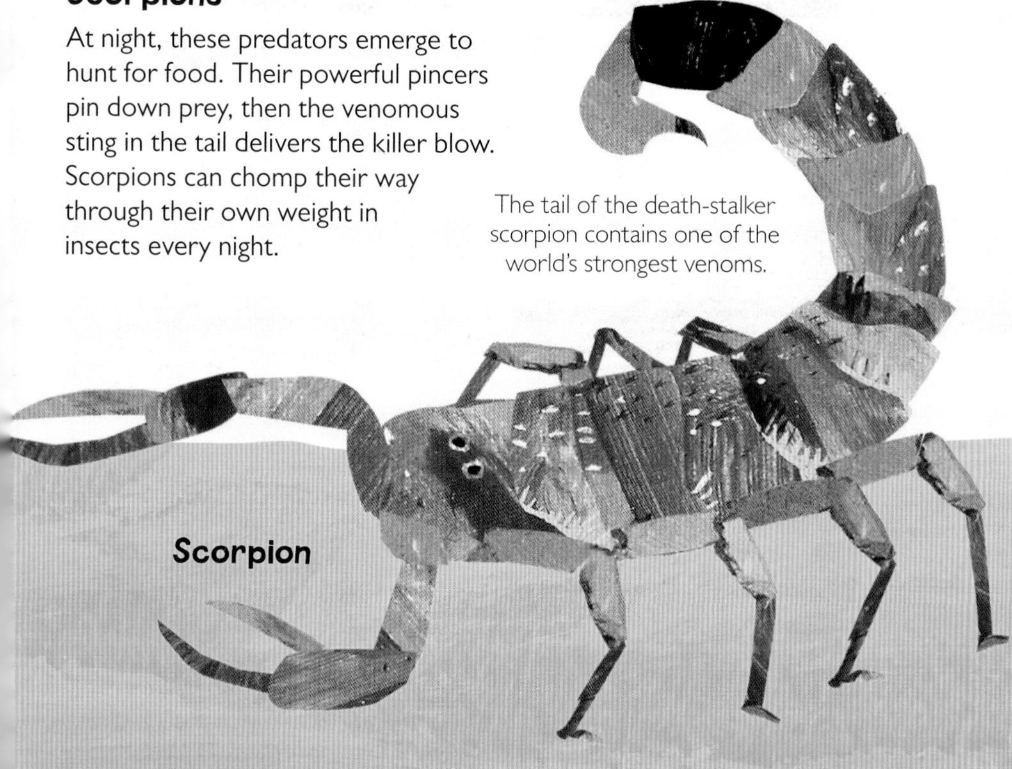

The tail of the death-stalker scorpion contains one of the world's strongest venoms.

Scorpion

Most scorpions are fluorescent, which means they glow in the moonlight!

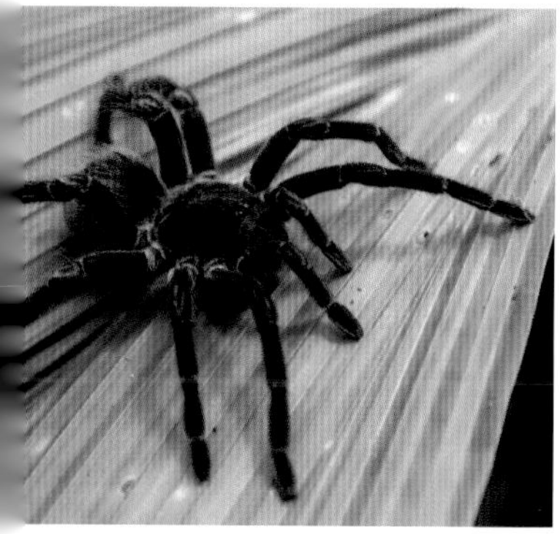

Goliath bird-eating tarantula

Living up to its name, this huge, hairy spider eats birds as well as bats, frogs, and mice. Instead of spinning a web, it hides, then ambushes passing prey.

Water spider

Most spiders are land-based, but the water spider lives in lakes and ponds. It builds a silky, air-filled home under the water, then chases prey such as water fleas and midge larvae.

Garden guests

Our gardens are full of inventive invertebrates. Some have no legs and make their way by slithering, sliding, wriggling, and writhing, while others have too many legs to count.

Snails

Soft-bodied, slow-moving snails carry their homes on their backs. Snails depend on their hard shells to protect themselves from predators.

The shell has a spiral pattern.
The eyes are on long stalks.
Soft body without any bones
Short feelers for finding food

Slimy trail

What's that silvery slime that trails behind a snail? Snails have one foot, which produces slime to help them glide over surfaces and stick to walls. When a snail moves, the slime is shiny and watery. When the snail stops moving, the slime becomes solid and sticky.

Snails and slugs don't just live in gardens. Some types live in ponds or in the sea.

Lots of legs!

While some garden visitors have no legs, others have hundreds. Centipedes have more than 50 legs and millipedes have up to 300. They both move their pairs of legs in gentle waves to make sure that the legs don't keep banging into each other.

Centipede

Millipede

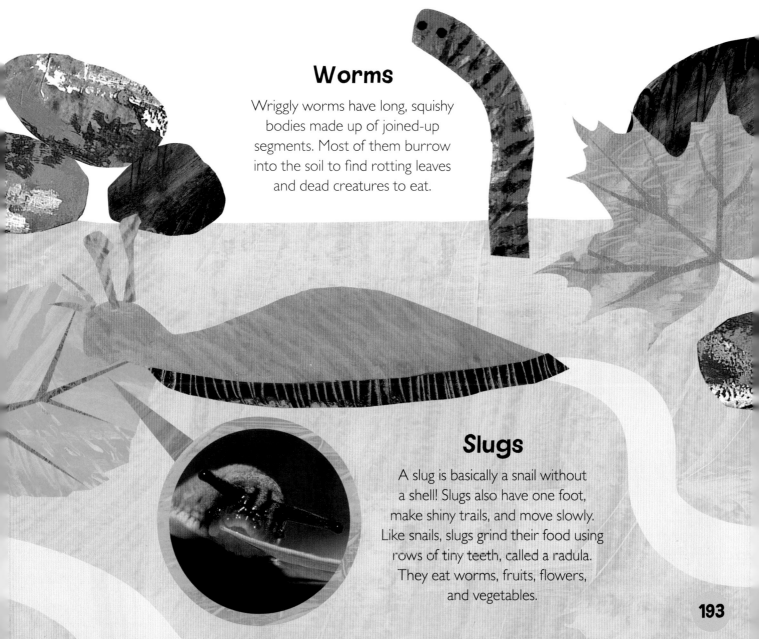

Worms

Wriggly worms have long, squishy bodies made up of joined-up segments. Most of them burrow into the soil to find rotting leaves and dead creatures to eat.

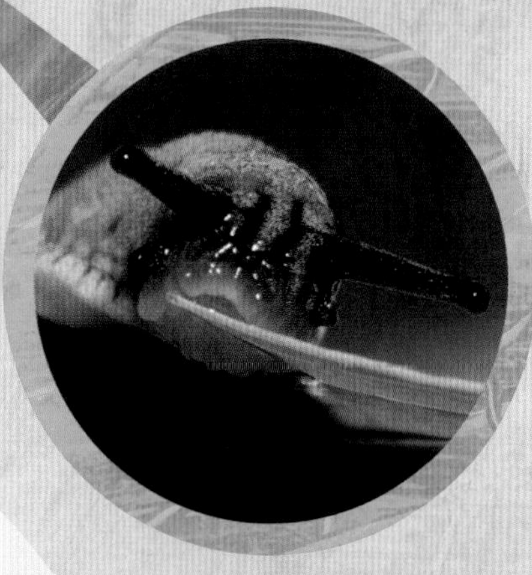

Slugs

A slug is basically a snail without a shell! Slugs also have one foot, make shiny trails, and move slowly. Like snails, slugs grind their food using rows of tiny teeth, called a radula. They eat worms, fruits, flowers, and vegetables.

Praying mantis

The praying mantis sits as still as a statue on a leaf, blending easily into its surroundings and waiting patiently for prey to pass. Then, quick as a flash, it snatches and swallows its victim.

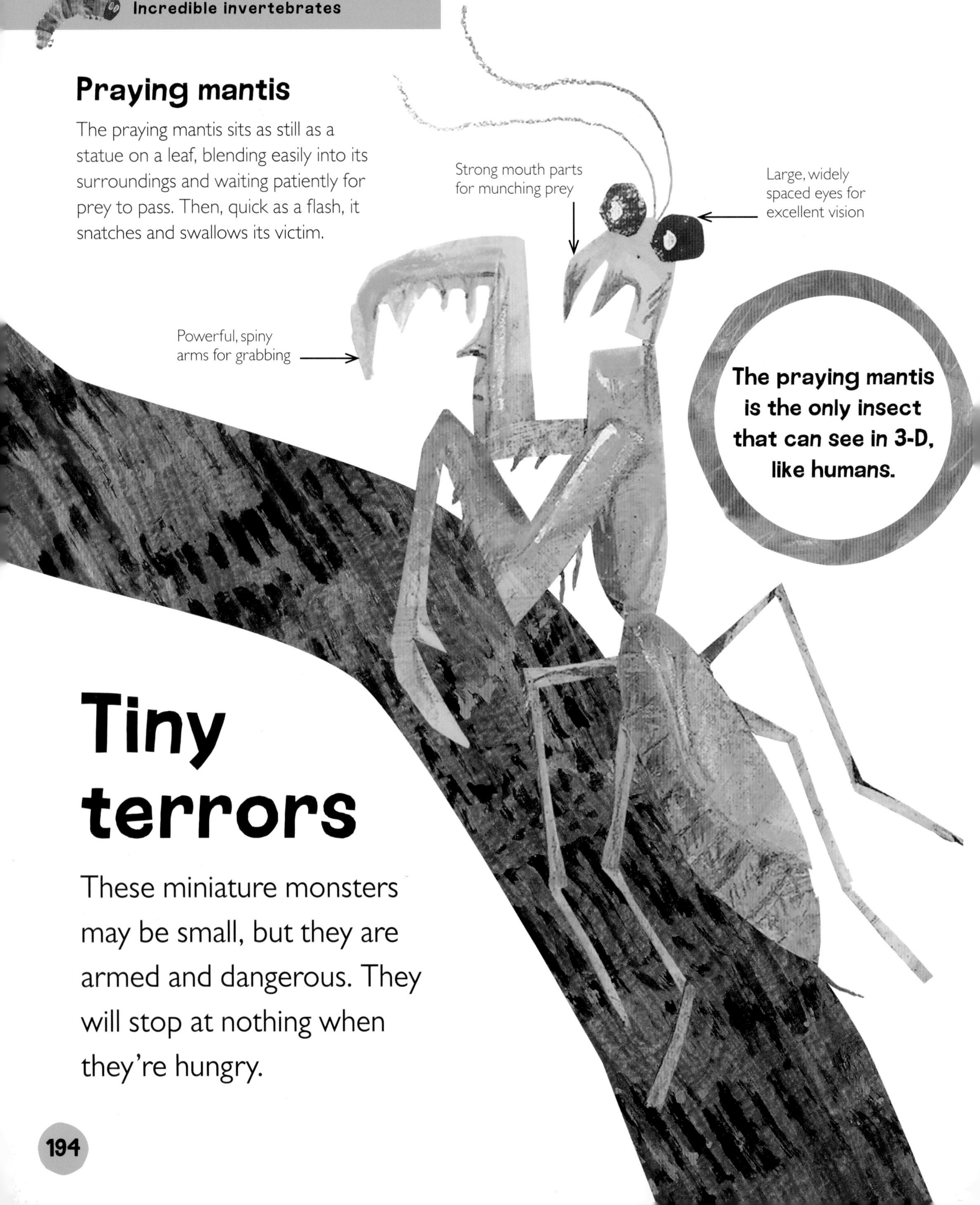

The praying mantis is the only insect that can see in 3-D, like humans.

Tiny terrors

These miniature monsters may be small, but they are armed and dangerous. They will stop at nothing when they're hungry.

Cockroach

This tough customer is the ultimate survivor. It will eat almost anything, including live prey or leftover human food. A cockroach can go without food or water for a month, and can even survive for three days without its head!

Bombardier beetle

When predators approach, bombardier beetles detonate their homemade bombs. They release a blast of steaming hot, super-smelly chemicals from their rear end to kill smaller enemies and scare off bigger ones. BOOM!

Assassin bug

Other insects try to steer clear of the assassin bug. This ruthless hunter pins down prey before jabbing repeatedly with its needlelike mouthparts. It then sucks out the victim's insides. Yuck!

Mosquito

Which animal is the deadliest risk to humans? It's not a scary shark or a hungry hippo, but the miniature mosquito. Female mosquitoes spread a serious disease, called malaria, by biting into human skin and sucking out blood.

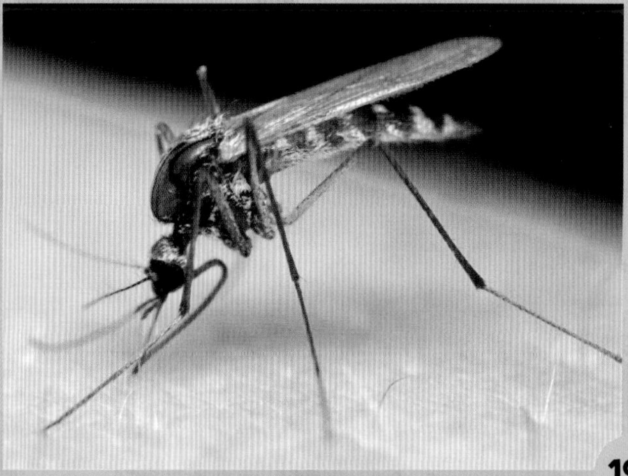

Suckers on the squid's tentacles help to grasp prey.

Giant squid

The giant squid is the world's biggest invertebrate. With superlong tentacles, it is five times longer than a human, and its eyes are the size of dinner plates.

Octopuses and squid can squirt clouds of ink from their bodies to confuse predators.

Soft bodies

Marine mollusks can be many different shapes and sizes, but their bodies are always soft. Some have a shell to protect them, but others use clever camouflage to escape ocean predators or to creep up on prey.

Squishy sea life

Meet the marine mollusks. These soft and squishy creatures live in seas around the world.

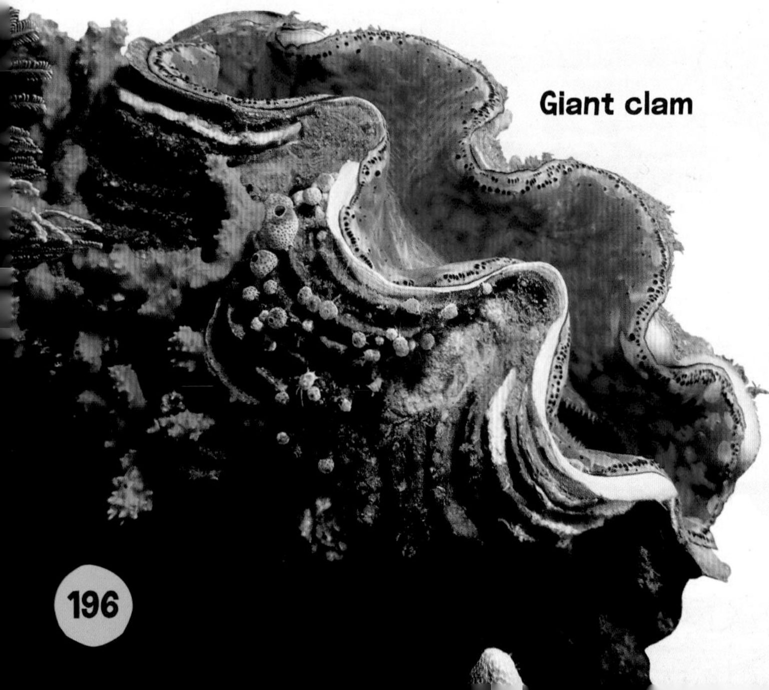

Giant clam

Bivalves

These animals have a shell that opens to let them breathe and eat and shuts to keep out predators. Members of the bivalve family include clams, mussels, oysters, and scallops.

Octopus

This unique animal has three hearts, eight arms, and blue blood. It also has nine brains and is amazingly clever. Scientists have found that these mollusks can solve complicated puzzles and even find their way out of mazes.

The eight tentacles have a mini-brain at the end of each one.
Arms grab prey and bring it up to the mouth.
Suckers to feel and taste surroundings

Sea snails

This family includes conches, whelks, and winkles. Often found in rock pools on the shore, sea snails have hard shells on their backs, just like snails on land.

Odd octopuses

The ocean is home to some truly incredible octopuses!

Mimic octopus

These amazing impersonators can mimic 13 different animals! This octopus is pretending to be a stingray.

Blue-ringed octopus

One of the deadliest marine animals, this tiny octopus carries enough venom to kill 26 people!

Caribbean reef octopus

To escape danger, this octopus can change color lightning-fast to match the surrounding coral reef.

Seaside shellfish

Crustaceans are a tough bunch of water-based invertebrates, with hard shells and snapping pincers that give a nasty nip.

Crustaceans

Almost all crustaceans live in oceans or rivers. Most have a hard shell to protect their soft bodies. Many have a pair of pincers that snap open and shut to grab food or attack enemies. Their eyes usually stand out on stalks.

Hard, flat shell
Crabs have 10 legs, with an extra-large front pair.

Crabs

On the beach, crabs scurry sideways over the sand. They can live on the seashore or the ocean floor. Their strong shells and powerful pincers give them double protection against predators.

Crazy crabs

Different types of crab look and behave differently, depending on their habitats and the food they prefer to eat.

Decorator crab

This crab loves to dress up. It covers its whole body with seaweed, sea sponges, and pieces of coral so that it merges into the background and avoids predators.

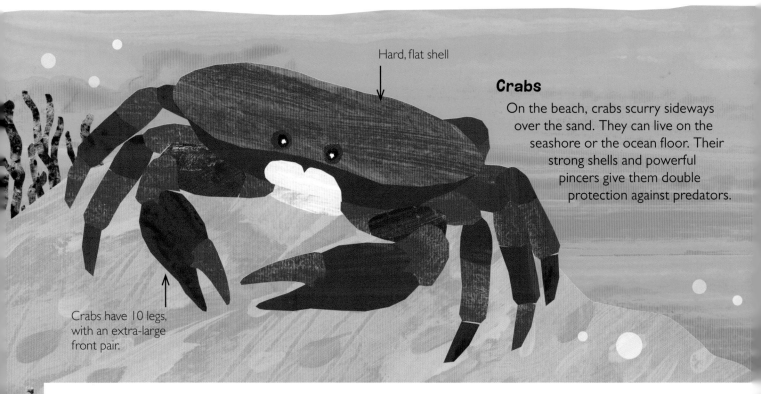

Barnacles

Seashore rocks are often covered in barnacles. As soft-bodied youngsters, they cling to rocks. Then they grow tough shells that affix them firmly in place.

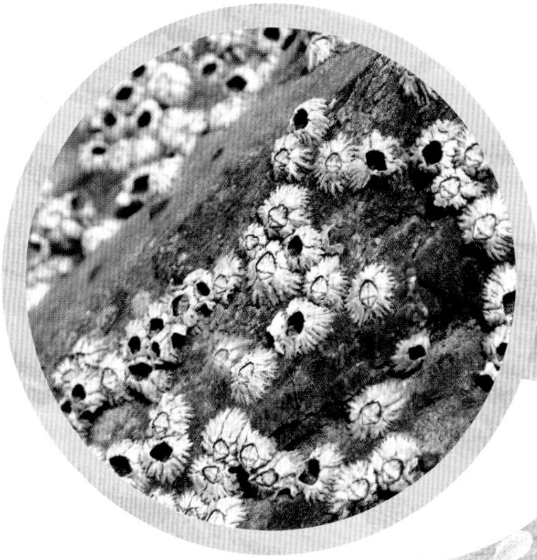

Barnacles stick to a rock for years without budging a bit!

Shrimp

These shellfish are super scavengers. They use their tiny pincers to pick up almost anything they come across, including fish, plants, snails, and worms.

Lobsters

These close relatives of the crab also have body armor and a pair of pincers. However, lobsters are a longer, slimmer shape and they crawl forward along the seafloor, instead of sideways.

Coconut crab

The world's biggest crab has the most powerful grip of any animal. It loves to eat coconuts and easily cracks open the shells with its huge pincers.

Fiddler crab

Size matters for male fiddler crabs. One pincer is much bigger than the other, to impress female crabs and to use as a weapon against rivals.

Jaw-dropping jellyfish

Dive deep to discover some strange, stunning marine stingers.

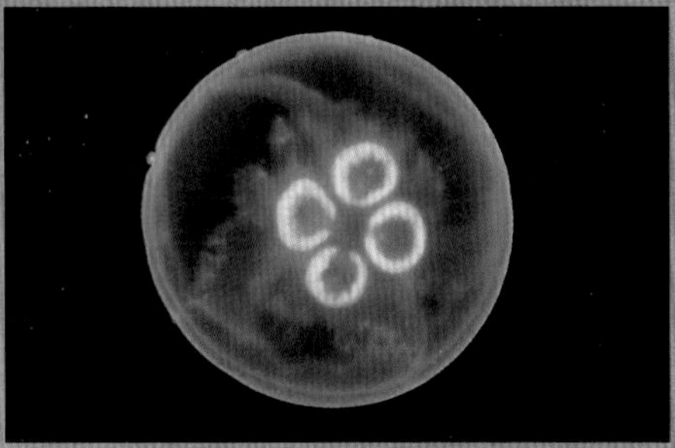

Moon jellyfish

The round body, or bell, of this jellyfish looks like a full moon shimmering in the dark water.

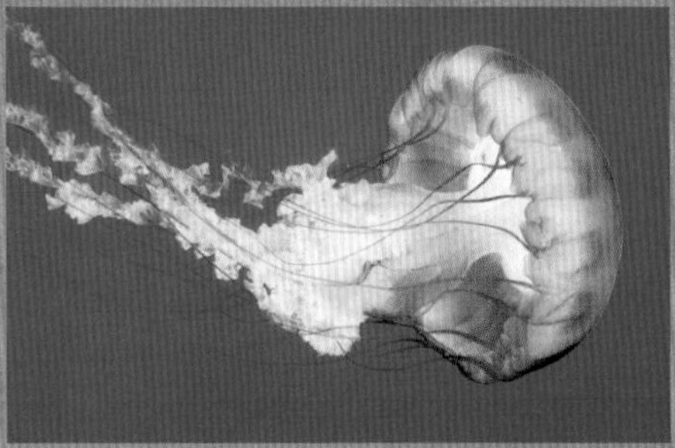

Pacific sea nettle

The long, venomous tentacles of this huge jellyfish are a bit like the wavy stalks of the stinging nettle plant.

Lion's mane jellyfish

The largest of all jellyfish has a mass of tentacles that spread out like the mane of a lion.

Simple stingers

Jellyfish, corals, and anemones look different but they are all closely related. These simple creatures are found in every ocean, and they all sting in self-defense.

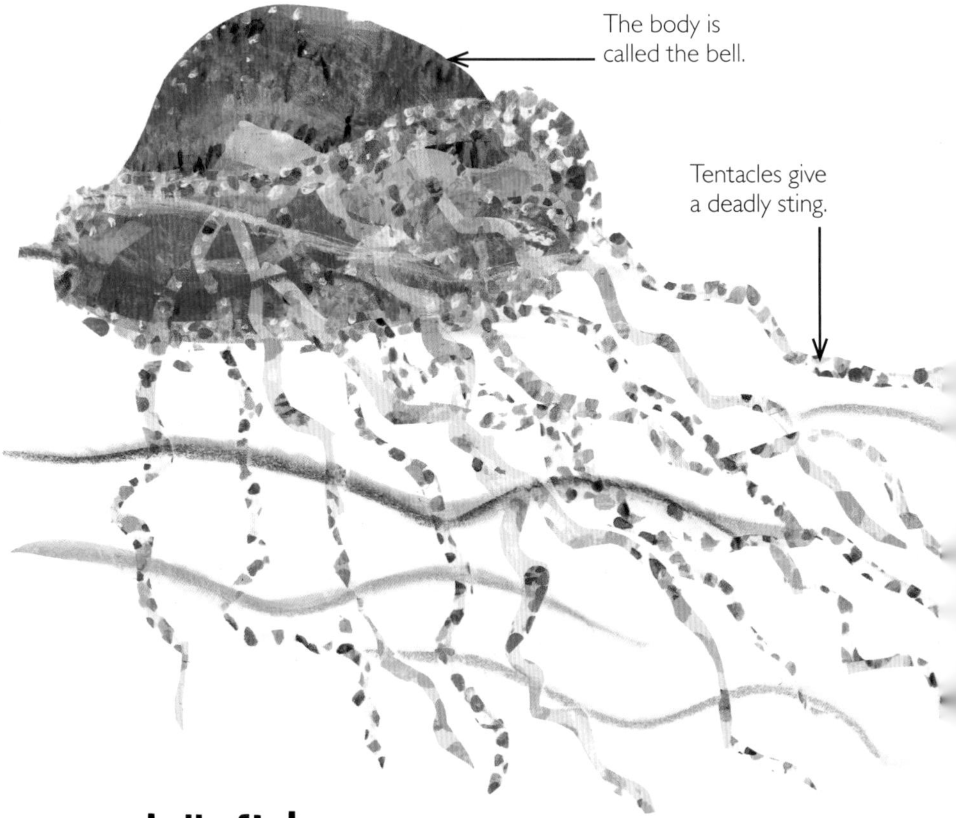

The body is called the bell.
Tentacles give a deadly sting.

Jellyfish

Looking like wobbly jelly molds, jellyfish have no bones, brain, eyes, or heart! They have three sections: a body, arms for pushing food into the mouth, and trailing tentacles that deliver a sting when they are touched. Jellyfish squeeze their muscles to push water in and out of their bodies, powering them through the oceans.

Sea anemone

They may look like flowers in an underwater garden, but sea anemones are actually animals. Their tentacles give a venomous sting to prey, including small fish and tiny plankton.

Anemones come in many different bright colors.

Coral

Vast underwater coral reefs look like rock, but the reefs are made up of masses of tiny animals called polyps. These microscopic invertebrates have the power to sting marine life and other corals.

Coral close-up

The surface of the brain coral is made up of millions of tiny polyps, each with a ring of stinging tentacles.

Brain coral has many folds, just like a human brain!

Marine magicians

Sea stars have the amazing ability to create a brand-new body. If a sea star is attacked and loses an arm, or sheds an arm on purpose to escape a predator, the detached arm grows into a new and complete sea star!

Sea stars

Sea stars used to be called starfish, but scientists renamed them because they are nothing like fish. Their bodies can be smooth or spiny. Most have five arms, but some sea stars have 40 arms.

The sea star's mouth is underneath its body.

Sea stars have existed on Earth for nearly 450 million years.

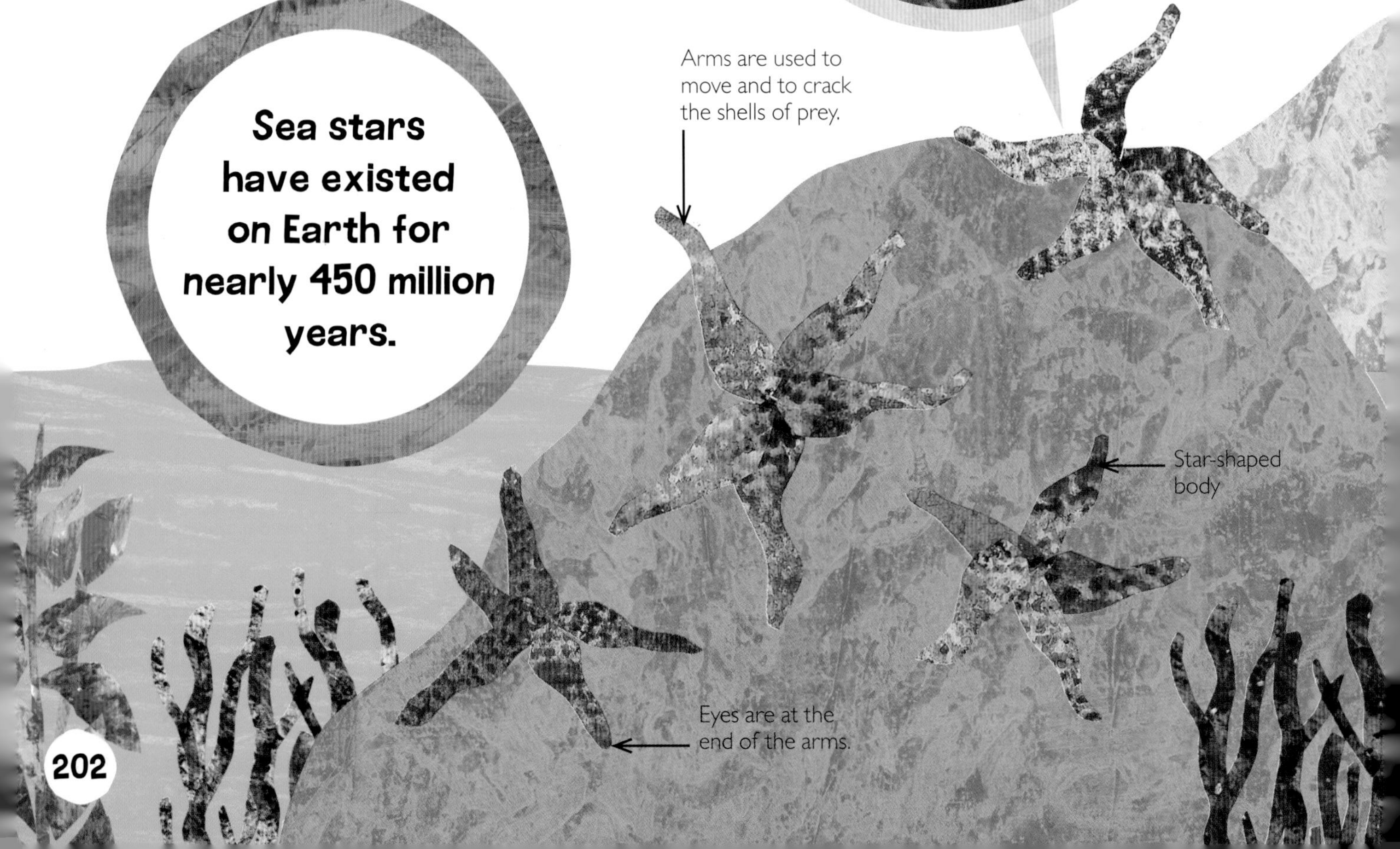

Arms are used to move and to crack the shells of prey.
Star-shaped body
Eyes are at the end of the arms.

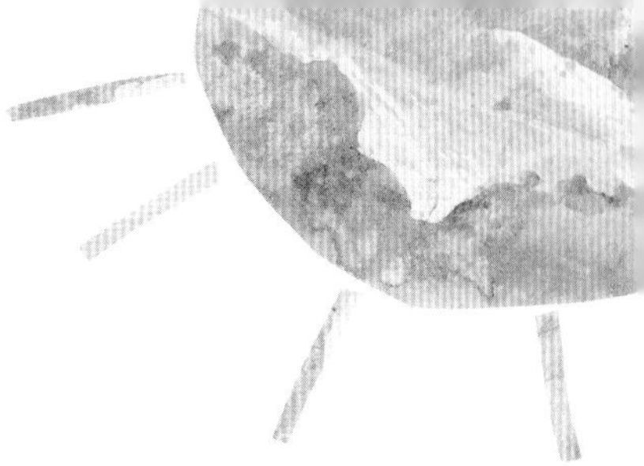

Stars and spikes

Sea stars, sea urchins, and sea sponges have no brains and they can't swim. However, they thrive in the ocean, and some even have the superpower to grow a whole new body!

Sea urchins

These simple spiked creatures are covered in sharp spines that protect their squishy bodies. Predators or human swimmers that get too close to the spines receive a painful sting.

The sea urchin has a round mouth and five pointed teeth.

Sea urchins are known as the porcupines of the sea.

Sea sponges

The simplest animals of all are sponges. They sit on the seabed, attached to rocks and hardly moving. They feed by soaking up the sea and filtering out the tiny plankton swimming in the water.

Animal activities

Animal champions

The animal kingdom is full of remarkable record-breakers. Three cheers for these champions!

World's strongest

The dung beetle can pull a dung ball 1,000 times heavier than its body. That's the same as you dragging six buses along a road!

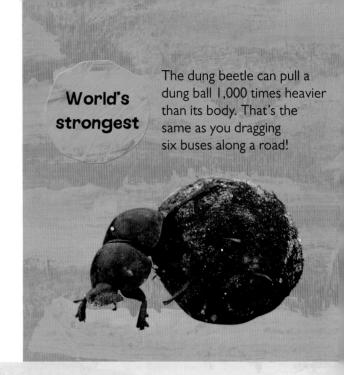

The wandering albatross beats all the other birds, with a whopping wingspan of 10 ft (3 m).

Longest wingspan

The Arctic tern makes the world's longest journey. Each year, it flies 44,000 miles (71,000 km) from the Arctic to Antarctica and back again.

Farthest flier

Fastest insect

Don't race a dragonfly! They can fly at 34 mph (54 kph), which is faster than any human has ever run.

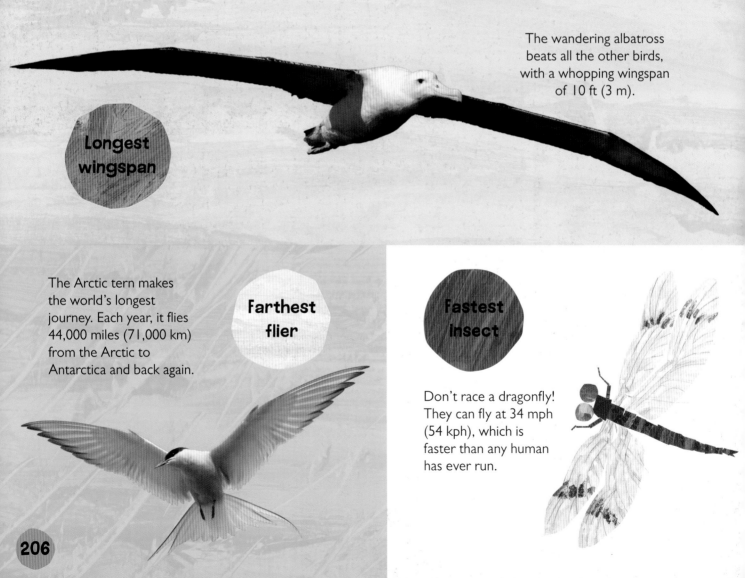

Slowest mammal

The sloth is the slowest-moving mammal. It would take more than four hours for a sloth to walk the length of one soccer field.

Deadliest stinger

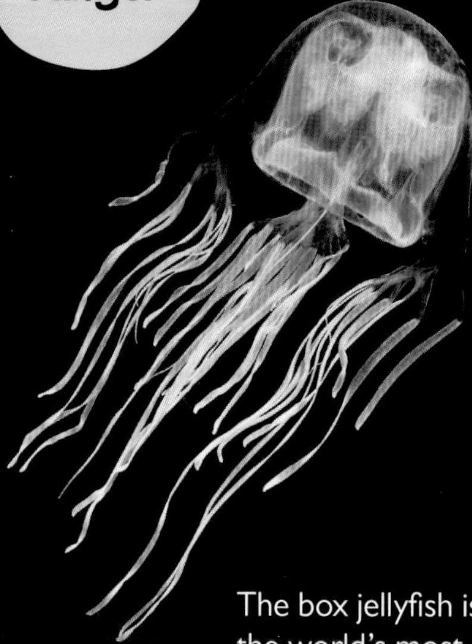

The box jellyfish is the world's most venomous creature. Its toxins can kill a human in minutes.

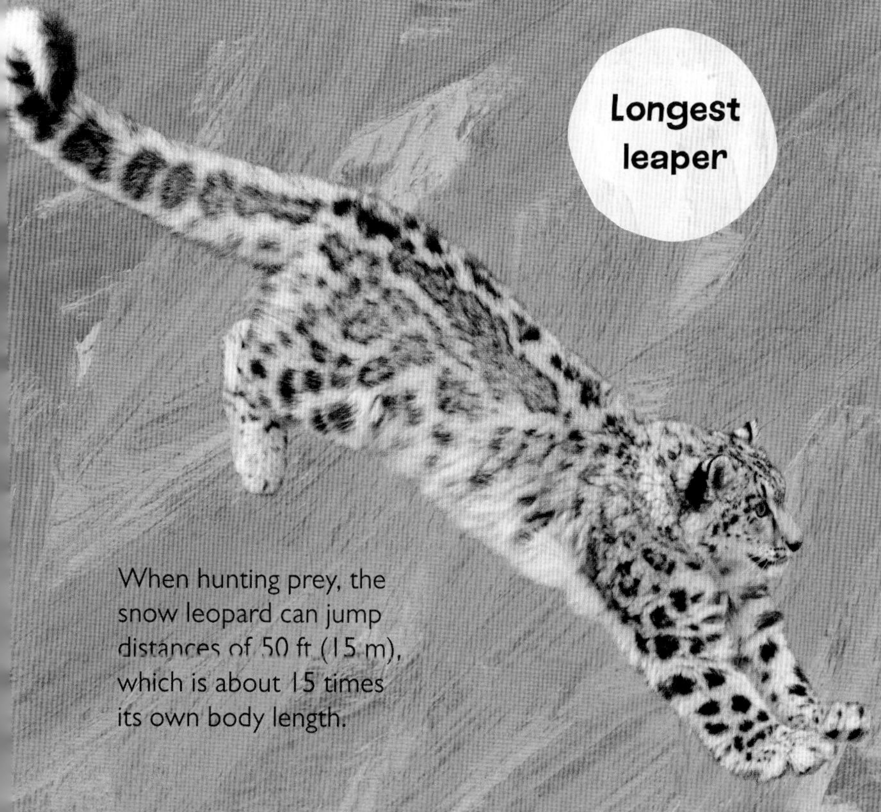

Longest leaper

When hunting prey, the snow leopard can jump distances of 50 ft (15 m), which is about 15 times its own body length.

Earth's fastest

The peregrine falcon flies at mind-blowing speeds of 240 mph (390 kph), making it the quickest creature on Earth.

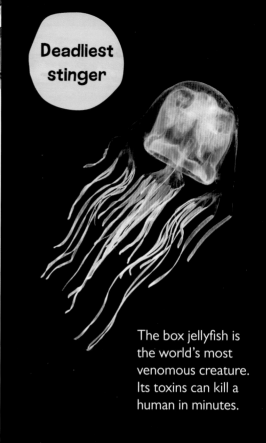

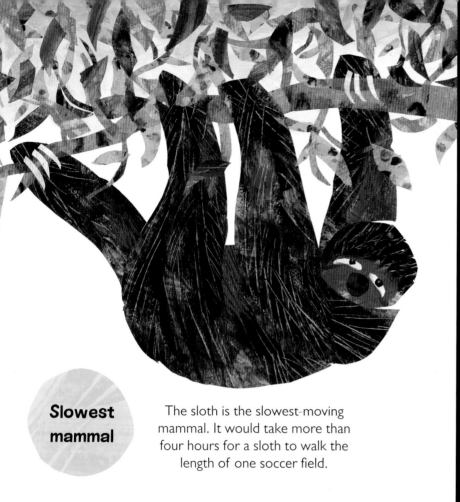

Helping animals

There are lots of different ways you can interact with animals, help wildlife, and play a part in protecting the planet.

Rescue pets

If you're lucky enough to be able to have a pet, try to find one at a local anmal shelter first. They often have family-friendly dogs, cats, and other animals in need of homes.

Neat and clean

Animals can get hurt if they swallow trash or get tangled up in leftover packaging. Put litter in a suitable container, or take it home with you if you are out and about. Help out with recycling at home by separating the paper, glass, and plastic.

Adopt an animal

If you can't have a pet at home, you could adopt an animal at your local zoo, rescue center, or wildlife park. From pandas to penguins, you can choose your favorite animal, find out lots of information about them, and perhaps even visit your new friend.

On your bike!

Instead of traveling in cars that pollute the atmosphere, walk or cycle wherever you can. This is healthier for you and much better for the environment, helping to preserve the different habitats where animals live.

Welcome wildlife

Make small changes to your backyard, balcony, or windowsill to help wildlife. Grow bee-friendly flowers, set up a bug hotel for insects, leave a water bowl for thirsty garden guests, or hang up a bird feeder. Then watch to see which visitors come flocking!

1. I can fly high in the sky, but I have no feathers.

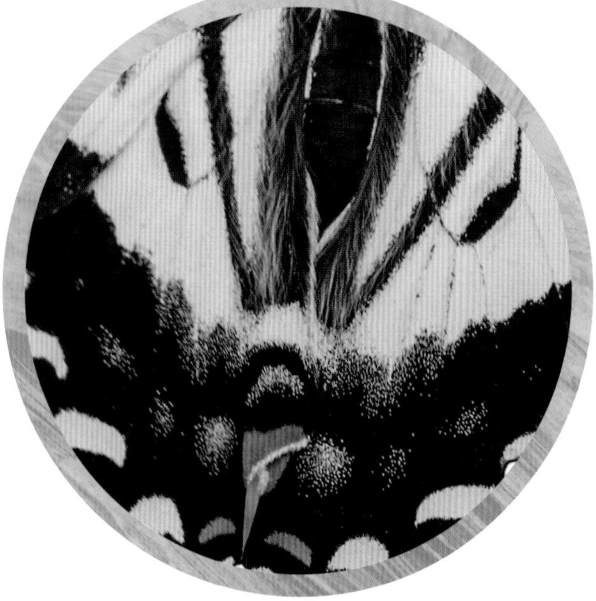

2. I'm the perfect traveling companion for a desert trek.

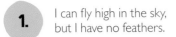

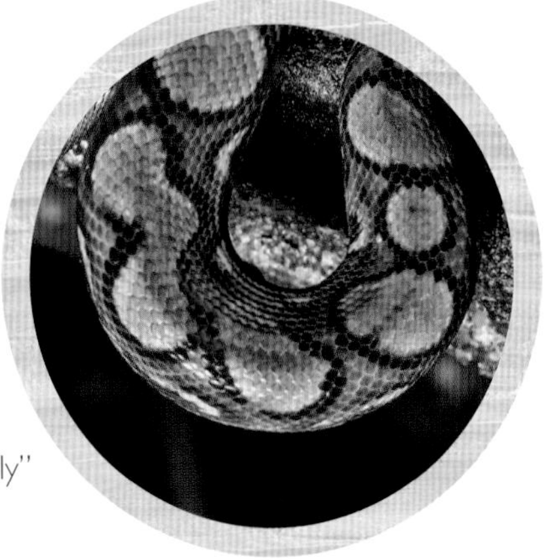

3. I love to give the animals I meet a "friendly" squeeze!

4. I'm an ocean-dweller who is always hungry like a wolf…

Guess who?

Can you name the animals from the clues? All the pictures are included somewhere in this book. When you've found them, check the answers at the bottom of the next page.

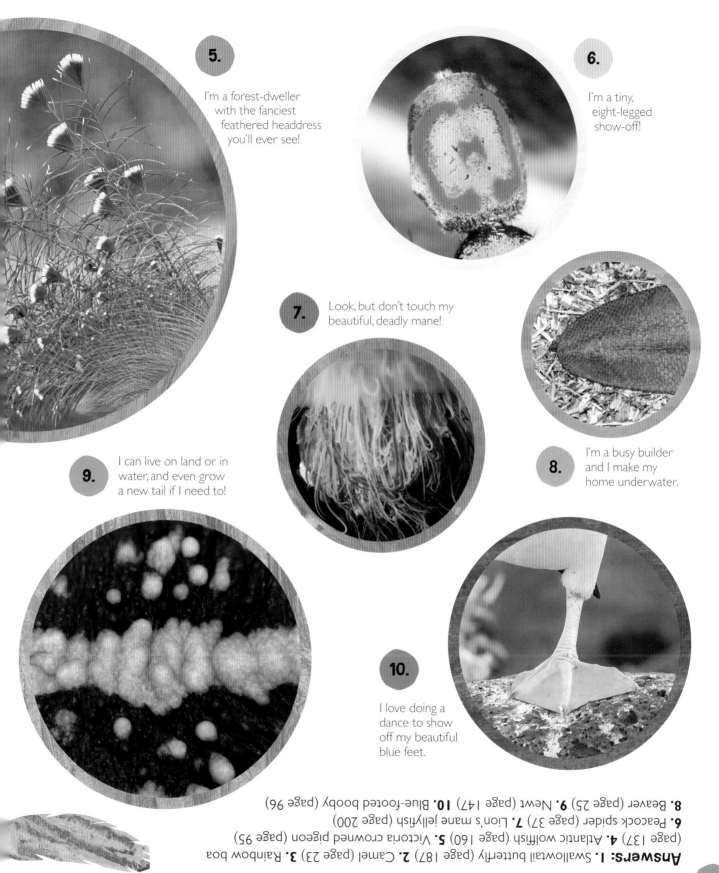

5.

I'm a forest-dweller with the fanciest feathered headdress you'll ever see!

6.

I'm a tiny, eight-legged show-off!

7.

Look, but don't touch my beautiful, deadly mane!

8.

I'm a busy builder and I make my home underwater.

9.

I can live on land or in water, and even grow a new tail if I need to!

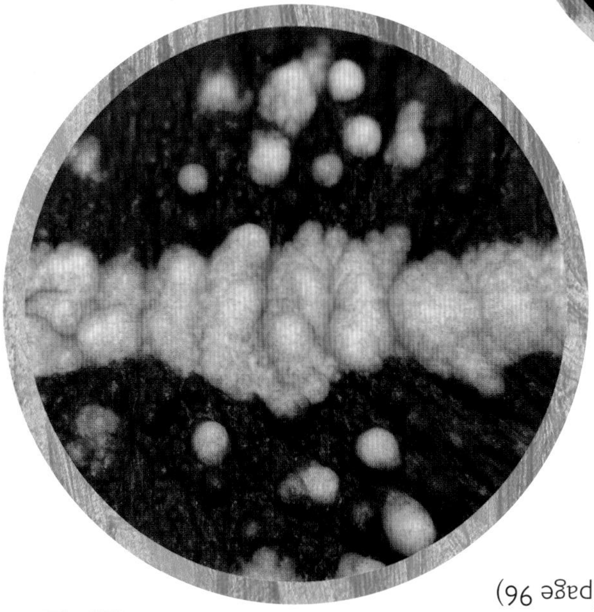

10.

I love doing a dance to show off my beautiful blue feet.

Answers: 1. Swallowtail butterfly (page 187) **2.** Camel (page 23) **3.** Rainbow boa (page 137) **4.** Atlantic wolffish (page 160) **5.** Victoria crowned pigeon (page 95) **6.** Peacock spider (page 37) **7.** Lion's mane jellyfish (page 200) **8.** Beaver (page 25) **9.** Newt (page 147) **10.** Blue-footed booby (page 96)

Crazy creature!

What have we here? This looks like the most extraordinary animal ever! But, look closely… it's actually a mishmash of five real-life creatures. See if you can spot them all.

Can you match this creature's body parts to the five animals shown?

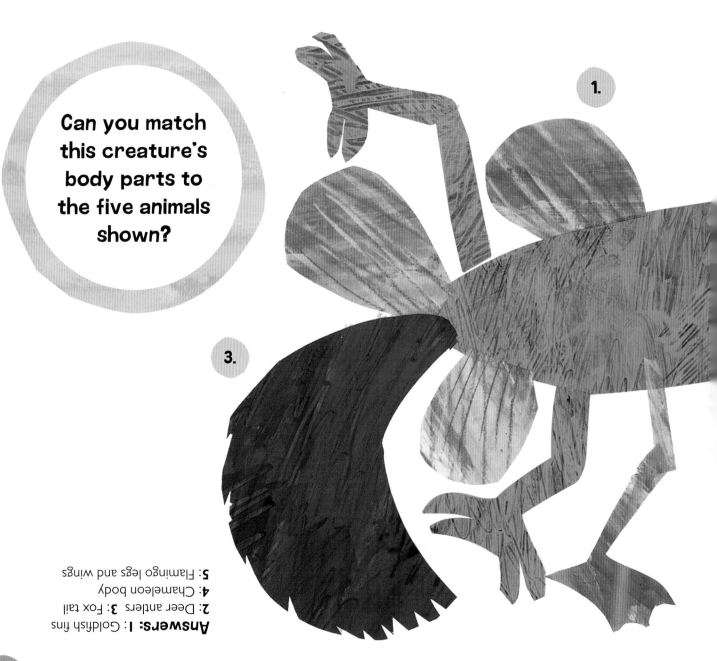

Answers: 1: Goldfish fins
2: Deer antlers **3**: Fox tail
4: Chameleon body
5: Flamingo legs and wings

Flamingo

Fox

Chameleon

Deer

Goldfish

Dragon

In European legends, flying, fire-breathing dragons spread fear and chaos. In Asia, however, serpentlike dragons like this one symbolize good luck.

Mythical creatures

Monstrous and magical creatures fill the pages of storybooks. Many are ancient legends shared by generations for centuries, but their roots are based firmly in the real animal kingdom.

Kraken

Beware giant tentacles wriggling from the water. This Norwegian sea monster was believed to capsize ships so that it could gobble up the sailors on board!

Phoenix

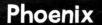

In ancient legends, this bird grew old, died, and was reborn from the ashes of a fire. The new phoenix that took flight was a symbol of hope and eternal life.

Cerberus

In Greek myths, this three-headed dog with a serpent's tail guarded the Underworld, making sure the dead could not escape.

Griffin

With the beak and wings of an eagle and the body of a lion, this creature was described as more powerful than 12 eagles and more dangerous than a pride of lions.

Unicorn

The unicorn is a magical pure-white horse with a horn growing from its forehead. One legend says that if a unicorn dips its horn into water, the water becomes instantly pure.

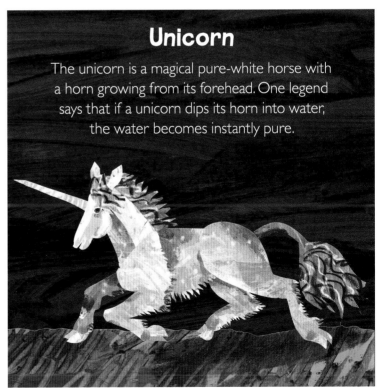

Animal quiz

You've read the book and you've met the animals. Now test your brain to see what you've learned. Good luck!

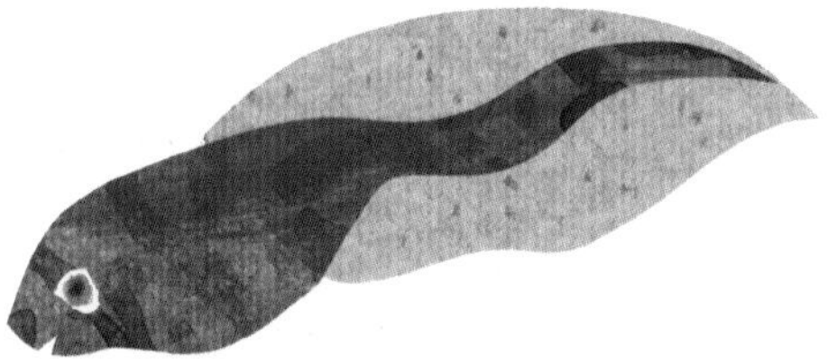

1. What does a tadpole turn into?

a) A fish
b) A frog
c) A tiger
d) A prince

2. What is the deepest zone of the ocean called?

a) Midnight zone
b) Hadal zone
c) No-go zone
d) Freezing!

3. Which animal lives for a record-breaking 2,300 years?

a) Greenland shark
b) Giant tortoise
c) Mayfly
d) Giant barrel sponge

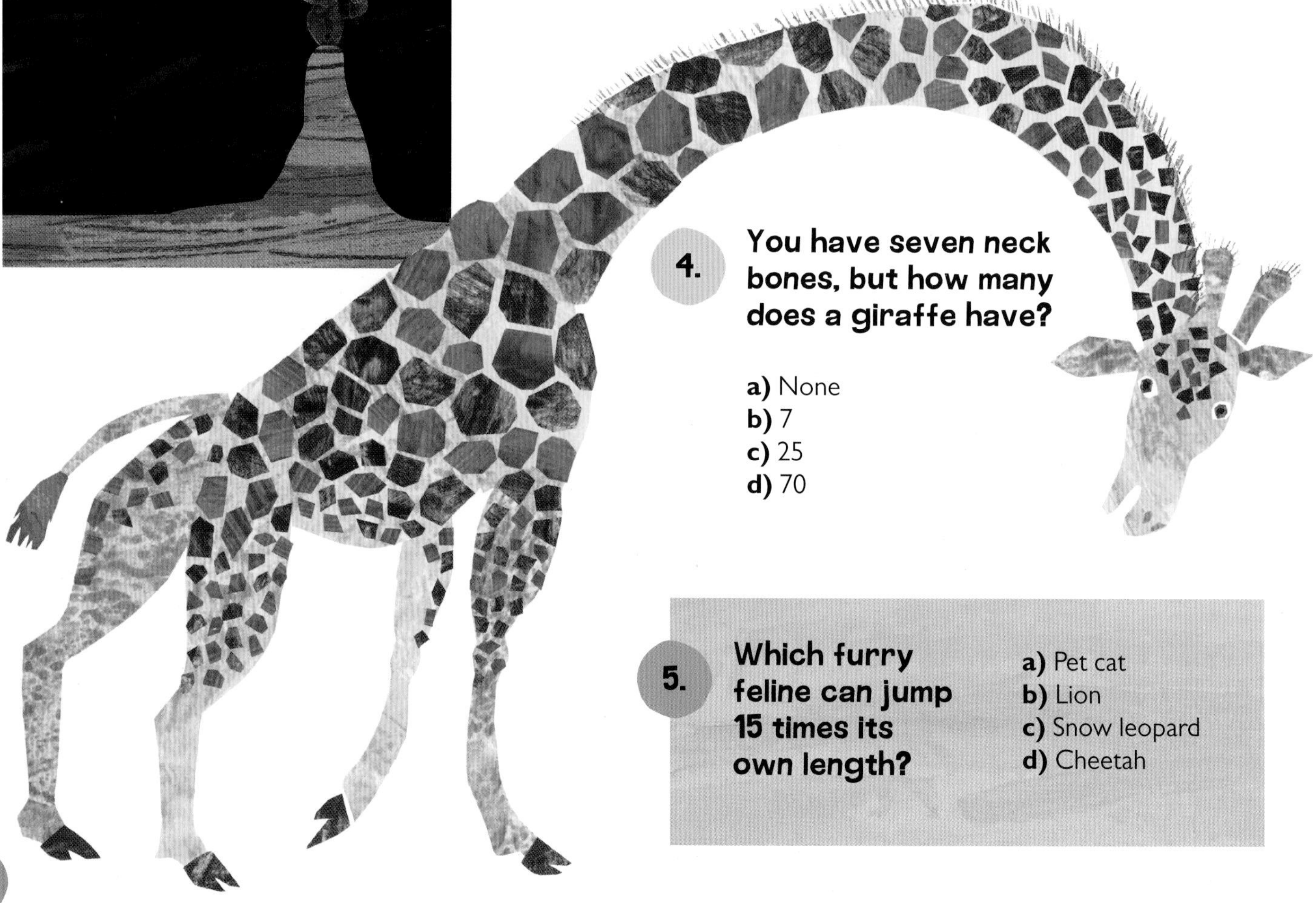

4. You have seven neck bones, but how many does a giraffe have?

a) None
b) 7
c) 25
d) 70

5. Which furry feline can jump 15 times its own length?

a) Pet cat
b) Lion
c) Snow leopard
d) Cheetah

6.

What do you call a mammal that carries her baby inside a belly pouch?

a) Rodent
b) Invertebrate
c) Amphibian
d) Marsupial

7.

What happens on Christmas Island?

a) People keep their Christmas trees up all year round
b) Santa Claus lives there
c) Red crabs migrate to the ocean
d) It is home to the Komodo dragon

8.

Which creature does 13 impressions of other animals?

a) Honeybee
b) Giant manta ray
c) Giant panda
d) Mimic octopus

9.

Which group of living things is big enough to be seen from space?

a) A family of blue whales that has just eaten dinner
b) A herd of African elephants
c) The Great Barrier Reef
d) Migrating monarch butterflies

10.

What is stored inside a camel's hump?

a) Fat
b) Lemonade
c) Water
d) Milk

Answers: 1. b; **2.** b; **3.** d; **4.** b; **5.** c; **6.** d; **7.** c; **8.** d; **9.** c; **10.** a.

Glossary

Amphibians
A group of cold-blooded animals that can live both in water and on land

Aquatic
Word that describes an animal or plant that spends most or all of its time in water

Birds
A group of warm-blooded animals that hatches from eggs, has a beak and feathers, and usually can fly

Breed
When a male and female animal mate and produce offspring

Camouflage
The color or pattern of an animal's skin, fur, or scales that helps it to hide in its natural habitat

Canine
Word used to describe any member of the dog family

Carnivore
An animal that eats only meat

Cartilage
Tough but flexible material that makes up the skeleton of some animals, including sharks and rays

Chrysalis
The hard shell that grows around a butterfly larva during metamorphosis. Also called a pupa

Cocoon
The hard shell that grows around a moth larva during the process of metamorphosis

Cold-blooded
Describes an animal with no control over its own body temperature

Echolocation
A way of using reflected sounds (echoes) to detect prey. Bats and dolphins hunt using echolocation

Exoskeleton
A hard skeleton on the outside of an invertebrate's body

Extinct
When a type of animal dies out, so there are no more left on Earth

Feline
Word used to describe any member of the cat family

Fish
A group of mainly cold-blooded animals; fish live in water and are usually covered in scales

Habitat
The natural place where an animal or plant lives

Herbivore
An animal that eats only plants

Invertebrate
Word that describes an animal without a backbone

Keratin
The substance that makes up animal claws, hair, hooves, nails, and scales

Larva
A young animal that looks totally different from its adult version. A caterpillar is the larva of a butterfly

Mammals
A group of warm-blooded animals with hair or fur covering their bodies. Mother mammals produce milk to feed their babies

Marsupial
A type of mammal whose females carry their babies in belly pouches

Metamorphosis
A total transformation that some animals go through as they grow from babies to adults. Tadpoles turn into frogs through metamorphosis

Migration
A long-distance journey that some animals make to find food, a mate, or warmer weather

Nocturnal
A word to describe an animal that is active only at night

Omnivore
An animal that eats both meat and plants

Predator
An animal that survives by hunting other animals to eat

Prehistoric
Word that describes ancient times, before people wrote down and kept records of things that happened

Prey
An animal that is hunted for food by another animal. Animals can be both predators and prey

Primates
A group of mammals that includes apes, lemurs, monkeys, and humans

Pupa
The hard shell that grows around a butterfly larva during metamorphosis. Also called a chrysalis

Reptiles
A group of cold-blooded animals that hatches from eggs; reptiles are covered in scales or bony plates

Savanna
A large area of hot, flat grassland with very few trees

Scavenger
An animal that feeds on dead animals, sometimes by taking them from predators

Temperate
Word that describes an area where the climate is neither very hot nor very cold

Vegetarian
A word to describe animals or humans that eat only plants

Vertebrate
An animal with a backbone and a skeleton inside its body

Warm-blooded
Describes an animal that can control its own body temperature

Index

Index

The World of Eric Carle nurtures a child's love of literature and learning, encouraging imaginative play and exploration. Trusted by parents, teachers, and librarians and beloved by children worldwide for generations, *The Very Hungry Caterpillar* and other timeless storybooks come to life in colorfully creative books and products, designed to inspire very hungry young minds. Eric Carle is acclaimed and beloved as the creator of brilliantly illustrated and innovatively designed picture books for very young children. Carle illustrated more than 70 books, many best-sellers, most of which he also wrote, and more than 170 million copies of his books have sold around the world. *The Very Hungry Caterpillar's Very First Animal Encyclopedia* introduces early learners to the key themes of animals and their habitats.

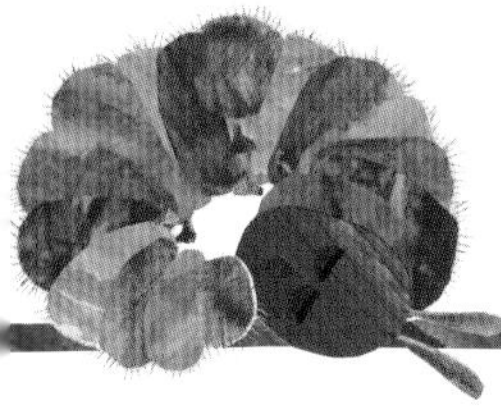

Acknowledgments

DK would like to thank Syed Md Farhan for DTP assistance; Vagisha Pushp, Bilal Ahmad, and Manpreet Kaur for picture research help; Caroline Hunt for proofreading; and Helen Peters for the index.

The publisher would like to thank the following for their kind permission to reproduce their photographs:

(Key: a-above; b-below/bottom; c-center; f-far; l-left; r-right; t-top)

1 123RF.com: Pavlo Vakhrushev (tc). **Dreamstime.com:** Isselee (cla, br). **6 Getty Images / iStock:** Dunning Imagery (ca). **7 Alamy Stock Photo:** Scenics & Science (cra). **Getty Images / iStock:** BanksPhotos (tc). **9 Dreamstime.com:** Andreykuzmin (2/tr); Natika (tr); Vikrant Deshpande (ca). **10 Dreamstime.com:** Yiu Tung Lee (c); Photographyfirm (cr). **Getty Images / iStock:** Searsie (cl). **11 Dreamstime.com:** Viacheslav Dubrovin (cr); Jordan Tan (cl); Thomas Lenne (c). **Getty Images / iStock:** E+ / lindsay_imagery (tl). **12 Getty Images / iStock:** stanley45 (c). **13 Alamy Stock Photo:** Anne Coastey (bl); Nature Picture Library (bc). **Getty Images / iStock:** Savany (br). **naturepl.com:** Gavin Maxwell (tc). **14 Alamy Stock Photo:** Mark Conlin (crb). **15 Alamy Stock Photo:** Blue Planet Archive (br); Adisha Pramod (cb). **Dreamstime.com:** Viacheslav Dubrovin (tr). **16 Dreamstime.com:** Leo Malsam (br); Natador (bl); Patricia Dubbeldam Wezel (bc). **17 Alamy Stock Photo:** Rosanne Tackaberry (br). **Dreamstime.com:** Jmrocek (bc); Miladrumeva (bl). **18 Dreamstime.com:** Kairi Aun (bc); David Steele (bl); Tarpan (br). **19 Dreamstime.com:** Joan Egert (tr); Isselee (tl); Hedrus (tc). **20 Alamy Stock Photo:** Nature Picture Library / Solvin Zankl (bl). **Getty Images / iStock:** BanksPhotos (tr). **21 Alamy Stock Photo:** Wildlife / Robert McGouey (tl). **Dreamstime.com:** Andreanita (br). **22 Getty Images / iStock:** E+ / Gerald Corsi (bl). **22-3 Dreamstime.com:** Stu Porter (t). **23 Dreamstime.com:** Ongchangwei (tr); Stedata (bc). **Getty Images / iStock:** Guillaume Regrain (br). **naturepl.com:** Ingo Arndt (cla). **24 Alamy Stock Photo:** Kenebec Images / Val Duncan (br). **Dreamstime.com:** Gordon Tipene (bc). **Getty Images / iStock:** Bazilfoto (bl). **25 Alamy Stock Photo:** Joe Blossom (br). **Dorling Kindersley:** Wildlife Heritage Foundation, Kent, UK (crb). **Dreamstime.com:** Joycemarrero (bl); Kcmatt (cra). **26 Dreamstime.com:** Jmrocek (tr). **Getty Images / iStock:** GoDogPhoto (cl). **27 Dreamstime.com:** Michel Arnault (cra); Itor (b). **28 Dreamstime.com:** Atalvi (bl). **29 Alamy Stock Photo:** Nature Photographers Ltd / PAUL R. STERRY (bl); Scenics & Science (crb). **Getty Images / iStock:** Dunning Imagery (cra). **30 Dreamstime.com:** Planetfelicity (cb). **31 Alamy Stock Photo:** Adisha Pramod (bc); Mike Robinson (crb). **Shutterstock.com:** Annmarie Young (cra); Shahar Shabtai (cb). **35 Dreamstime.com:** Lianquan Yu (bl). **36 Dreamstime.com:** Michael Smith (bc). **Getty Images / iStock:** reptiles4all (br). **37 Alamy Stock Photo:** BIOSPHOTO / Adam Fletcher (bl). **Dreamstime.com:** Stormcastle (bc). **38 Dreamstime.com:** Hannah Babiak (ca); Slowmotiongli (cla); Photographerlondon (cra); Natalia Bubochkina (bc). **39 Dreamstime.com:** Volodymyr Byrdyak (ca); Chdecout (cla). **naturepl.com:** Steve Gettle (cra). **40 Alamy Stock Photo:** WaterFrame_fba (tr). **Dreamstime.com:** Wayan Sumatika (clb). **41 Alamy Stock Photo:** Nature Picture Library / Michael D. Kern (cra). **42 Dreamstime.com:** Irina Orlova (br). **43 Dreamstime.com:** Jmrocek (tr). **44 Getty Images / iStock:** JHVEPhoto (tr). **45 Alamy Stock Photo:** Colin Marshall (crb). **Dreamstime.com:** Ndp (cl). **46 Getty Images / iStock:** s-cphoto (cla). **47 Alamy Stock Photo:** Minden Pictures / Kevin Schafer (cra). **48 Dreamstime.com:** Goce Risteski (cla). **49 Alamy Stock Photo:** Blickwinkel / Schmidbauer (cr). **Dreamstime.com:** Positive Snapshot (cra); Lukas Vejrik (crb). **51 Dreamstime.com:** Jeffrey Banke (cb); Lynn Watson (bc); Daniel Bellhouse (br). **52 Alamy Stock Photo:** Tierfotoagentur / m.blue-shadow (cr). **52-3 Getty Images:** Stone / Ignacio Palacios (t). **53 Getty Images / iStock:** Hannes Lochner (clb). **54 Getty Images / iStock:** s-cphoto (cl). **55 Dreamstime.com:** Johan Reineke (clb). **Getty Images / iStock:** Andyworks (tr). **56 Alamy Stock Photo:** Minden Pictures / Kevin Schafer (bl). **Dreamstime.com:** Eric Gevaert (br). **57 Alamy Stock Photo:** Chris Craggs (bl). **Dreamstime.com:** Edwin Butter (br). **58 Getty Images / iStock:** E+ / DmitryND (bl); E+ / HuntedDuck (bc). **59 Dreamstime.com:** Simon Eeman (bc); Julian W (bl). **Getty Images / iStock:** E+ / serengeti130 (tl). **61 Alamy Stock Photo:** Amar and Isabelle Guillen - Guillen Photo LLC (c). **Dreamstime.com:** Volodymyr Byrdyak (tr); Lucaar (cla); Pär Edlund (1/ca); Ondřej Prosický (cra); Sorin Colac (tc). **Getty Images:** Moment / Arun Roisri (cl). **Getty Images / iStock:** ytwong (ca). **63 Depositphotos Inc:** 2630ben (cla). **Dreamstime.com:** Ecophoto (bl); Anke Van Wyk (tc). **64 Dreamstime.com:** Joanne Eastope (crb); Yodke67 (tr); Stu Porter (clb). **Getty Images:** EyeEm / Nurdin Nurdin (cb). **65 Dreamstime.com:** Bennymarty (clb); Adam Edwards (cb). **Getty Images:** Moment / Wokephoto17 (crb). **67 Dreamstime.com:** Maurizio Camerin (ca); Janian Mcmillan (cla). **Getty Images / iStock:** Stockbyte / Tom Brakefield (cra). **70 naturepl.com:** Eric Baccega (bc); Klein & Hubert (tr). **71 Alamy Stock Photo:** PA Images / Andrew Milligan (bc). **Dreamstime.com:** Gnomeandi (bl). **naturepl.com:** Mark Carwardine (cl). **72 Dreamstime.com:** Hotshotsworldwide (cl). **73 Alamy Stock Photo:** Rick & Nora Bowers (clb). **Dreamstime.com:** Bernhard Richter (cla). **74 Alamy Stock Photo:** Reinhard Dirscherl (bc). **75 Alamy Stock Photo:** Rolf Hicker Photography (tl). **Dreamstime.com:** Mirage3 (cr). **76 Alamy Stock Photo:** Gon2Foto / Richard Mittlema (cl). **79 Alamy Stock Photo:** blickwinkel / M. Woike (cra); Steve Bloom Images / Joe McDonald (bc). **Getty Images:** Moment / Nicolas Reusens (crb). **Science Photo Library:** Merlintuttle.org (c). **80 Getty Images / iStock:** Aaprophoto (clb). **Getty Images:** EyeEm / Christina Shaskus (crb). **81 Getty Images / iStock:** FRANKHILDEBRAND (crb); photos_martYmage (clb). **Getty Images:** Moment / Picture by Tambako the Jaguar (tr).

83 Dreamstime.com: David Dirga (tl); Lesya Marchuk (bl); Miroslav Hlavko (bc); Edurivero (br). **86 Dreamstime.com:** Ziga Camernik (ca); Flownaksala (cra). **87 Getty Images / iStock:** Equilibrium99 (cra). **89 Dreamstime.com:** Photowitch (br). **Getty Images / iStock:** E+ / 4FR (cra). **90 123RF.com:** Corey A Ford (ca). **91 Dreamstime.com:** Jolanta Dabrowska (crb); Richard Espenant (tc); Zuzana Randlova (cra); Torikell (cr). **92 Alamy Stock Photo:** Michael Fritzen (bl). **Dreamstime.com:** Gabe9000c (bc); Liam O Hara (br). **93 Dreamstime.com:** Jillian Cain (br); Kojihirano (bl); Dee Carpenter (bc). **95 Alamy Stock Photo:** Nature Picture Library / Tui De Roy (bc). **Dreamstime.com:** Riverrail (cr). **96 Dreamstime.com:** Ken Griffiths (bc). **Getty Images / iStock:** E+ / guenterguni (bl). **97 Dreamstime.com:** Johannes Gerhardus Swanepoel (bc). **Getty Images / iStock:** CraigRJD (bl). **98 Dreamstime.com:** Malgorzata Morawska (bc). **99 Dreamstime.com:** Rinus Baak (cra, br). **101 Dreamstime.com:** Daniel Budiman (tl); Sahatdreams (bl). **Getty Images:** Moment / Michele D'Amico supersky77 (crb). **103 Dreamstime.com:** Ziga Camernik (1/cl); Prapass Wannapinij (cr); Theohrm (1/cr); Nikita Maykov (cl); Vasyl Helevachuk (bl); Isselee (bc). **Getty Images / iStock:** Bebedi (ca). **104 Alamy Stock Photo:** Paul Miguel (br). **105 Alamy Stock Photo:** David Tipling Photo Library / David Tipling (cla); John Warburton-Lee Photography / Nigel Pavitt (br). **Dreamstime.com:** Sander Meertins (cra). **Getty Images / iStock:** THEGIFT777 (ca). **107 Alamy Stock Photo:** FLPA (tl). **Dreamstime.com:** Awcnz62 (cra); Corners74 (cr); Flownaksala (cl). **Getty Images:** Moment / Darwin Fan (crb). **108 Dreamstime.com:** Wayne Marinovich (bc); Oleg Troino (br). **109 Getty Images / iStock:** Johnson Martin (tc). **110 Dreamstime.com:** Igor Batenev (cra). **111 Dreamstime.com:** Liam Gutierrez Huamani (tr). **Getty Images / iStock:** Equilibrium99 (cr); Manakin (l). **112 Dreamstime.com:** Javarman (tr); Vladimir Seliverstov (tc); Alexey Sedov (1/tc). **113 Alamy Stock Photo:** Minden Pictures / Otto Plantema / Buiten-beeld (cr). **Dreamstime.com:** Inaras (tc); Tarpan (cra, br). **115 Alamy Stock Photo:** L. Kurtze (tr); Nature Picture Library / Alex Mustard (ca). **Dreamstime.com:** Frank Fichtmueller (crb); Johncarnemolla (clb). **Getty Images:** The Image Bank / Oliver Strewe (cb). **116 Dreamstime.com:** Jgade (tc); Matthijs Kuijpers (clb). **117 Getty Images / iStock:** anankkml (cra). **118 Getty Images / iStock:** Mark Kostich (cr). **119 Dreamstime.com:** Leonello Calvetti (cra). **Getty Images / iStock:** Jarib (crb). **120 Dreamstime.com:** Ozflash (br). **121 Dreamstime.com:** Tjkphotography (tc). **Getty Images / iStock:** anankkml (br). **122 Dreamstime.com:** Beautifulblossom (bl); Zachzimet (br). **123 Alamy Stock Photo:** Minden Pictures / Ch'ien Lee (bl). **Dreamstime.com:** Tarpan (cla). **Science Photo Library:** Nature Picture Library / Bence Mate (br). **125 Dreamstime.com:** Andrey Gudkov (br); Robin Winkelman (tl). **Shutterstock.com:** reptiles4all (tr). **126 Dreamstime.com:** Isonphoto (clb); Jay Pierstorff (tr). **naturepl.com:** John Cancalosi (crb). **127 Dreamstime.com:** PeterWaters (tr). **Getty Images:** Stone / Paul Starosta (tl). **129 Shutterstock.com:** AP / Frank Glaw (bc). **131 Alamy Stock Photo:** Design Pics Inc / Keith Levit (cra). **132 Alamy Stock Photo:** Michelle Gilders (bc). **133 Alamy Stock Photo:** Scubazoo (bc). **Dreamstime.com:** Jdazuelos (bl). **135 Alamy Stock Photo:** Nature Picture Library / MYN / Gil Wizen (bc). **Dreamstime.com:** Adogslifephoto (tc); Amwu (cl); Matthijs Kuijpers (crb). **Getty Images / iStock:** RibeirodosSantos (cra). **136 Alamy Stock Photo:** John Cancalosi (crb). **137 Alamy Stock Photo:** Minden Pictures / Thomas Marent (tc); WaterFrame_fba (tr). **Getty Images / iStock:** Agus Fitriyanto (tl); Sstaton (br). **138 Dreamstime.com:** Alexander Shalamov (tr). **Getty Images / iStock:** foryouinf (cr). **naturepl.com:** Daniel Heuclin (c). **139 Alamy Stock Photo:** Andrew Newman Nature Pictures (tr); Geordie Torr (cr). **Dreamstime.com:** Tjkphotography (c); Aekkaphum Warawiang (cl). **141 Dreamstime.com:** Isselee (tc); Jgade (1/tc); Verastuchelova (br). **naturepl.com:** Todd Pusser (bc). **142 Alamy Stock Photo:** Eyal Bartov (cla). **143 Alamy Stock Photo:** Bel (crb). **Getty Images / iStock:** pjmalsbury (cr); Michel VIARD (cra). **144 Alamy Stock Photo:** Zoonar GmbH / DiKKY_O (bc). **145 Alamy Stock Photo:** Design Pics Inc / Thomas Kitchin & Victoria Hurst (bc). **146 Alamy Stock Photo:** DP Wildlife Vertebrates (tr). **147 Alamy Stock Photo:** Roberto Nistri (tr). **Dreamstime.com:** Isselee (br); Henk Wallays (cb); Voislav Kolevski (crb). **Getty Images:** Moment / Pedro H. Bernardo (bl). **149 Alamy Stock Photo:** Scenics & Science (tr). **Dreamstime.com:** Lunamarina (cla). **150 Alamy Stock Photo:** Buiten-Beeld / Ron Offermans (br). **Getty Images / iStock:** Andrea Izzotti (bc). **151 Alamy Stock Photo:** Minden Pictures / Fred Bavendam (cr); SeaTops (crb). **Dreamstime.com:** Mirkorosenau (cra). **152-3 Dreamstime.com:** Tennesseewitney (t). **152 Dreamstime.com:** Lunamarina (clb). **153 Dreamstime.com:** Oreena (bl); Mirecca (cr); Tazdevilgreg (crb). **154 Getty Images / iStock:** frameyazoo (bc). **154-5 Getty Images / iStock:** Placebo365 (b). **155 Alamy Stock Photo:** Nature Picture Library / Alex Mustard (bc). **Dreamstime.com:** Bennymarty (ca); Corey A Ford (tr). **156 Alamy Stock Photo:** BIOSPHOTO / Gerard Soury (bc). **Dreamstime.com:** Andrey Gudkov (bl). **157 DESCNA:** (bl). **Dreamstime.com:** Hbuchholz (tc). **naturepl.com:** David Shale (bc). **158 naturepl.com:** Brandon Cole (c). **159 Dreamstime.com:** Maria Dryfhout (tc). **Getty Images:** Premium Archive / Field Museum Library (bc). **160 Alamy Stock Photo:** WaterFrame_fba (bl). **161 Dreamstime.com:** Jakkapan Prammanasik (cra). **163 Alamy Stock Photo:** Minden Pictures / Norbert Wu (ca); VWPics / Kelvin Aitken (cr); Nature Picture Library / David Shale (br). **164 Alamy Stock Photo:** Joe Austin Photography (bc). **164-5 Alamy Stock Photo:** Biswa1992 (b). **165 Alamy Stock Photo:** Minden Pictures / Stephen Dalton (tr). **naturepl.com:** Piotr Naskrecki (bc). **166 Getty Images:** Photodisc / Mark Webster (tr). **167 Dreamstime.com:** Irko Van Der Heide (cra); Wrangel (crb). **naturepl.com:** Georgette Douwma (clb). **169 Dreamstime.com:** Wrangel (clb). **Getty Images:** Moment / Douglas Sacha (crb). **171 Alamy Stock Photo:** imageBROKER / Norbert Probst (cra). **Getty Images:** Moment / by wildestanimal (crb). **172 Alamy Stock Photo:** Stephen Frink Collection / Stephen Frink (cra). **173 Alamy Stock Photo:** imageBROKER / . / . (tl); Nature Picture Library / GEORGETTE DOUWMA (c). **Dreamstime.com:** Bin Zhou (cra). **175 Alamy Stock Photo:** blickwinkel / F. Hecker (cra). **176 Alamy Stock Photo:** Scenics & Science (clb). **178 Dreamstime.com:** Andrey Burmakin (tl). **179 Dreamstime.com:** Filip Fuxa (clb). **Getty Images / iStock:** Kaphoto (tc). **180 123RF.com:** Andrzej Tokarski (clb). **Getty Images / iStock:** Kaphoto (bl). **181 Getty Images:** 500Px Plus / Leighton Lum (cra). **Getty Images / iStock:** Delpixart (br); vojce (cr); Irina Kulikova (crb). **183 Dreamstime.com:** Icefront (tl). **184 Getty Images / iStock:** Backiris (tr). **185 Dreamstime.com:** Andrey Burmakin (br). **186 Dreamstime.com:** Isselee (cra). **187 Dreamstime.com:** David Burke (cla); Filip Fuxa (tl); Jens Stolt (tc); PeterWaters (tr); Isselee (cra). **189 Dreamstime.com:** Dariusz Szwangruber (br). **190 Dreamstime.com:** Tomatito26 (bc). **191 Alamy Stock Photo:** FLPA (bc); Ivan Kuzmin (tl); K.D. Leperi (bl). **Dreamstime.com:** Leonidikan (cra). **Getty Images / iStock:** ebettini (cr). **193 Dreamstime.com:** Artushfoto (bl); Dwi Yulianto (tc); Dannyphoto80 (tr). **195 Dreamstime.com:** Claffra (br); Roberto Junior (cla); JustNatureChannel (clb). **naturepl.com:** Nature Production (tr). **196 Dreamstime.com:** Ara Pintos (bl). **197 Dreamstime.com:** Aquanaut4 (cra). **Getty Images:** Corbis / Hal Beral (cr); Stocktrek Images / Ethan Daniels (crb). **198 Dreamstime.com:** John Anderson (bc). **198-9 Dreamstime.com:** Yisi Li (b). **199 Dreamstime.com:** Chirawan (bc); Tan Kian Yong (tc). **200 123RF.com:** Pavlo Vakhrushev (cl). **Getty Images / iStock:** Warren A Metcalf (clb). **naturepl.com:** Shane Gross (cla). **201 Alamy Stock Photo:** Nature Picture Library / Pascal Kobeh (bl). **Dorling Kindersley:** Natural History Museum, London / Colin Keates (crb); Linda Pitkin (br, bc). **202 Dreamstime.com:** Wessel Cirkel (cla); Sergey Skleznev (ca). **203 Alamy Stock Photo:** Nature Picture Library / Sue Daly (cr). **204 Dreamstime.com:** Luis Leamus (cra); Duncan Noakes (cr). **205 naturepl.com:** Oceanwide / Gary Bell (cla). **206 Alamy Stock Photo:** Ray Wilson (c). **Dreamstime.com:** Luis Leamus (bl); Duncan Noakes (cra). **207 Getty Images / iStock:** June Jacobsen (bl). **naturepl.com:** Oceanwide / Gary Bell (cra). **209 Alamy Stock Photo:** A ROOM WITH VIEWS (cla). **210-1 Dreamstime.com:** Riverrail (t). **210 Alamy Stock Photo:** Minden Pictures / Thomas Marent (cl); WaterFrame_fba (c). **Dreamstime.com:** David Burke (tl); Stedata (tc). **211 Alamy Stock Photo:** BIOSPHOTO / Adam Fletcher (tc); Joe Blossom (cra). **Dreamstime.com:** Isselee (bl). **Getty Images / iStock:** E+ / guenterguni (crb); Warren A Metcalf (c)

Cover images: *Front:* **123RF.com:** Pavlo Vakhrushev tc; **Dreamstime.com:** Isselee br, cla; *Back:* **Dreamstime.com:** Filip Fuxa cla, Mirecca cra

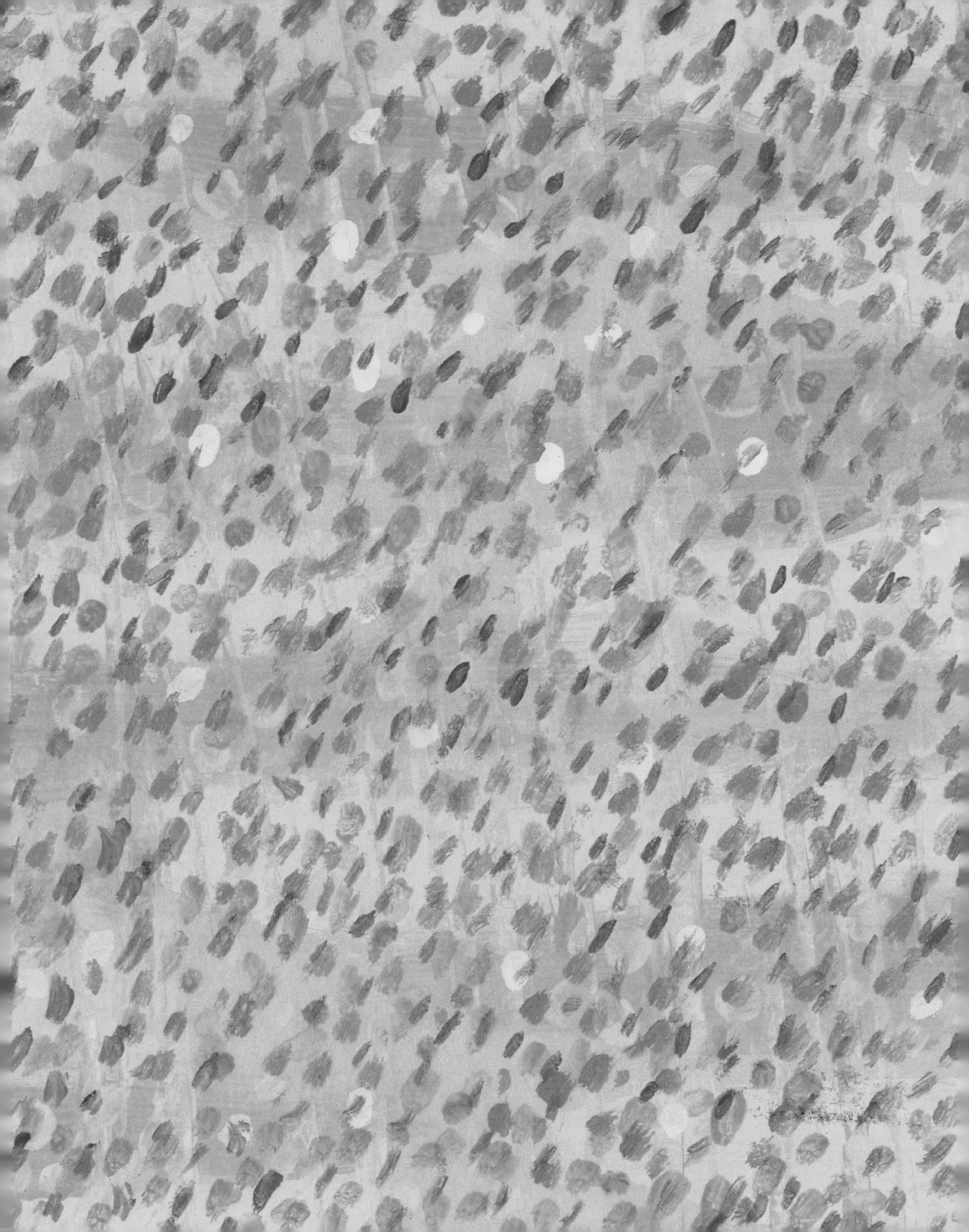